SED CARS
1st
YOUR SATISFACTION
IS IMPORTANT TO US
PAINT
FENDER REPAIR
MASSEY MOTORS
TAMPA
JACKSONVILLE
GARLITS' DODGE
MASSEY MOTORS

MOPAR
FACTORY
DRAG CARS
1962-1972
CRAGAR
JEG'S
CarTech®

DODGE & PLYMOUTH'S QUARTER-MILE DOMINATION

Steve Holmes

CarTech®

CarTech®, Inc.
6118 Main Street
North Branch, MN 55056
Phone: 651-277-1200 or 800-551-4754
Fax: 651-277-1203
www.cartechbooks.com

Edit by Wes Eisenschenk
Layout by Monica Seiberlich

ISBN 978-1-61325-722-7
Item No. CT688

Library of Congress Cataloging-in-Publication Data Available

Written, edited, and designed in the U.S.A.
Printed in China
10 9 8 7 6 5 4 3 2 1

All photos are courtesy of author Steve Holmes unless otherwise noted.

Front Flap: Photo Courtesy Peewee Wallace Family Archives

Frontispiece: Photo Courtesy Don Garlits Collection

Publisher's Note: In reporting history, the images required to tell the tale will vary greatly in quality, especially by modern photographic standards. While some images in this volume are not up to those digital standards, we have included them, as we feel they are an important element in telling the story.

DISTRIBUTION BY:

Europe
PGUK
63 Hatton Garden
London EC1N 8LE, England
Phone: 020 7061 1980 • Fax: 020 7242 3725
www.pguk.co.uk

Australia
Renniks Publications Ltd.
3/37-39 Green Street
Banksmeadow, NSW 2109, Australia
Phone: 2 9695 7055 • Fax: 2 9695 7355
www.renniks.com

Canada
Login Canada
300 Saulteaux Crescent
Winnipeg, MB, R3J 3T2 Canada
Phone: 800 665 1148 • Fax: 800 665 0103
www.lb.ca

TABLE OF CONTENTS

ACKNOWLEDGMENTS

Quite simply, this book couldn't have been created without the help of some remarkable people.

My sincere thanks go (in no particular order) to Dan Roney, Jim Schild, Steve Reyes, John Rogers, Lou Hart, Geoff Stunkard, Tony Thacker, Don Webber, Charlie Suggs, Tom Bettencourt, David McWilliams, Rob Carley, Charles Milikin Jr., Mike Cook, Alan Lewis, James Handy, Bret Kepner, John Hellmuth, and Revs Institute. These incredible enthusiasts came forward to provide information, photos, period magazine articles, and a myriad of priceless drag racing artifacts to help pull this project together. This is simply an amazing group of people, and I could not have completed this project without them. I'm forever grateful.

In addition, thank you to Wes Eisenschenk and the team at CarTech for making this project possible in the first place.

Last but certainly not least, thank you to my amazing, incredibly understanding, and patient wife, Helen, who barely saw me during the last three months of this project. Seven-day weeks and long hours were standard fare, and I think she almost forgot what I looked like during that time.

FOREWORD BY HAYDEN PROFFITT

Labor Day 1962 was a day that propelled me into the national spotlight. I was at the U.S. Nationals going rounds and had just one race left. I had just got back from my semifinals run and had five minutes to cool down the 409 and face the Ramchargers in the finals for Mr. Stock Eliminator.

In the days prior, the large contingent of members on the Ramchargers were bumping their gums at us Chevrolet racers. They thought their 413, which they had been using to stomp everyone, was going to load all the Chevys up on the trailer. As we sat there trying to pack ice onto our water pumps, radiators, and engine blocks, I kept thinking about the trash talking that took place the days prior.

As we pulled up to the line and waited for the flag to drop, I saw the flag man look over at Jim Thorton and then over at me. I gave the head nod and steadied the tachometer at 2,000. As soon as it dropped, I let the

(Photo Courtesy Larry Davis Collection)

clutch out, and she bit. Between the low-to-2nd shift, I looked over and noticed I had about 3 feet on him. With each shift, I glanced over and saw that I was starting to gap him. As I shifted from 3rd to 4th, I saw I had a couple car lengths on him, so I reached back with my right hand and gave the Ramchargers the one-finger solute! Little did I know that in a few short months I too would be bumping my gums at the Chevys as a Super Stock Plymouth driver.

After Chevy pulled out of drag racing, I had the good fortune of running into my friend Lou Baney in Downey, California. Lou knew about Chevy quitting and wanted to know if I was looking for sponsorship and a car. Before I knew it, we were in Detroit, and Chrysler was giving me two haulers, two race cars, and $274,000! By June of 1963, we had set a new Super Stock automatic record running 11.87 at 119.44 mph at Lions Drag Strip. I think I made the right choice. In fact, we had our Plymouths running so well at Beeline Factory the AHRA Winternationals in February of 1964 that I won the finals in Mr. Top Stock Eliminator. I was in my S/SA 1964 Plymouth going against my other car running S/S driven by Roger Caster!

I had a lot of success running the Plymouths. In mid-1964, the Hemi debuted, and I received one of the very first cars as a factory-backed driver. We had those hardtop Wedge cars dialed in so well that it took the Hemi a while to catch up. By August, we had it singing when we went out East for a match race against Malcolm Durham and his 1964 Chevelle at Vineland Speedway in New Jersey. I rung the Hemi out with the lowest elapsed time of the meet with an 11.31 and swept the best-of-five from Durham.

However, with a new year came a new opportunity, and I left Plymouth for Mercury in 1965. Unfortunately for me, it was the wrong move. It seemed to be that every week we were fixing something that was broken. That Mercury just wasn't reliable like those Plymouths were.

I've got a lot of great memories from my time with Plymouth. I thoroughly enjoyed racing against Ronnie Sox and the young up-and-comer Butch Leal. It was always a treat to put "Dyno" Don Nicholson on the trailer as well. Man, that guy knew how to make horsepower! I'd always have to beat him on the tree.

I really hope you enjoy this book, *Mopar Factory Drag Cars: Dodge & Plymouth's Quarter-Mile Domination 1962–1972*. Having lived through racing these cars and against great competition, you'll need to put a lap belt on your rocking chair after reading it!

INTRODUCTION

The 1950s were subject to a power race in the world of motorsport. The public flocked to racetracks in droves, and with them came the manufacturers. But the decade was blighted by a series of fatalities within the sport with losses of both drivers and spectators.

Certainly, the darkest hour was the 1955 24 Hours of Le Mans race, when the Mercedes-Benz of Pierre Levegh struck Lance Macklin's Austin-Healey at speed on the front straight. Macklin swerved to avoid Mike Hawthorn's Jaguar, which pulled across and slowed in front of him to make a pit stop. The ensuing carnage saw Levegh's Mercedes fly into the air, clear a protective earth embankment, and propel through a spectator area, where it impacted twice before disintegrating.

Levegh and 83 spectators were killed, and another 80 or more were injured. Mercedes-Benz withdrew immediately from the sport and didn't return until 1987. Certainly, the late 1950s was not a good time for manufacturers to be associated with motor racing.

In 1957, two years after the Le Mans tragedy, the Automobile Manufacturers Association (AMA), consisting of members representing major American automotive companies, agreed to a withdrawal from all forms of motorsport. This agreement was essentially self-imposed, as manufacturers feared Congress may intervene and force their hand had they not acted. With motorsport suffering an increasingly negative reputation, the manufacturers agreed racing limitations may likely be imposed, and these would be far more draconian than anything they themselves could inflict.

However, automotive manufacturers are in the business of selling cars. The more cars they shift, the more money they make, and at the core of every manufacturer is the need to make money. In the late 1950s, increasingly, motor racing was proving to be a highly effective tool for achieving this.

Motor racing had a stigma, but the manufacturers benefitted from their involvement with racing. So, while they all agreed to openly step away from the sport, they all came back one by one. At least initially, involvement had to be achieved covertly.

In motor racing terms, no other decade, before or since, has witnessed such widespread revolution as the 1960s. The transformations this era introduced to the racing world have left lasting impressions, many of which continue to influence the sport to this day.

The 1960s boasted massive innovation that propelled forward at breakneck speed. Phil Hill won the 1960 Italian Grand Prix aboard a Ferrari 256, which was the last front-engined car to win a Formula 1 World Championship race as the rear-engined revolution swept in. The same was about to happen at Indianapolis. There was further fast-paced development in virtually every other aspect of the sport, including tire technology, brakes, suspension, aerodynamics, and even the core design of the vehicles themselves.

It wasn't just engineering for speed and efficiency that changed during the 1960s. Indeed, the relationship that automotive manufacturers had with the sport was also transformed—the results of which filtered down to the consumer. In no other country did this immense level of change play out more than the United States. In 1960, American car manufacturers were reserved, at best, in their involvement with racing. Ten years later, their commitment was absolute.

Motor City Action and Reaction

Growing popularity in both drag racing and stock car racing ultimately forced Detroit's hand. Indeed, both disciplines dated back several decades, but it was the restructuring of these forms of the sport by the leading promoters in each (the National Hot Rod Association [NHRA] and National Association for Stock Car Auto Racing [NASCAR]), and their proactive inclusion of late-model, stock-based, and mass-produced domestic vehicles that forced the manufacturers to take action.

Essentially, the strengths and weaknesses of the products they produced were being showcased in public. Obviously, it was better that their products be faster and more robust than those of their competition.

In terms of entertainment and competition in its purest form, there can be no equal to quarter-mile drag racing and bullring dirt and pavement oval racing. These amphitheaters provide spectators an uninterrupted view of the action with the entire show played out in front of them. Furthermore, the atmosphere produced by these ready-made stadiums can be electrifying. That atmosphere drives emotion. Emotion sells cars. Throughout the 1950s, examples of both were sprouting up across the country, seemingly in every town, so drag racing and speedway events were hugely accessible.

For the manufacturers, competitions where thousands of potential customers congregate to witness these head-to-head scrimmages became too hard to resist. General Motors and Ford were the first companies to break ranks. Their initial involvement followed an under-the-table approach, quietly assisting specific teams and drivers with parts, engineering support, and even money.

By 1961, both manufacturers were offering specialized high-performance engines in their full-sized models. Those very same models were contesting NASCAR Grand National and NHRA Stock competitions. Then, they reaped the rewards when their products won in front of large audiences of highly emotional race fans.

The 1961 Daytona 500 was won by Marvin Panch, driving a Pontiac Catalina built and entered by Smokey Yunick. Nearly 100,000 race fans were in attendance. "Dyno" Don Nicholson, aboard a Chevrolet Impala, won Mr. Stock Eliminator at the 1961 NHRA Winternationals at Pomona. He then backed it up by scoring Top Stock (only to be disqualified for illegal valve springs) at the U.S. Nationals at Indianapolis. Indeed, GM products were stealing the headlines at most of the big racing events in 1961.

Chrysler Corporation, by contrast, was notable for its absence. Despite a lack of official support for teams racing its brand, Chrysler still enjoyed some good results in 1961, most notably, Frank Dade's win in Stock A/S (Chrysler didn't have a vehicle eligible for Super Stock) at the U.S. Nationals at Indianapolis and Al Eckstrand's victory over Nicholson's Chevy in a hastily concocted grudge match at the same event.

The 1961 NHRA Nationals at Indy proved to be the catalyst for Chrysler. The automaker finally unleashed itself from its self-imposed no-racing policy and set about producing its first dedicated drag packages in preparation for the 1962 season.

When Ford Motor Company went racing in the 1960s, it did so on a massive scale. By 1964, the majority of its passenger cars were involved in some specific area of the sport. The Falcon contested European endurance rallies, the Fairlane and Mercury Comet focused on drag racing, and the Galaxie and Mercury Marauder were represented in NASCAR Grand National stock car racing. Ford supported Carroll Shelby's efforts with the cottage industry Cobra sports cars in both domestic and international GT racing. Ford was itself embarking upon its most ambitious racing program to date: the GT40 Le Mans project.

Ford didn't embark on its wildly expensive Le Mans venture because it wanted to sell GT40s. It wanted to showcase itself as a global heavy weight that could succeed in any discipline it set its sights on. The company wanted to display the qualities and durability of its products and their sporting attributes.

Yes, the program was a little emotionally charged too. Enzo Ferrari had agreed to sell his company to Ford so Ford could win the 24 Hours of Le Mans but withdrew at the eleventh hour. Ford, therefore, decided it would topple Ferrari from his perch by going to Le Mans with its own cars and beating "il Commendatore" in the very arena he'd made his own. However, a colossus like Ford doesn't make knee-jerk decisions. The GT40 project was both calculated and closely managed, and after the company won Le Mans in 1966 and again in 1967, it promptly withdrew. The point had been made.

Much like Ford, General Motors took a broad approach to its motorsport involvement. As well as its stock car and drag racing commitments, it also supported the Chevrolet Corvette in sports car racing. In 1963, however, General Motors promptly withdrew from the sport once more and opted instead to showcase its sporting qualities through its street cars. But while officially out of racing, unofficially, it couldn't afford to leave.

When the Sports Car Club of America (SCCA) launched the Trans-Am pony car series in 1966, the Ford Mustang won the coveted Manufacturers Championship (there was no Drivers Championship). The Mustang had been a game changer in the automotive world, ringing up record sales upon its launch in April 1964.

Ford commissioned Carroll Shelby to produce a fleet of special Mustang fastbacks aimed at tackling the small-block Corvette in SCCA B/Production sports car racing. After dominating the category with the Shelby GT350 in 1965, Ford turned its attentions to the new Trans-Am series in 1966. Chevrolet, in response to the Mustang, released its new Camaro pony car in September 1966 and immediately produced a small batch of special Z28 street cars brimming with the tools racers needed to take the model Trans-Am racing. It beat the Mustang.

Chrysler Returns to Motorsports

When Chrysler Corporation finally re-entered racing, it opted for a highly concentrated program: a two-pronged attack dedicated to drag racing and stock car racing. It did so with absolute unwavering intensity.

Chrysler's 1960s drag racing program celebrated a series of technically impressive factory race cars. Furthermore, the company was willing to adapt to the constantly moving target of the Stock drag racing regulations. Early ventures focused upon the larger, more conservative sedans, typifying the era for purely promoting the mechanical qualities of the brand.

Styling

As the decade trucked on, Chrysler's attention changed and so did the products representing it. There followed a switch to smaller, more compact bodystyles and sporty body shapes, notably its hardtop models with their fastback roof lines. Certainly, these were purely focused cars designed to win races, but more importantly, they carried a level of youthful styling that nailed the target market.

As well as a gradual shift to sporty pony and muscle cars, Chrysler also took advantage of some of the styling cues appearing on its factory-supported race cars and carried these across to its street cars: racing stripes, hood scoops, spoilers, and mag wheels. Furthermore, as its rivals produced bigger, heavier, and more lavish muscle cars that drifted further away from the original concept, Chrysler remained true to form, and its road cars carried a swagger and reputation that commanded respect on the street just as they did on the track.

Handicapping Chrysler in Racing

The introduction of the new NHRA Pro Stock formula in 1970 removed the need to produce highly specialized street cars to homologate for racing. But Chrysler still continued on its path of creating high-performance factory hot rods that transitioned into winning race cars. As such, it was victorious in the first two Pro Stock championships. Moreover, Chrysler dominated, winning 12 of the 15 national events throughout 1970 and 1971. Ultimately, the NHRA chose to intervene and imposed new weight-break rules for 1972 that canceled Chrysler's advantage and then some.

The original golden era of high-performance muscle cars was all but over by the early 1970s. It was forced to end by an impending energy crisis, crippling insurance premiums on high-performance cars, and new government-mandated anti-smog regulations. The final nail in the coffin arrived in the form of new frontal impact regulations that made upgrading many of the existing fleet simply unviable. By the mid-1970s, the American factory high-performance market was already dead and buried. Regardless, the 1960s and early 1970s produced a bevy of Chrysler factory drag cars and performance street cars that are some of the most coveted in today's collector car market.

The late 1970s and early 1980s were a grim time for the U.S. performance car industry, and the muscle car market had all but dissolved. Despite the severe restrictions imposed upon it, Chrysler Corporation was still a company of petrol heads who still loved to build fast and exciting cars. Indeed, its brash *Lil' Red Express Truck*, produced in small numbers in 1978 and 1979, was the fastest accelerating American-made vehicle at the time it was produced. It could out-accelerate a Corvette.

Chrysler engineers cottoned on to the fact the D150-based pickup could sidestep car emissions regulations and, as such, wasn't required to drudge around a catalytic converter. The market may have changed, but Chrysler engineers and marketers still loved fast cars.

The 1980s and early 1990s (as a whole) continued a low ebb for the American performance market. Chrysler still sought to add color to the grayness with products such as the unhinged but incredibly charismatic V-10-powered Dodge Viper and the completely outrageous Plymouth Prowler. But it wasn't until the Dodge Charger name was resurrected in 2006 and the Dodge Challenger returned in 2008 that Chrysler finally went full circle and tapped into the DNA of its 1960s racing roots. That it continues to produce wild, fast, and powerful examples of what are essentially family sedans "just because" has been a decision not just accepted by loyal Chrysler customers but also one that is wholeheartedly celebrated.

They say that to know where you're going, you need to know where you've come from. This is the story of Chrysler's factory drag racing in the 1960s.

CHAPTER 1

1924-1961

THE EMERGENCE OF PREWAR SPEEDWAY RACING

"Big" Bill France was the colossus that polished and repackaged the once-shady, down-and-dirty sport of stock car racing and delivered it to the masses, building a billion-dollar empire along the way. He was as opportunistic as he was savvy and ambitious. France was an old stock car racer who emerged from the gnarly bull ring dirt ovals, and he recognized a wealth of untapped potential in the sport that seemingly no one else had spotted.

Born in 1909, France spent his early years carving out a career as a race car driver, slinging a modified Model T around his local Baltimore-Washington Speedway, a hairy-chested 1.125-mile timber velodrome. His racing aspirations continued in 1935, when he moved his young family to Daytona, Florida, to escape the Great Depression and build a better life. He worked a series of odd jobs before finally opening a service station/automotive repair shop.

In 1936, France entered a local race for late-model, strictly stock cars that was promoted by Sig Haugdahl and contested on the freshly created Daytona Beach Course. The course was comprised of a simple 3.2-mile layout connecting a pair of long straights (one being a section of road running adjacent to the beach and the other a stretch of the beach itself) linked by a pair of tight 180-degree bends at each end.

Daytona Beach was a popular destination for speed events and benefitted from funding by a local council that viewed racing as a tourist attraction, and as such, it was eager to see high-profile contests take place. Indeed, eight consecutive world land speed records were set on Daytona Beach between 1927 and 1935.

France went on to finish fifth in that first Daytona Beach Race, claiming a healthy share of the rich $5,000 purse. The race itself was chaotic. The deep sand in the tight bends scuppered several competitors and soon resembled a car wrecking yard with carcasses piled high.

Financially, the event was a disaster, as the council lost a reported $22,000. Unphased, however, Haugdahl pushed ahead for a repeat performance in 1937, this time with France joining him at the controls. When the race lost money again, Haugdahl jumped ship, and France went it alone in 1938. In his first year at the helm, Daytona Beach hosted two events and expanded to a third in 1939. France's promotional commitments continued until 1942, when the Japanese invaded Pearl Harbor and the United States entered the war.

Even by 1961 full-sized Super Stock terms, the latest Dodge was a sizeable drag car. However, it was quick. Al Eckstrand drove the Ramchargers entrant all the way to the Mr. Stock Eliminator final at the 1961 NHRA U.S. Nationals. He chased "Dyno" Don Nicholson's Chevy across the stripe, but was ultimately awarded victory when Nicholson's car failed post-race inspection. This high-profile victory finally prompted Chrysler to wade into Super Stock drag racing with all its might. (Photo Courtesy David Rockwell)

Postwar Speedway Racing

France continued racing his own cars at local speedway events until peace finally resumed in 1945. At that time, he hung up his helmet and made the commitment to focus his energies purely on promotion. He ran events at the local Seminole Speedway before building the 0.9-mile Occoneechee Speedway in 1947 on the site where there once nestled a horse racing track.

France established the National Championship Stock Car Circuit (NCSCC) in late 1946, pouncing on the unruliness and disorganization that was rife throughout the sport and bringing some much-needed order. By organizing a racing series using a stable set of regulations that carried across all his events, France looked to assemble a field of unified drivers in a traveling road show. When the American Automobile Association (AAA) rejected his proposal for financial backing, he went it alone, cobbling together a $1,000 prize for the series winner.

The 1947 NCSCC series was contested over 40 events, starting on the Daytona sands in January and concluding in December in Jacksonville. Fonty Flock was declared the winner.

With the 1947 NCSCC series run and won, France brought together various racers, car owners, and mechanics and shared his grand plan for an organized racing group, involving universal rules, guaranteed appearance and prize money, and insurance coverage. At a time when disorder and dubious track promotion was commonplace in stock car racing, France's proposal could be seen as a shining beacon, a bright new future. He wanted to name the organization the National Stock Car Racing Association, but with this already taken by a rival sanctioning body, car builder Red Vogt suggested the National Association for Stock Car Auto Racing. NASCAR was formally founded in February 1948.

The Birth of NASCAR Grand National

For its first year, NASCAR catered to two divisions: Modifieds and open-wheel Roadsters. Modifieds were firmly established in a collection of guises among dirt tracks across America, and stringing together full grids was

"Suddenly it's 1960." That was the ad slogan promoting Chrysler's new Virgil Exner-designed 1957 models, which were said to be three years ahead of their time. Wally Parks and Ray Brock at Hot Rod *magazine thought it would be fun to attempt some record runs as part of an expansion of the NASCAR Daytona Beach event. Through their connections at Chrysler, they were loaned this brand-spanking-new Plymouth Savoy, and they rebuilt it with a Hilborn fuel-injected Hemi running on alcohol and producing 448 hp. In addition to other modifications,* Suddenly, *as the team called the car, recorded 153.453 mph with Parks at the wheel. On his return run, he reached 166.989 mph for an average of 160.175, which was a new class record. Then they took it to Bonneville, where, with Brock at the wheel,* Suddenly *hit 178 mph and was running 183 when the motor broke. Parks always had a soft spot for* Suddenly, *and 40 years later, the* Hot Rod *magazine crew had a replica built, which they ran on the salt in 1995. (Photo Courtesy Revs Institute/William Hewitt)*

easy pickings. However, France had grander ambitions. He wanted to grow NASCAR into a titan. He wanted to attract the automotive manufacturers and their money. To that end, a new category was established, catering to showroom stock cars—those to which the public could relate and those they themselves drove on the street. The new division, named Strictly Stock, was launched in 1949.

Stock car racing was not a new concept, and the stock car races held on Daytona Beach were not the first of their type. Indeed, in the early 1930s, a large B-shaped course was carved into the dirt (on which the Los Angeles Municipal Airport [now LAX] sits) created by William Hickman and funded by Earl Bell Gilmore of the famous Gilmore family. On this course, which was named the Mines Field Speedway, high-profile events for late-model stock cars were held, including 1932–1934 Ford and

Stock car racing made a popular, if brief, appearance at the temporary Mines Field Speedway, which is on the site where Los Angeles Municipal Airport now sits. With the fenders removed, Ford and Chrysler (car #32) roadsters battled on the dusty B-shaped track from 1932 to 1934. The cars were entered by dealerships, although the manufacturers also got involved. (Photo Courtesy Revs Institute/Bruce R. Craig)

Chrysler roadsters, bereft of fenders. The stock car races were big, drawing as many as 75,000 spectators.

During its formative years, NASCAR survived on the popularity of the feral Modifieds. The Roadster division bombed while Strictly Stock (rebranded as the Grand National in 1950) was slow to gather momentum. But France had a vision, and although popular with the fans, the Modifieds held limited long-term potential. Throughout the 1950s, the NASCAR Grand National series grew in stature as the manufacturers came one by one. Hudson was first to take the bait, but others ultimately followed.

1957 AMA No-Racing Policy

In 1957, France's path to world domination hit a speed hump when the major automotive manufacturers announced their plans to withdraw from racing. The agreed AMA racing ban went into effect in June.

While Ford upheld its part and stepped back, General Motors (through its Chevrolet, Pontiac, and Oldsmobile brands) remained involved. Indeed, even its sales catalogs continued to promote performance products.

While GM marques rode roughshod through the 1958 and 1959 NASCAR Grand National, Ford began to regret its decision to withdraw. But its desire to honor the AMA racing ban meant that if it were to return, it had to do so covertly. It had to project the image that Ford vehicles were so good, they could win without any factory assistance.

Daytona International Speedway

In February 1959, Bill France further added to Ford's no-racing dilemma with the unveiling of his colossal new Daytona International Speedway introduced to replace the chaotic beach course race. The monstrous superspeedway received prodigious media attention—this, in a pocket of the sport largely shunned by the press.

In 1953, France met with Daytona Beach engineer Charles Moneypenny to discuss his ambitious plans for the biggest and fastest racetrack in the world. He wanted stock car racing to hit the giddy heights and speeds previously only seen in Indy car racing. Moneypenny approached Ford Motor Company, which provided him reports on the design and construction of its high-banked Ford Proving Grounds test track in Michigan. France, meanwhile, was busy hustling, pulling together the vast sums of money required to fund the project, which extended well north of $600,000.

Ground was first broken in 1957, and the inaugural Daytona 500 Stock Car race at the epic 2.5-mile structure took place on February 22, 1959, in front of an audience of 42,000 astonished race fans. With the opening of Daytona International Speedway, France now had three prominent paved Grand National events: the Daytona 500, the Rebel 500 at Darlington, and the Charlotte 600. Most other Grand National races were still contested on the ballistic little dirt ovals.

The Crown Jewels

In 1960, the NASCAR Grand National totaled 42 events plus an additional two qualifying races at Daytona. The season began in November 1959 and concluded the following October. Chevrolet driver Rex White emerged as the champion.

But for most teams, and more so for the manufacturers, victory in the Daytona 500, Rebel 500, and Charlotte 600 carried more weight than winning the Grand National. Indeed, many of the top teams didn't actually run the full schedule. They focused on the races attracting the most media attention, the biggest crowds, and the richest prize purses. It just so happened that Daytona, Darlington, and Charlotte were the fastest tracks.

To win the big races in the NASCAR Grand National, manufacturers were required to build the fastest and most powerful cars. The push to win these races meant that factory engines became larger. The manufacturers began producing low-volume specials aimed purely at achieving success in the big NASCAR races. The growing success of NASCAR had Ford back on the hook. While this was good for NASCAR Grand National, it also produced an unlikely benefactor.

The Ramchargers, a team of engineers working for Plymouth, spent its weekends at the drag strip. Having raced their own cars, the individuals on the team pooled their resources in the late 1950s to build a heavily modified 1949 Plymouth named The High & Mighty. *Among its extensive list of unique features was a Chrysler Hemi above which towered a pair of 4-barrel carburetors mounted atop a tall intake manifold that fed the cylinder banks via eight long runners. In addition, the old Plymouth sported a chopped roof and shortened frame over which the body was slid forward, resulting in the driver sharing cabin space with the Hemi. (Photo Courtesy John Hellmuth)*

Before Arnie "the Farmer" Beswick became synonymous with Pontiac, he campaigned a pair of potent Coronets. The D-500 (left) and D-501 (right) were Hemi Dodge offerings for a hard-core performance enthusiast. Beswick found great success with them when they weren't broken down. (Photo Courtesy Arnie Beswick)

"Dyno" Don Nicholson has good reason to smile. He and his Chevy Impala scooped up most of the big national trophies in 1961. (Photo Courtesy Doug Boyce)

Stock Car Drag Racing's Popularity Boom

While stock car racing grew in stature during the 1950s, so did drag racing. Crowds packed into drag strips across the country every weekend to watch in awe at the bravery and bravado of those piloting a variety of sling-shot dragsters. The dragsters were, of course, the headline act. They were the fastest cars in existence, and they were shattering records continuously. But almost as popular were the Gassers and whacky short-wheelbase Altereds. Every single car was a technical marvel, and each completely bespoke an extension of its creator's wildest imagination and budget.

At the other end of the spectrum were the Stock class cars, which were the showroom street machines. The Stock cars were regularly the most prominent for pure numbers at any given event. It was common for their ranks to swell up past 100 cars. But many fans of 1950s drag racing viewed the Stock cars as an opportunity to go grab a hot dog or avail themselves of the conveniences. The great majority of race fans didn't attend a drag racing event to see the Stock cars. That all changed in 1961, with the emergence of Super Stock with its headline-grabbing races and increasingly intensive factory involvement.

The big two NHRA events of 1961 were the Winternationals at Pomona, California, in February and the National Championships (U.S. Nationals) at Indianapolis Raceway Park in early September. It was here that the factory-supported heavy hitters from General Motors and Ford truly strutted their stuff. Suddenly, everyone stood up and took notice of Stock-based drag racing.

With more than 60 percent of the competition at any given event coming from the Stock classes (the 1961 Winternationals Stock entries had to be closed at 200 cars), the NHRA was keen to boost the profile of this segment. Of course, it was not lost on the NHRA that, just as in the NASCAR Grand National, here was a class that was obviously benefitting from increased manufacturer involvement. It was something that needed to be nurtured.

1961 NHRA Winternationals

At the 1961 Winternationals, in front of 40,000 race fans on Sunday, NHRA Field Director Ed Eaton devised a plan to parade the top 50 cars, running in pairs side-by-side

Long before it entered drag racing in an official capacity, Chrysler marketing was already onboard with using motorsport events as a means to promote its products. Here at the 1959 NHRA Nationals at Detroit Dragway, Chrysler displays a new 1960 Plymouth Sonoramic Commando motor with long-ram intake manifold. (Photos Courtesy John Hellmuth)

from the shut-off end. A similar spectacle had been organized at the National Championships in 1960. *Hot Rod* magazine wrote of the procession in its event coverage: "During this parade, a wild and spontaneous ovation erupted from the crowd for favorites they recognized. The frenzy that followed was enough to keep any drag enthusiast, or just an interested passerby, on the edge of his seat."

Factory performance engines from Ford and Chevrolet were now hovering around the 400-hp mark. Pontiac, previously the high-water mark, was suddenly feeling the heat. The Pomona drag strip had been resurfaced prior to the Winternationals in an effort to help the dragsters reach new speeds. And the trickle-down effect was benefitting all the classes.

Earlier in the weekend, the top Fords and Chevys were knocking out passes at more than 105 mph with high-13-second elapsed times (ETs), which was impressive enough. Then, "Dyno" Don Nicholson blasted his 409 bubble-top Chevy through the traps at more than 108 mph with a low-13-second ET, and the crowd went berserk. Saturday saw an all-Chevy affair in the Super Stock finals with Nicholson going up against Frank Sanders in the Rudolph Chevrolet entry. Sanders's Chevy (incidentally, tuned by Nicholson) narrowly took the win. Bill Paterson, in another Chevy, took top honors in A/Stock.

Mr. Stock Eliminator

On the Sunday, and with the record crowd whipped up to fever pitch, the battle for the Mr. Stock Eliminator kicked off. This epic race, which combined all the Stock classes together, saw the big field face off against one another in two-by-two action, whittling the entry down until only the two fastest cars remained.

Having taken out the 1961 Ford of Les Ritchey in the semifinals, Don Nicholson once again faced Frank Sanders in the final. From the start, Nicholson bolted out of the hole and held a narrow lead down the track, crossing the line ahead.

Away from the headline-grabbing Super Stock and Mr. Stock Eliminator features, there were a handful of Chrysler pilots quietly achieving some good things of their own. Sheldon Lowrie took the honors in D/SA with his Plymouth, running a 14.66 at 94.33 mph, while Larry Burnett abord a Dodge claimed victory in G/SA with a winning 17.01 at 82.34 mph. Certainly, it was not enough to garner a photo in any of the main media outlets but something to celebrate nonetheless.

Suddenly, the Stock classes were the darlings of drag racing. The crowds were immensely enthusiastic, and the top drivers emerged as heroes. The investments made by General Motors and Ford in both NASCAR Grand National and in drag racing was now paying for itself.

1961 NHRA U.S. Nationals

At the NHRA U.S. Nationals in September, the Stockers were again the starring act. Hayden Proffitt came out swinging in Mickey Thompson's Pontiac followed closely by Nicholson as the cars made their first passes on Friday. These full-sized behemoths both looked and sounded superb. Proffitt went on to win Optional/Super Stock, while Arnie Beswick, in another of the Pontiacs, won Super Stock. Ford driver Don Turner took Optional/Stock Automatic.

Mr. Stock Eliminator

For Monday's action, as was now a tradition, the top 50 Stock cars made their two-by-two parade run prior to Mr. Stock Eliminator. Proffitt took himself out of the competition during eliminations, while Al Eckstrand in the 1961 Ramchargers Dodge met Don Nicholson in the final.

Eckstrand had shifter trouble in the big Dodge, and Nicholson reached the line first. However, on teardown, the Chevy was revealed to have a list of illegalities and was subsequently disqualified from the event.

Of the extensive 28 different Stock classes competing at the 1961 U.S. Nationals, the vast majority saw a Ford or a GM product roll into victory circle. But they didn't have it all their own way. Sure, Eckstrand scooped the big one, but a fleet of lesser-known Mopar campaigners also went home winners. Frank Dade won A/Stock with his 1961 Dodge, Charles Cross won H/S with his 1960 Valiant, and Ray Christian won A/SA with his 1960 Plymouth. Certainly, the Ford, Chevy, and Pontiac racers in the commanding Super Stock ranks were benefitting from a healthy dose of factory involvement.

Eckstrand's successes in the Mr. Stock Eliminator competitions were rare highlights in an era of relative anonymity for Chrysler Corporation in both the NASCAR Grand National and in Super Stock drag racing. The lure of parading the qualities and sporting capabilities of its products in front of tens of thousands of buzzing race fans was too much for the company to ignore. Shortly after the conclusion of the 1961 NHRA Nationals, Chrysler launched into a racing program that transformed the very nature of its image into that of a performance powerhouse, not just during the 1960s but forevermore.

Chrysler Corporation's Formative Years

Quality engineering and affordable performance were virtues that stood at the core of the Chrysler Corporation when the company was first founded by Walter Chrysler from the reorganization of the ailing Maxwell

In 1925, two Chrysler 70s entered the Le Mans 24 Hours race in just the third time the French epic took place. The Chryslers were entered by Grand Garage Saint-Didier Paris. Of the two, this car, driven by Henri Stoffel and Lucien Desvaux, was the only one to start the race. Although running at the finish, various delays deemed it hadn't completed enough laps to be classified. Regardless, this was the first American car to compete in the famous French classic. (Photo Courtesy Revs Institute/Albert R. Bochroch)

Motor Company in 1925. Within five years, Chrysler had introduced its Plymouth and DeSoto brands and purchased the Dodge Brothers company. As such, it carefully positioned each of its marques within the clearly defined American automotive class system.

Throughout its early history, Chrysler achieved a number of automotive breakthroughs. Indeed, its very first offering, the Chrysler Model 70, was the first medium-priced American car fitted with a high-compression (4.7:1) motor and four-wheel hydraulic brakes. Production of the Model 70 actually began in 1924 before Chrysler Corporation was officially formed. Ralph de Palma delivered early Chrysler racing success by driving a Model 70 to overall victory in the 1924 Mt. Wilson Hill Climb.

Improving the Breed through Racing

Chrysler was quick to embrace motor racing as a tool for promoting the performance and engineering qualities of its products. In 1925, two Chrysler Model 70s were entered in the 24 Hours of Le Mans race by French Chrysler agent Grand Garage Saint-Didier Paris. Therefore, Chrysler Model 70 became the first American car to compete at La Sarthe. Three years later, Grand Garage Saint-Didier Paris guided a pair of the latest Chrysler 72s to third- and fourth-place finishes.

Creation of the Mopar Brand

In 1937, the name MOPAR (MOtor PARts), which was already used internally within the company, launched as an official brand name for parts and accessories. It all started with its revolutionary antifreeze product, which became Mopar Antifreeze.

Enter the Hemi

Throughout the 1930s and 1940s, Chrysler continued to excel in its engineering achievements. In 1951, its top-of-the-line Saratoga, New Yorker, and Imperial models bristled with the impressive new 331-ci V-8 with overhead valves and hemispherical-shaped combustion chambers. The Chrysler Hemi had nearly 40 hp more than the executive Cadillac and Oldsmobile models from rival General Motors.

Chrysler in NASCAR Grand National

Naturally, with the emergence of stock-based racing that was spearheaded by the new NASCAR Grand National, racing teams gravitated toward the powerful Chrysler. Privateer Oldsmobiles won the Grand National from 1949 to 1951 before Hudson arrived as the first manufacturer to shove its weight behind the series. Hudson then proceeded to dominate the championship, taking the lion's share of victories over the next two years. Hudson drivers Tim Flock and Herb Thomas emerged as the Grand National Champions in 1952 and 1953.

Lee Petty finally toppled the Hudson juggernaut in 1954 and recorded the first NASCAR Grand National championship for Chrysler. The Petty name would become synonymous with the Chrysler brand, but Lee's crown was achieved with no notable manufacturer support. Indeed, his was a low-budget campaign carved out through consistency rather than pure speed.

At odds with Petty's modest program was millionaire Carl Kiekhaefer's 1955 operation. Founder and owner of Kiekhaefer Marine (later Mercury Marine), the hard-nosed businessman was not a motor racing enthusiast. However, he noted the number of fans turning up to watch NASCAR races and figured this to be a good outlet to promote his business. Indeed, he was no stranger to racing. He'd entered a pair of Chrysler Saratogas driven by Tony Bettenhausen and John Fitch in the 1951 La Carrera Panamericana, the crazy Mexican endurance road race. He returned in 1953, this time with a pair of Chrysler New Yorkers.

Kiekhaefer waded into the 1955 season, spending money at will. He had a fleet of the latest Chrysler C-300s prepared with the best parts and people available. He chose the Chrysler because, quite simply, this was the best and most powerful car on the market. Kiekhaefer arrived at the Daytona Beach Race with a car and no driver but convinced recently retired Tim Flock out of retirement for the princely sum of $40,000. Flock won on debut, and then went on a winning spree, claiming 18 victories from 38 starts, and ended the 1955 season as Grand National Champion.

Flock won three Grand Nationals early in the 1956 season, including Daytona, before he and Kiekhaefer fell out

Resting on the Daytona sands prior to the 1956 Daytona Beach Race is the fleet of Chrysler C-300s owned by millionaire Carl Kiekhaefer. The owner of Kiekhaefer Marine, better known as Mercury Marine, Kiekhaefer entered six cars in the race, and the 300-A driven by Tim Flock took the win. The mid-1950s was a time of total domination in NASCAR Grand National for Chrysler products. (Photo Courtesy Revs Institute/Tom Burnside)

and parted ways. Kiekhaefer entered multiple cars at most events, including one for Buck Baker, who was emerging as a contender. Baker went on to take 14 victories on his way to winning the 1956 NASCAR Grand National.

Kiekhaefer's team thundered aggressively through the NASCAR Grand National, showing up to each event with his immaculate race cars strapped to a trailer towed by a box truck packed to the gunnels with spare parts, wheels, tires, and tools. He tested at the tracks, took dirt samples of the surface, and even hired a weather specialist to check conditions so that his cars could be fitted with the right tires. This was done at a time when many of his rivals flat-towed their cars to the track on an A-frame or simply drove them.

Bill France was not amused. He had carefully constructed his kingdom through a controlled management style, but he couldn't control Kiekhaefer. He had Kiekhaefer's cars torn down at every opportunity, but no irregularities were found.

France and Kiekhaefer weren't particularly fond of one another. In the end, France got his way and the millionaire left. But it wasn't so much because of anything that France did. Such was the devastation with which Kiekhaefer's armory ripped through the Grand National that people just got tired of seeing the rich guy's team win everything. They started booing his cars and even threw bottles at them. Kiekhaefer entered the Grand

National to promote his business and to sell his outboard motors, but the lack of respect displayed by the fans was not what he'd bargained for. His investment had backfired.

Kiekhaefer's departure coincided with the ramped-up efforts of Ford and General Motors in 1957. Both manufacturers recognized the sales potential within the growing sport and the benefits awarded to the manufacturer whose products were unquestionably faster and tougher than those of their competitors.

Despite the AMA no-racing policy agreed to by the manufacturers in early 1957, the momentum had already swung. Indeed, Ford went on to take 26 victories, Chevrolet 21, Oldsmobile 4, and Pontiac 2. While Chrysler, champion of the last 3 years, didn't score a single win.

Chrysler again went winless in 1958, while Lee Petty achieved seven victories in 1959, having switched from Dodge in 1956, to Oldsmobile in 1957, and finally to Plymouth after 19 races in 1959. Between them, Lee and his young son Richard scored eight victories in 1960 and three in 1961. The Pettys were winning the smaller races often in the absence of the heavily funded factory teams from Ford and General Motors.

Junior Johnson's Chevy won the 1960 Daytona 500, Joe Lee Johnson's Chevy won the Charlotte 600, and Buck Baker's Pontiac won the Rebel 500 at Darlington. Marvin Panch won the big one at Daytona in 1961 driving Smokey Yunick's Pontiac, while David Pearson's Pontiac won the Charlotte 600, and Ford driver Nelson Stacy took an impressive victory in the Rebel 500.

Chrysler Corporation, of course, became profusive in its approach to 1960s stock car and drag racing. But in late 1961, when it finally got serious, the company was starting on the back foot.

Lee Petty (#42) and his son Richard, sandwich Banjo Matthews's Thunderbird in their Petty Enterprises Savoys during the 1960 Daytona 500, which was the second running of the race on the new superspeedway. Petty Jr. was in just his third season in the Grand National, and he would go on to become the all-time most successful NASCAR driver with much of his success achieved aboard a Plymouth. Here at the 1960 Daytona 500, he finished third while the old man trailed home one spot behind. (Photo Courtesy Revs Institute/Tom Burnside)

THE 413 MAX WEDGE TAKES CHRYSLER DRAG RACING

"Big Daddy" Don Garlits (left) was a Top Fuel pioneer who occasionally did a little Super Stock racing. Among the displays in his incredible Museum of Drag Racing is a 1962 Max Wedge Dodge. (Photo Courtesy Don Garlits Collection)

Chrysler launched its initiative for a 1962 drag racing assault shortly after the conclusion of the 1961 NHRA National Championships at Indy. The new drag racing program was part of a much larger strategy spearheaded by Chrysler president Lynn Townsend to introduce a more youthful and performance-focused identity for the company.

Chrysler's 1962 Intermediates

Concurrently, Chrysler was also in the throes of downscaling several of its models for 1962, including the Dodge Dart and Polara and the Plymouth Belvedere, Fury, and Savoy. These models were reduced in wheelbase from 118 to 116 inches with an overall length reduction of around 7.5 inches. The trimming of bulk also benefitted in a sizeable weight loss of up to 300 pounds depending on the model. Sadly, the shedding of inches and pounds didn't result in a more sporty, svelte silhouette. In fact, quite the opposite was true.

The drastic changes were the outcome of a misunderstanding prompted by Chrysler executive vice president William C. Newberg. While attending a garden party of automotive bigwigs in 1960, he overheard Chevrolet's Ed Cole talking to a companion about his company's plans to introduce a midsized model for 1962. Newberg, only weeks into his new role, was convinced Cole's reference related to the full-size Impala. In fact, Cole had been talking about the new compact Nova.

The late 1950s and early 1960s spawned widespread uncertainty within the automotive industry as to the market's future direction. The belief that compact cars were the way forward was gathering traction; the era of extravagant land yachts was nearing an end.

Chrysler, its styling department headed by the celebrated Virgil Exner, was well advanced in composing its 1962 designs. By all accounts, they were typical Exner creations: bold and groundbreaking. With Newberg now second-guessing his company's direction, he immediately ordered the downscaling of Chrysler's fleet to match the route he perceived the market was now heading. Upon Newberg's directive, wholesale changes were implemented.

Further adding to the carnage was the financial predicament Chrysler found itself in following a late-1950s recession, which greatly impacted new-car sales. Indeed, the impossibly tight timeframe didn't allow for a fully committed redesign and neither did the puny budget.

Therefore, the 1962 B-Body models were based on a stretched version of the compact Valiant platform. Various styling themes from the planned Exner models were awkwardly shoehorned in it to fit. The end results were not well received. An enraged Exner famously referred to them as "plucked chickens."

Perhaps unfairly, Exner was relieved of his position. His designs had invariably polarized opinions. His 1961 styling creations had drawn public and media criticism particularly on the full-size models with reversed fins, rear fender scallops, and a concave grille. The taillights were likened to ingrown toenails. Controversial as his designs might have been, the haphazard 1962 results could not be laid at his doorstep.

Ironically, the downsized models tended to lend themselves better to Lynn Townsend's inspiration for the company's youth performance image overhaul. The reduced heft ultimately benefited Chrysler's new competition programs, including its upcoming initiative in the fast-accelerating Super Stock drag racing phenomenon.

While the 1962 styling drew mixed reactions, Chrysler's intermediate B-Body offerings were actually very good cars beneath the surface, boasting several improvements over their 1961 counterparts. The chassis was of

RAM INDUCTION

When the RB-Block first appeared in 1959, it was fitted to Chrysler 300s, New Yorkers, and Imperials. With its raised deck producing an increased stroke (from 3.18 to 3.75 inches), its intention was that of a torque-monster designed to effortlessly propel the significant mass of Chrysler's substantial land yachts that were encroaching 5,500 pounds fully laden. But in 1960, Chrysler began offering its latest technical (and aesthetical) masterpiece: the Ram Induction (branded as the Sonoramic Commando on Plymouths and the D-500 Ram Induction on Dodges) as a performance option.

The Ram Induction was an extravagant cross-ram system incorporating a pair of long-tube aluminum runners (one for each cylinder bank of the V-8) each with a Carter AFB 4-barrel carburetor mounted at either end, feeding the system. The air-fuel charge that builds when the intake valve closes can be greatly increased if the length of the intake passage is itself increased at the engine's desired operating RPM.

Chrysler had been experimenting with various competition themes on the Ram Induction system for years. One option was a beautiful ram-horn setup fitted to a 331-ci Hemi in the early 1950s for a planned Indianapolis 500 assault that never happened.

Several years later, in 1959, a group of Chrysler engineers with a passion for drag racing built its own race car as an after-hours project. The club called itself the Ramchargers, and its creation was an eccentric and quite ungainly looking 1949 Plymouth fitted with a Chrysler Hemi. The low-buck enterprise was designed for C/Altered competition.

Dubbed *The High & Mighty*, the captivating old Plymouth sported a chopped roof and shortened frame while the body was slid forward on the chassis, resulting in the back half of the Hemi imposing itself inside the driver's compartment. Its two most distinctive features were its blunderbuss megaphone exhaust system (four pipes exploding out through C-cuts above the front wheel openings) and its impossibly tall intake with an aluminum hat cramming gobs of air to a pair of 4-barrel carburetors that then fed the cylinder banks via eight long runners. The concept was similar to the Ram Induction system that would find its way onto Chrysler production cars, only without the limitations of having to fit it beneath the factory hood.

The new Ram Induction system, including carburetors, spanned 4 feet, and with its 30- to 31-inch-long runners (the length arrived at after intensive research). Chrysler claimed a performance improvement of 10 percent was achieved. The sinewy long ram greatly improved torque, which aided Chrysler's full-size leviathans to waft along effortlessly, providing greatly improved driving quality. The added torque resulting from the long-ram setup also proved to be a benefit in NASCAR Grand National stock car racing.

However, stock car racing and drag racing are two completely different monsters. The 1962 Maximum Performance Wedge 413 motor, therefore, didn't feature the long ram. Instead, it employed much shorter runners with two Carter carburetors mounted diagonally on a large cross-ram intake manifold.

The Max Wedge had been blossoming since 1959. Indeed, Chrysler product planning engineer Tom Hoover headed its development. Hoover was a key member of the Ramchargers club. The short-ram system was found to produce better top-end horsepower. The intake runners were virtually half that of the long-ram system, at 15 inches.

unibody design, whereas the 1961 models featured a separate front subframe. The unibody construction provided greater body rigidity. Front suspension was an independent arrangement with torsion bars (Torsion-Aire) and hydraulic tube shocks, while leaf springs and hydraulic tube shocks suspended the rear end. Brakes were four-wheel drums measuring 10x2.5 inches, although cars equipped with the Pursuit Package were equipped with 11-inch drums.

Upon launch in September 1961, standard engine choices for the new 1962 Dodge and Plymouth models ranged from a 225-ci Slant 6 to a 361-ci V-8 based on the B-Series block producing 310 hp with a single 4-barrel carburetor. A special order high-performance 389 based on the B-Series block produced 325 hp with a 4-barrel carburetor and twin exhausts or 330 hp with the long-ram intake. But much more was to come.

The First Max Wedge

In May 1962, Chrysler unleashed its new 413-ci Maximum Performance Wedge motor, which was aimed specifically at thrusting the company to the forefront of Super Stock drag racing. The 413 Max Wedge used Chrysler's RB-Block. The RB was a raised-deck evolution of the B-Block, itself introduced in 1958 as Chrysler sought to phase out the Hemi, which had been in production since 1951.

While a masterpiece of engineering, the Hemi, with its domed combustion chambers and splayed valves, was both complex and expensive to produce. The performance advantages it enjoyed early in its production had wilted by the late 1950s, despite continual capacity increases over its original 331-ci configuration.

The B-Block followed a more conventional wedge-shaped combustion chamber with its intake and

Chrysler's 1962 Super Stock package was all business and strictly bare bones. (Photos Courtesy Geoff Stunkard Collection)

exhaust valves arranged in a line. Its greatest appeal to Chrysler was that it was cheaper to produce than the Hemi but without any loss in performance. Indeed, torque figures actually increased. Upon launch, the B-Block was installed in DeSoto and Dodge models.

Two heavy-duty variations of the 413 were available to order. One was listed under sales code 500, and it had an 11:1 compression ratio, producing 410 hp at 5,400 rpm and 460 ft-lbs of torque at 4,400 rpm. The second, listed under sales code 509, had a 13.5:1 compression ratio, punching out 420 hp at 5,400 rpm and 470 ft-lbs of torque at 4,400 rpm.

The cylinder head design differed from that of the regular RB motor and featured 25-percent-larger ports and bigger valves. A high-lift camshaft was used, along with double valve springs, forged connecting rods, forged pistons, and a baffled oil pan.

The 413 Max Wedge came equipped with a set of superb upswept exhaust headers that not only helped the big motor breathe to its best ability but also were themselves simply a joyful sight to behold.

The Max Wedge was available as an option only on the B-Body Dodges and Plymouths. The Dodge variant was named the Ramcharger 413, while the Plymouth was, most appropriately, the Super Stock 413. New-for-1962 NHRA rules required the cars competing in the Super Stock division be actual factory-produced stock cars. Therefore, the engines used in the race cars had to be installed on a manufacturer's assembly line. Cars couldn't sport magical over-the-counter racing parts that weren't true production items. However, there was still a place for such creations within the NHRA ranks: the new Factory Experimental (FX) class.

The year 1962 also marked the release of Chrysler's latest variant of its trademarked TorqueFlite automatic: the meaty new 3-speed A-727. The A-727 featured stronger internals plus an aluminum case, providing a weight savings of 60 pounds more than the previous TorqueFlite. Buyers could also opt for a 4-speed manual transmission, but this unit wasn't tough enough for drag racing purposes.

Of course, the Max Wedge 413 was completely impractical on the street. It was purely a drag racing engine. However, Super Stock regulations required that the cars raced on the track had to be factory stock and available to be ordered at any dealership like any other factory production car. Super Stock rules were stringent and teams had to work with what the manufac-

turer produced. This ensured, therefore, that the race cars were only as good as the street cars. As such, success on the track was directly linked to each manufacturer's level of commitment. Thus, a golden era of drag racing began that inspired the creation of some of the most brutal factory hot rods in history.

1962 Drag Racing Highlights

Ultimately, the Max Wedge was given life so that Chrysler could win on the track. Therefore, its success was dictated by its achievements in Super Stock drag racing. Beyond the charisma of the Max Wedge, its brutal cross-ram intake and its sweeping headers, the bottom line for Chrysler was to sell more cars. This is the reason any manufacturer enters the world of motor racing.

1962 Super Stock Regulations

Despite the name, teams running in the Stock divisions were allowed to make a select number of changes to their cars for the sake of performance and common sense. Cylinders could be bored 0.060 inch, engines could be balanced, the clutch and flywheel could be replaced by items offered over the counter by the same manufacturer, provided they were of the same weight. Exhaust systems could be subjected to limited changes, and traction bars could be installed.

The 1962 NHRA Super Stock rules used a sliding-scale power-to-weight ratio of 9.59 pounds for every advertised horsepower. Did the manufacturers really advertise the true horsepower of their performance cars?

As the manufacturers began involving themselves in Stock drag racing, a variety of mystery parts began appearing on select cars. The manufacturers claimed these components could be ordered over the counter or were due to be installed on next year's cars, but invariably, they weren't. They were essentially experimental parts that

Roger Westberg's Jolly Roger *Super Stock Automatic Plymouth, out of Salem, New Jersey, gets pulled to the line to face an Impala at York U.S. 30 Drag-O-Way in 1962. (Photo Courtesy Geoff Stunkard Collection/Kramer Automotive Archive)*

were produced in very small numbers and gifted to the teams closely associated with each manufacturer.

For 1962, however, the cars were required to be truly stock. That meant the parts on the race cars had to be available on the street cars as they rolled off the assembly line. Several cars in 1961 sported non-factory hood scoops or flexible ram-tubing feeding the carburetors, but in 1962, these were strictly prohibited.

Wheel and tire rules were relatively relaxed and only required that they fit within the factory wheel wells. The tires had to be treaded, and magnesium wheels weren't allowed.

In the name of safety, a heavy-duty pressure plate or flywheel could be installed, and these items became mandatory in the Factory Experimental class. In addition, for the first time, safety belts were a requirement.

1962 NHRA Winternationals

The midyear introduction of the Max Wedge ensured Chrysler teams were missing in action at the first big NHRA event of 1962: the second running of the Winternationals at Pomona. The 1962 Winternationals boasted 26 Stock classes, extending through to the screaming 6-cylinder Chevrolet Corvairs running in J/Stock. But the headliner was the emerging Super Stock ranks.

By 1962, the Super Stock division had become big business, and it was attracting both manufacturer money and professional racers. The Stock cars were no longer the hot dog and fries class of drag racing. Now, the punters were completely captivated. Indeed, *Motor Trend* magazine, in its review of the 1962 Winternationals, opened with the headline: "Stockers Steal the Show."

Nearly 39,000 fans packed the Pomona facility in February 1962 to soak up the action and drama, living the emotional highs and lows with the teams and drivers that were providing the entertainment. Of the 26 Stock classes, Chevrolet emerged as the big winner, taking 10 victories, followed by Pontiac with 9. Ford, Buick, and Dodge trailed with 2 apiece, and Oldsmobile scored just a solitary win.

The Super Stocks (or Super-Super/ Stocks as some were now calling them) were the headline act. Hayden Proffitt highlighted the growing significance of the Stock car division by switching from his ballistic dual Chevy-powered (with twin superchargers) A/Dragster to Pontiac's factory Super Stock program in 1960. He beat all comers in Saturday's action.

Dick Landy was an early Chrysler recruit when the company got serious about drag racing in 1962. Although "Dandy" Dick would become forever linked with Dodge, his first factory Mopar was a Plymouth. (Photo Courtesy Geoff Stunkard Collection/Landy Family Archive)

Proffitt, who worked for Mickey Thompson, was aboard a self-tuned 421-ci Pontiac Catalina. He faced off against the 409-ci Chevy of Dave Strickler in the SS/S finals on Saturday, pulling off a barnstorming 12.37 at 116.27-mph run to take the victory.

In Sunday's Mr. Stock Eliminator contest for the fastest 50 Stock cars at the meet, Proffitt didn't make the final. Instead, it was the pair of white 409 Chevys of Strickler and the bespectacled "Dyno" Don Nicholson that were the only cars still standing after all the eliminations had been fought. Nicholson cut a dynamite start and held a slight margin right down the chute. The two big bubble-top Chevys with their thunderous open headers had the massive crowd in raptures. Nicholson's race-winning 12.84 at 109.22 mph made for a joyous trip home, complete with a sky-scraping trophy and a color TV.

1962 NHRA U.S. Nationals

The May release of Chrysler's big 413 Max Wedge drag motor package put the factory GM and Ford teams on notice.

Although this photo takes place at York U.S. 30, the Ramchargers' 1962 Dodge was runner-up to Hayden Proffitt's Chevrolet at the U.S. Nationals. (Photo Courtesy Geoff Stunkard Collection/Kramer Automotive Archive)

THE RAMCHARGERS

It was perhaps the greatest team name in all of drag racing and almost certainly the most famous and recognizable. The Ramchargers was a group of 1957 graduates from Chrysler Institute that enjoyed racing cars on the street and the track. Given they worked together and shared a common passion, in 1958 they formed an NHRA-sanctioned Hot Rod Club, a common theme among young hot rodders and drag racers at the time.

Early members of the club, which totaled about 25 people, included Tom Hoover, Dan Mancini, Jim Thornton, Richard E. Maxwell, Dan Knapp, Tom Coddington, and Herman Mozer, among others. In 1959, they decided to focus their energies and build a car together rather than race a fleet of individual cars.

They decided on a 1949 Plymouth that they modified to extreme measures, including a chopped roof and a shortened frame upon which the body was slid forward. It was powered by a Chrysler Hemi, which ended up sharing cabin space with the driver due to the body being moved forward. It sported a mad-looking megaphone exhaust system with four pipes bursting out each side through the front wheel openings. Meanwhile, the Hemi carried a pair of 4-barrel carburetors mounted atop a tall intake manifold, feeding the cylinder banks via eight long runners. It was initially named the *Ram Rod* but very soon became *The High & Mighty* (after a John Wayne movie).

As the team began enjoying success with *The High & Mighty*, Dodge public relations became interested in improving the sporting image of the company. Although they talked to Plymouth also, Plymouth wasn't too interested in racing. Thus, the Ramchargers would forever be synonymous with Dodge.

The Ramchargers began racing in the Stock division before Chrysler officially entered the sport. But as Chrysler waded in, the Ramchargers were at the epicenter of development. They spearheaded the company's successes on the track. By 1964, not only were the Ramchargers the top dogs among the Dodge and Plymouth contingent but they were also claiming a good portion of all the Super Stock silverware.

Although considered a factory race team, there was little if any money trickling down the pipe from Chrysler. Certainly, cars and parts were a given, including the latest developments, but the Ramchargers afforded its racing through sponsorship, and the bigger partnerships came from Chrysler dealers. Hodges Dodges of Ferndale, Michigan, appeared on several Ramchargers cars.

This beautiful photo of the Ramchargers' Dodge fully illustrates exactly what a drag car should look like in 1962. It was very common to see the rears of the car slung low to the ground to gain traction at launch. (Photo Courtesy Clinton Wright)

As the altered-wheelbase and A/FX cars began gaining popularity from 1965, the Ramchargers went in that direction. The group was also at ground level during the birth of the Funny Car phenomenon before it was an official class. In addition, the team began racing a Top Fuel slingshot dragster in 1966 and focused much of its attention there throughout the next three years.

In 1970, the NHRA officially recognized the Funny Car division and positioned it as one of its three top-drawer classes for its new Super Season along with Top Fuel and Pro Stock. With that, the Ramchargers focused their attention on Funny Car racing with a Dodge Challenger. The last car to carry Ramchargers sponsorship was a 1970 Plymouth 'Cuda Super Stock built by Ramcharger Dean Nicopolis and campaigned by him from 1974 through 1997.

The Ramchargers name was trademarked in 1970 (officially Ramchargers Racing Engines Inc.) and was developed into a brand that became a business enterprise supplying performance engines and aftermarket parts.

From 1958 through 2004, there were 48 Ramchargers members in total—plus another 10 or so who were also actively involved with the group in some form.

As for the name, they initially called themselves the Ram Chargers. Ram referred to Chrysler's 1931 radiator emblem, on "ram tuning" or "charging," and to propel straight ahead at speed. It was intended to be two separate words, but it's believed an early typo mashed the two words into one, and it stuck.

The 1962 NHRA National Championship Drags at Indianapolis Raceway Park pitted all the big factory squads against one another. There were 60,000 fans in attendance. With General Motors maneuvering Pontiac out of racing, Hayden Proffitt had switched to a 409 Chevy for Indy, joining the similar cars of Nicholson and Strickler at the head of the SS/S division.

Chrysler entries, as expected, were strong and included the Ramchargers club, Al Eckstrand, Bill "Maverick" Golden, Bud Faubel, and countless others. Indeed, even *Hot Rod* magazine entered its own 413 Max Wedge Plymouth. The top Chrysler entries contested the SS/SA class.

With so much at stake, and with increased factory money and participation funneling into the sport, NHRA officials ramped up their vigilance in their pre-race inspections prior to each round. Among their arsenal of tools were magnets to check that body panels were correct and legal.

Proffitt and Strickler repeated their Winternationals head-to-head final in SS/S, although this time Strickler turned the tables on his GM rival, getting the jump and holding on with a 12.97 at 113.35 mph. In SS/SA, Eckstrand and Faubel emerged as the two top dogs, with Eckstrand's Dodge scoring a narrow victory with a 12.72 at 113.35 mph.

The close times throughout the top Super Stock classes were building for an epic showdown in Mr. Stock Eliminator for the fastest 50 stock cars, and the boisterous crowd was not disappointed. The big field was whittled down to four cars, including Proffitt, Strickler, Jim Thornton (in the Ramchargers Dodge), and Eckstrand. The semifinals had the two Chevys pitted against one another in one matchup and the two Mopars in the other. Proffitt exacted his revenge on Strickler to march forward into the final, where he'd go up against Thornton.

As if to underline the intensity of the Super Stock wars by late 1962, Proffitt was quoted many years later by historian Alex Gabbard regarding his battle with Thornton as saying, "We had over a hundred cars at Indy that year, and they were all factory backed. There were 33 factory-backed Mopars, and man, I had to go through them. I kicked the hell out of all their asses and sent them home licking their wounds, and remembering that makes me feel good.

"Mopars, Fords, anything that pulled up there. The last two to run were a Ramcharger, Jim Thornton, and myself with the 409 red Chevrolet. Everything had to click to win these kinds of things. I don't think I can stress this enough; the factories were trying to get the jump on the other one. The drivers were good, and the tuners had to be good.

"I moved first, and his was automatic coming up beside of me. I went to second, and I pulled him about a half of a car. Then I went to third, and I pulled him about another half. I knew then if I got it in fourth gear, I had a couple o' miles per hour on the top end. As soon as it went in fourth gear, everything was straightened out, and I turned around and I gave him the bone. That was the first time I'd ever done that, and I never will do it again."

Proffitt ran a 12.83 at 113.92 mph to take the win.

By the end of 1962, the Super Stock drag racing division was rightly being touted as one of drag racing's big drawcards. And it was the participation of the manufacturers that made it so. As well as the focused drag racing packages they were producing under the guise of stock street cars, they were also pumping money and parts into the teams, which was attracting all the top professional racers.

Things were set to get bigger, faster, glitzier, and quite rightly, an awful lot crazier.

Bob Frederick's brand-new 1962 Dodge Dart promotes Chrysler's new 413 Maximum Performance packages. Frederick owned a Dodge dealership in Canfield, Ohio, and raced a fleet of fast Mopars that carried bold "Big Bad Dodge" lettering along the flanks from 1963 onward. His 1962 variant was a little more modest. (Photo Courtesy Geoff Stunkard Collection/Kramer Automotive Archive)

CHAPTER 3

1963

A NEW LOOK AND MORE CUBIC INCHES

Not surprisingly, Chrysler's B-Body lineup was the subject of a major styling overhaul for the 1963 model run. As if to fully shake off the hangover of the polarizing Virgil Exner designs bestowed upon its early 1960s fleet, Chrysler went ultra-conservative for 1963—all except the nose treatments. In some cases, the 1963 snouts were almost the same as those of 1962. The Plymouth Sport Fury convertible and a few other models might even be described as attractive, which was not a tagline generally associated with the 1962 offerings.

Despite the visual differences, the B-Body Dodge and Plymouth models remained largely unchanged beneath the skin from their 1962 predecessors. The Dart nameplate was moved to a smaller compact A-Body model based on a 111-inch-wheelbase platform. The 1963 Dodge B-Body range included the 330, 440, and Polara, while Plymouth's lineup featured the Savoy, Belvedere, and Fury/Sport Fury.

Due to product placement of its various lines, Chrysler positioned Dodge further up the food chain than Plymouth, and because of this, its models had to reflect this. While the 1963 B-Body Plymouths maintained their 116-inch wheelbase, their Dodge counterparts were stretched to 119 inches.

1963 Super Stock Regulations

Chrysler's entry into the ever-evolving world of Stock and Super Stock drag racing in 1962 thrust it into the sporting spotlight. Tens of thousands of race fans packing drag racing arenas across the country were responding to the fast-growing popularity of the category. In response,

Bob Harrop's gorgeous Atco Dragway Special *1963 Dodge 330 poses while sporting the fabled dual-snorkel Max Wedge hood scoop. (Photo Courtesy Clinton Wright)*

Chrysler kicked its 1963 program into overdrive.

The NHRA Super Stock regulations were the subject of a constantly moving target, changing with each new year, and 1963 was no exception. A new 427.2-ci maximum engine size rule was introduced, while the awkward weight-versus-advertised-power rule of previous years was replaced by a much more sensible weight-per-cubic-inch rule. For 1963, this was 7.5 pounds per cubic inch and a minimum 3,200 pounds. Meanwhile, the American Hot Rod Association (AHRA), the NHRA's rival sanctioning body, allowed a maximum of 430 ci.

Another difference was the opening of the exhaust headers. In 1962, the opening was required to be the same diameter as the factory exhaust pipe. Rules in 1963 allowed a 3.5-inch diameter regardless of the factory size.

In 1962, many teams were raising the nose of their cars and lowering the tail to help gain a weight-shift

The Goodies Speed Shop Dodge 330 sedan equipped with the latest 415-hp 426 engine is pictured at Half Moon Bay drag strip in January 1963. The 1963 models, such as this, had only been launched a matter of weeks prior. This car was put straight to work. (Photo Courtesy Tom Bettencourt)

The Lucky Larsen's Metropolitan Dodge 1962 Dart rests in the Half Moon Bay pit area in early 1963. It was pretty rare to see a drag car fitted with hubcaps. (Photo Courtesy Tom Bettencourt)

Dick Landy continued running his 1962 Plymouth into the early part of 1963. The big Plymouth is shown here resting in the Pomona pit area during the 1963 NHRA Winternationals. (Photo Courtesy Geoff Stunkard Collection/Landy Family Archive)

advantage. The 1963 rules limited this to 2.5 inches front or rear.

Scattershields were now mandatory in all manual-transmission Stock cars down to E/Stock. Transmission options available included the T85 3-speed, BorgWarner T10 4-speed, and A727 TorqueFlite automatic. Most Mopar teams opted for the auto.

1963 Chrysler Super Stock Packages

Feeling bullish about its 1962 accomplishments, Chrysler came out swinging for the fences in 1963. It stretched its 413-ci RB-based Max Wedge out to 426 ci by increasing bore size by 0.0625 inch. Once again, two versions were offered: 415 hp (with 11:1 compression) and 425 hp (13.5:1 compression). Improvements

A superb-looking Dodge 330 sedan launches hard at Quaker City Dragway. Note the lack of hood scoop, suggesting this car hasn't yet been fitted with the lightweight front end. (Photo Courtesy Gary Ralston)

Two 1963 Mopars go at it. Even before the new lightweight package was launched in March, Mopars were already a popular choice among Super Stock racers across the country. (Photo Courtesy Geoff Stunkard Collection/Kramer Automotive Archive)

Dick Landy gets set to take on a bubble-top Chevy at San Fernando Raceway. Automotive Research was Landy's own company and appeared on all of Landy's race cars. Chromed steel wheels were a cool look on the Stockers before lightweight aluminum and magnesium wheels began appearing. The primer paint on the rear quarters suggests some massaging of the wheel openings had taken place to clear the tires. (Photo Courtesy Geoff Stunkard Collection/Kramer Automotive Archive)

The Horsepower Engineering Dodge 330, driven by Don Roberts, rests in the Fremont pit area. Chrysler's new lightweight front-end package had yet to arrive when this photo was taken in early March. (Photo Courtesy Tom Bettencourt)

The Garlits Dodge, pictured at Fremont Dragstrip in March 1963, was a long way from home. Garlits's Dodge ran Super Stocks for a few years in the early 1960s. For the most part, this car was driven by Jim Kaylor. As well as racing the big Dodge and working the spanners on Don Garlits's Top Fuel car, Kaylor also raced a Chevy-powered Austin A40 in B/Gas. (Photo Courtesy Tom Bettencourt)

The Yeakel Bros. had multiple new-car franchises, including Yeakel Plymouth Center in Downy, California. As well as sponsoring the Top Fuel dragster owned by Lou Baney (Yeakel Plymouth's general manager) and driven by Tom McEwen, the company was also highly active in Super Stock competition. This is the Yeakel Plymouth Belvedere at Fremont Dragstrip, where it was driven by Bruce Morgan. (Photo Courtesy Tom Bettencourt)

were made in the bottom end of the motors to assist high-speed lubrication.

The remainder of the engine, including the intake manifold, carburetors, the exhaust system, and the driveline, was largely unchanged from that of 1962. The standard rear-end ratio was 3.91:1 with a variety of various options offered ranging from 2.93 to 4.89:1.

Unlike the 1962 Maximum Performance Wedge package, which arrived midway through the model year, the 1963 Ramcharger and Super Stock factory packages were available by late 1962. They were ready for an all-out assault on the 1963 schedule.

1963 Drag Racing Highlights

The 1963 national drag racing season kicked off on February 17 at the annual NHRA Winternationals. It ended with the NHRA U.S. Nationals on September 2, bookending an increasing number of high-profile events. The AHRA held its Winternationals on February 24, the AHRA Summer Championship in early June, and the AHRA Nationals at Green Valley Raceway took place the same weekend as the NHRA U.S. Nationals in early September.

1963 NHRA Winternationals

The new Max Wedge package was still in the production stage when the 1962 NHRA Winternationals were being fought, and therefore the event was mostly lacking in competitive Chrysler contestants. However, the 1963 event was awash with an army of strong-running Mopars.

Tom Grove, aboard the *Melrose Missile*, was the top stick-shift pilot, taking out S/S (the not-so-catchy Super

Super/Stock phrase of 1962 had since been dropped) and blitzing the existing record with a blazing 12.50 ET. A Dodge built by Jim Nelson of Dragmasters fame and driven by Bob Simmerly took the top speed record in S/S with a 115.32 mph.

In S/SA, Tom Ritchie's 1963 Plymouth driven by his son Darrel set new ET and top speed records with 12.33 at 115.03 mph.

Mr. Stock Eliminator had Al Eckstrand in the Ramchargers Dodge facing off against Bill Shirey in the Golden Commandos Plymouth in the final. Eckstrand took the win with a 12.44 at 115.08 mph.

The Winternationals results didn't tell the whole story. To some extent, Chrysler's domination in the Super Stock ranks was a series of hollow victories, prompted by a lack of serious involvement by General Motors and Ford.

Throughout the late 1950s and into 1962, General Motors had evolved into a motor racing powerhouse. The company invested heavily in producing performance packages that resulted in an extensive list of race victories and championships in NASCAR Grand National, NHRA Stock, and even into SCCA road course racing. Its drag racing programs extended to offering its small-block 327 ci with big valve heads, 11.25:1 compression, hot solid-lifter cams, and Rochester fuel injection as an over-the-counter crate package for fitting to its new Chevy Nova/Chevy II for the new NHRA Factory Experimental class.

But in March 1963, GM's racing involvement met an abrupt end. Top brass within the company decreed that racing offered minimal benefit to its financial bottom line and did little to help improve the breed. Therefore, the costs and resources required to fund a racing program could not be justified.

General Motors had already committed to the 1963 racing season before its self-imposed racing ban was enforced, and some of its fast parts did manage to sneak across the line. Its Chevrolet Impala RPO Z11 package received a handful of upgrades, while Pontiac's contribution was a set of high-dome pistons.

Within GM's walls were countless racing enthusiasts who continued to design and produce parts, mostly on their own time, which then filtered through to select teams. But in 1963, most of the Chevy and Pontiac drag cars were forced to contest the Factory Experimental classes because they didn't qualify for Super Stock.

Ford, by contrast, was still very much in the racing game. Indeed, it ramped up its commitment. Initially, the new 1963 Galaxie sported the same 406 that propelled the outgoing model. But a new 427-ci Galaxie was in the works and offered midyear. It featured a special fastback roof profile that greatly aided its top speed on NASCAR superspeedways.

The Powers Automotive Belvedere, driven by Ron Powers, is pictured at Half Moon Bay in late May 1963. (Photo Courtesy Tom Bettencourt)

Yeakel Plymouth Center appeared at Half Moon Bay in May with a new car to match its new driver, and what a beautiful car it is! The black paint is complimented with yellow and red lettering, chrome wheels, and skinny whitewalls on the front. When 1963 dawned, Proffitt was a Chevrolet factory driver, and raced a Z11 Impala at the Winternationals. When General Motors suddenly withdrew from racing, Proffitt was quickly snapped up by Chrysler. On the C-pillar of the Yeakel Belvedere is painted "1962 Mr. Stock Eliminator," referring to Proffitt's victory at the 1962 NHRA U.S. Nationals. Never mind that he was aboard a Chevy when he took the win. (Photo Courtesy Tom Bettencourt)

BUD FAUBEL

Bud Faubel was one of the true gentlemen of drag racing and was extremely competitive with little factory assistance. Faubel had a pilot's license and was a fighter pilot during the Korean War. In racing, he was one of a handful of people campaigning Mopars in Stock drag racing competition before Chrysler decided to enter the sport. Despite his monstrous Dodge Phoenix lacking the factory speed equipment assisting competitors of rival manufacturers, he made the finals of A/SA at the 1961 U.S. Nationals.

For Faubel, racing was purely for enjoyment. He was vice president of Coldbrook Motors, a Chrysler/Plymouth dealership that was part of the Shively Motors empire in Chambersburg, Pennsylvania. He was a businessman first; racing was his hobby. But he was fiercely competitive, always had the latest machinery, and was usually there or thereabouts come Eliminations at the big events. But more so, he was a huge enthusiast of racing, and he loved to see Chrysler products winning.

Invariably, his cars carried the name *Honker* or *Hemi Honker*—and they were bright. Faubel's Mopars were either painted red or red and white. He regularly showed up to the track wearing a suit and tie that matched the color of his car.

In 1965, Faubel acquired one of the limited-edition altered-wheelbase Dodge Coronets. But rather than have it shipped to Pennsylvania, he opted to fly to Detroit and drive the car home. He wanted to spend time hanging out with the Ramchargers.

Before he left, they hung a license plate on the Coronet. On the way home, he carried out a few gentle test passes. Heading through the tollbooths on the turnpikes, he had to coast in, as there were often traffic cops policing them. Driving away, he clicked the Coronet into high gear and idle, so the open exhaust pipes didn't attract any unwanted attention. He was a genuine enthusiast.

Faubel led an active social life and was said to be aboard the light airplane that famously landed on the main street in a small town just so its occupants, which included the larger-than-life stock car racer and track owner Curtis Turner, could purchase some booze.

As drag racing grew more serious in the late 1960s, Faubel stepped away. He always maintained his enthusiasm for the sport and was a regular guest at vintage racing events in later years.

Bud Faubel died in 2013 at age 86.

Bud Faubel was quick to arm himself with the latest lightweight package on his Honker 1963 Dodge 330 *sedan. Once again, Faubel flew the Chrysler flag at the major NHRA and AHRA events. (Photo Courtesy Geoff Stunkard Collection/Kramer Automotive Archive)*

Likewise, Ford produced a drag racing–focused version of the Galaxie with a pair of 4-barrel Holley carburetors (NASCAR only allowed a single 4-barrel) perched atop the big 427. Although the fastback roof was much less effective in drag racing than it was on superspeedways, the drag package was put on an aggressive diet. The car was fitted with fiberglass front fenders, inner fenders, hood, and decklid, while bumpers were punched from lightweight Dural. Further weight savings came from an aluminum transmission case; the deletion of the sound deadener, heater, radio, and clock; and extended to the fitment of a thin rubber floor mat in place of carpet. All-in, the efforts saved around 700 pounds.

The big Galaxies would have made competitive Super Stock racers if only they would have been built in sufficient numbers. Instead, they ran in Factory Experimental.

Local Legends

Aside from the high-profile national events, Mopar Super Stock pilots were carving up local drag strips right across the country. Drivers, such as Billy Jacobs, Phil Carroll, Bill Tanner, Bud Faubel, Bob McIntyre, Emmitt Austin, and countless others, were pummeling opponents and further underscoring Chrysler products as the hottest thing in factory performance.

Jacobs was a multiple winner at Phenix City Drag Strip, as were Austin and Tanner. Carroll's *White Lightning* Dodge fended off Don Nicholson's Chevy at Houston Bros. Drag Strip in Fairburn, Georgia. McIntyre set a new A/Stock record at Blaney Drag Strip and also won at Mooresville, North Carolina.

Faubel clocked up a string of victories with a fleet

Its go-time at Half Moon Bay drag strip. Hayden Proffitt is in the far lane and Tommy Grove is in the near lane, in Melrose Missile IV. The Missile *is so new it hasn't yet been adorned in the missile artwork. Charlie Di Bari was running the* Missile III *at this same event. Note the hump on the hood of* Missile IV. *It's been fitted with the new lightweight front end complete with its sizable hood scoop. Proffitt's Yeakel Plymouth is still wearing the stock steel nose. On this occasion, the* Missile *won. (Photo Courtesy Tom Bettencourt)*

of Dodges contesting a variety of classes. He won Super Stock Automatic, Top Stock Eliminator, Middle Eliminator against the A/Gassers and altered coupes, Stock Eliminator, as well as Modified Stock Eliminator with his A/FX Dodge at Mason-Dixon Dragway, and A/FX and Little Eliminator at York U.S. 30 Drag-O-Way. He was crowned Mr. Stock Eliminator of the East Coast at York U.S. 30 Drag-O-Way in a multi-race series with his 1963 Dodge, and he finished second in the same competition with his 1962 Dodge!

1963 Chrysler Lightweight Packages

Regardless of the direction its rivals were taking, Chrysler pushed ahead with its next drag racing phase: a new lightweight package. Released in March 1963, the lightweight package was only available for order on the Dodge 330 and Plymouth Savoy two-door sedan body optioned with the 425-hp 13.5:1 maximum-performance motor.

The package consisted of aluminum front fenders, splash shield, and front bumper brackets and bar. A special custom hood featured a pair of front-opening snorkels (actually a single scoop with a pronounced ridge in the middle) that directed air straight to the carburetors via passages and hood intake cutouts. The hood, in particular, was a sensational-looking piece that completely transformed the appearance of the otherwise docile-looking intermediate sedans. In addition, the battery was relocated to the right rear of the trunk to further nudge weight toward the back of the car.

A Better Wedge

In June, Chrysler announced a new engine package. It was a "better breathing" version of its 426-ci maximum-performance powerhouse, which it dubbed the Maximum Performance Acceleration engine. The cylinder heads had been further developed, while the package also included a new higher lift camshaft, larger intake manifold risers, and the primary openings in the Ram Intake manifold were increased by 0.250 inch.

In its carefully worded bulletin, Chrysler stated, "Because it does not offer the stable, even idling of other high-performance engine options offered by Chrysler Corporation, the new '426' is not recommended for everyday driving."

In less subtle terms, Chrysler had built a full-blown race motor that was almost impossible to use on the street, even though these were technically street cars. Most certainly, this was truly a golden era of performance street machines.

1963 AHRA Summer Championship

While the NHRA was the clear leader in national drag racing, it had competition. The American Hot Rod Association (AHRA) featured slightly more liberal rules in its Stock divisions than those of the NHRA. As such, the 1963 AHRA Summer Championship featured Z11 Impalas facing off against lightweight

Sites Brothers Plymouth operated out of Kansas City, Missouri, and in 1963, it began racing Plymouth Super Stocks. Suction II *has been fitted with the latest lightweight aluminum front end, complete with its twin-snorkel hood. (Photo Courtesy Geoff Stunkard Collection/Kramer Automotive Archive)*

The 1963 Melrose Missile III, *pictured at Half Moon Bay in May, was the first of the Melrose Motors Plymouths to carry the famed missile artwork down the flanks. It was a total standout. Note the promotion of the team's success at the NHRA Winternationals earlier in the year. It was all about bragging rights. (Photo Courtesy Tom Bettencourt)*

Galaxies and the new Chrysler heavy hitters.

Malcom Durham won Super Stock driving a Z11 Impala, while Pontiac's larger-than-life ad man Jim Wangers raced the Royal Oak Pontiac Catalina to victory in A/Stock. The Sites Brothers Plymouth Savoy (*Suction II*) won Super Stock Automatic. Meanwhile, Top Stock Eliminator matched Wangers against Dick Lawrence in the Kansas City Plymouth, and the Mopar came away with the win.

1963 Detroit Dragway National Championship

If the AHRA could be considered liberal, the National Championship at Detroit Dragway on August 25 was a veritable free-for-all. Held in late August, this unsanctioned event was cleverly positioned to attract competitors making their way to the NHRA U.S. Nationals at Indy. To sweeten the

Bill Shirey in the Golden Commandos Plymouth and Roger Lindamood in the Color Me Gone *Plymouth get set to battle. Both cars are running the latest aluminum lightweight front end with 426 maximum-performance motors. The Golden Commandos emerged in 1963 as one of the best and fastest of the Chrysler contingent. Much like the Ramchargers, the Commandos relied on dealer sponsorship to fund their racing, in this case, Hamilton Motors of Detroit, Michigan. (Photo Courtesy Robert A. Carley/Rob Carley Collection)*

Al "Lawman" Eckstrand started the year 1963 aboard a Ramchargers Dodge and finished it at the helm of his own Plymouth. Eckstrand worked as a lawyer for Chrysler, but he was a demon wheelman. He reached the final in Mr. Stock Eliminator at the NHRA U.S. Nationals in this car, narrowly losing to Herman Mozer in the Ramchargers' Candimatic Too. *(Photo Courtesy Robert A. Carley/ Rob Carley Collection)*

pot, track owner Gil Kohn offered a $4,000 prize for the winner of the Top Stock competition.

Naturally, the ploy worked, and a quality field of A/FX, Super Stock, and Stock entries assembled. In the end, Hayden Proffitt, having switched to Chrysler after the GM racing withdrawal earlier in the year, won Super Stock Eliminator in the handsome Yeakel Plymouth Savoy. The Ramchargers took home the big prize by beating Proffitt in Top Stock.

New Chrysler Recruits

As 1963 lurched forward, Chrysler stacked the decks with quality teams. Some were coaxed across from rival manufacturer programs, including Hayden Proffitt. Others were forged by enthusiasts within its own ranks.

The Ramchargers (formed in 1958) had around 11 core members by 1963, including Tom Hoover, Jim Thornton, Dick Maxwell, Tom Coddington, Wayne Erickson, Dan Knapp, Gary Congdon, Dan Mancini, and Hartford "Mike" Buckel. Very soon, they were fending off another in-house team from within Chrysler Corporation: the Golden Commandos. Headed by Ray Kobe, a fuel specialist at the company, the Commandos also boasted factory dyno operators Troy Simenson, Steve Baker, Forrest Pitcock, John Dallafior, and others.

Naturally, an inter-tribe rivalry between the Ramchargers and Golden Commandos emerged. The Ramchargers referred to the Commandos as the "Commodes," while the Commandos shot back with the "Rumchasers."

With the Ramchargers having already established themselves with Dodge, the Commandos ran Plymouths.

Much like the Ramchargers, the Commandos were largely self-funded. There were not bags of money being delivered from the mother ship.

There was, however, a third party in the Chrysler mix: Corporate lawyer Elton "Al the Lawman" Eckstrand. Eckstrand performed legal duties for Chrysler and was well known and respected in the big offices. Aside from his day job, Eckstrand was also a racing enthusiast and a highly accomplished one at that. He kicked off the 1963 season driving a Ramchargers Dodge and won Mr. Stock Eliminator at the NHRA Winternationals. He was a demon peddler, for sure.

Eckstrand and the Ramchargers split following the Winternationals, after Eckstrand secured sponsorship from Stanford Dodge; the proceeds from which went to him and not the team. Now a free agent, he started his own team, running a new lightweight Plymouth campaigned as the "Lawman."

Further heavy artillery bolstered the Chrysler camp including Bill "Maverick" Golden in a Dodge and Roger Lindamood in the striking *Color Me Gone* Plymouth. Most of the Chrysler top dogs, at the very least, received support from Chrysler dealers or drove cars owned by Chrysler dealers.

1963 NHRA U.S. Nationals

A few weeks after the Detroit spectacular came the Big Go, the NHRA National Championships at Indianapolis Raceway Park. The U.S. Nationals showcased the very best of the best, attracting all the factory-backed machinery in both the Stock classes and Factory Experimental, which was becoming immensely popular. It was also the first major national event in which the new Dodge and Plymouth lightweight cars competed in NHRA Super Stock.

Around 100,000 fans packed the Indy circuit, and the atmosphere was electrifying. Adding further intrigue was the first appearance at an NHRA event of a light stand starter (or Christmas tree, as it was quickly dubbed) in place of a guy waving a flag. The new-fangled system tripped up several competitors, including a bunch of veterans, and was not overly popular. It also lacked the theatrics of a human flag waver. But it did ensure that early jumpers were caught.

With the Z11 Chevys forced to run in A/FX, the Super Stock ranks were without some of the heavyweights.

"DANDY" DICK LANDY

Californian "Dandy" Dick Landy was signed up as a Chrysler factory driver in 1962, making him one of the very first to be offered manufacturer support.

Landy began drag racing at age 19, driving a Ford pickup. Like so many of his era, his mechanical skills allowed him to go racing in the first place. In Landy's case, he studied mechanical engineering at San Fernando Valley Junior College. He established his company Automotive Research in 1961.

While racing his brother Mike's 1960 Ford, he came to the attention of a local Van Nuys Ford dealer, which raised his profile. Chrysler then swooped in, and he started racing a factory Plymouth in 1962.

In 1964, Landy switched from Plymouth to Dodge, and throughout, was supplied the latest Mopar racing machinery. But he was a tinkerer, constantly experimenting and constantly improving. Following the 1964 NHRA Winternationals, Landy stripped his Hemi-powered Dodge 330 Super Stock and massively modified it for A/FX competition, shifting the rear axle forward 8 inches and the front 6 inches. Furthermore, the entire factory front-end setup was replaced with the beam axle and parallel leaf springs from a Dodge A-100 van.

Although Chrysler produced four altered-wheelbase cars earlier in the year, Landy's version was by far the most dramatic. It was credited by many as being the first Funny Car.

Like most factory Chrysler racers, Landy drifted away from Super Stock racing in 1965 to surf the altered-wheelbase craze. Even though the NHRA wanted nothing to do with them, there were plenty of governing bodies and event promoters that did. As such, these cars and drivers were spoiled with many choices.

After two years running altered-wheelbase cars that were getting increasingly radical, Chrysler and its factory drivers shifted back to a more sedate Super Stock package for 1967 with the handsome RO/WO cars, and Landy went with them. Throughout his career, Landy campaigned multiple cars at once, running a variety of classes (his good friend Bob Lambeck drove several of them, as did his brother Mike), and that continued into the first year of NHRA Pro Stock in 1970. Although Landy's main priority was his new Pro Stock Dodge Challenger, he also continued to campaign Super Stock cars.

Dick Landy's beautiful new 1963 Plymouth Belvedere is shown with its lightweight front-end package. This angle perfectly showcases the gaping hood scoop, which was a sensation in 1963. Landy equipped the big Plymouth with lightweight front mag wheels. (Photo Courtesy Geoff Stunkard Collection/Landy Family Archive)

One of Landy's greatest racing achievements was winning the 1970 NHRA Summernationals, beating off a fierce grid of cars in what had become an immensely tight competition.

When the NHRA pulled the rug from under the Mopar fleet in 1972, Landy battled against the current. Like many of his Chrysler contemporaries, he found more success racing with other governing bodies, such as the AHRA and IHRA. By the late 1970s, he stepped down as a driver, and after 1980, he ceased fielding teams.

Landy was always an important asset to the Chrysler Corporation, and he was approachable, clean cut, and charismatic. Between racing and running his growing business, he also conducted Dodge Supercar Clinics at Dodge dealerships around the country and appeared constantly in the company's advertising. The ABC television network's *Wide World of Sports* program made a film called *The Age of Drag Racing* in 1971 and followed Landy's plight at the NHRA Supernationals at Ontario Motor Speedway. This single film brought drag racing to the attention of millions of new viewers.

Landy famously held an unlit cigar between his clenched teeth. It was always there, in the pits and in the car, but he didn't actually smoke. His friend Andy Andrews handed him a cigar for luck, back when he was racing Fords and the habit just stuck. He apparently went through more than 50 boxes of cigars a year, but they were never lit.

Dick Landy died in 2007 at age 69.

Ford's new lightweight Galaxie was eligible to run in Super Stock as of March 1963, but the big fastbacks with their 4-speed transmissions ran in the S/S division. Most of the TorqueFlight-equipped Mopars were in Super Stock Automatic.

Indeed, S/SA quickly developed into a Mopar motorcade, albeit a blisteringly fast one. The Ramchargers arrived with two Dodges resplendent in their white with candy apple red stripes and lettering for Herman Mozer and Jim Thornton. The two Ramchargers Dodges were identical in all respects except tires. One was fitted with M&H Racemasters, while the other rolled on a set of Goodyear cheater slicks.

The Ramchargers' two cars were punching out low 12s in the early running, as was the Lawman. Proffitt, Maverick, and Bud Faubel were a couple of tenths slower. The real pacesetter, though, was Forrest Pitman in the Golden Commandos' Plymouth, which was cranking out 11.90-second runs and looked to have it in the bag.

In the S/SA finals, however, Thornton blasted his way through the 40-strong field, including his teammate Herman Mozer, to score the decadent winner's trophy. Then, two-by-two, the big Stockers came out swinging in Mr. Stock Eliminator with the vast crowd being whipped into a frenzy by track announcer Bernie Partridge.

The Stock cars were now generating mass appeal in drag racing circles, being fast, loud, and spectacular. They also clearly related to the cars many fans drove to the track. Nothing drives emotions like brand loyalty, and nothing creates brand loyalty like racing.

The combatants whittled their way down to four cars, and they were all Mopars. The Lawman blitzed the Golden Commandos in one round, winning on a holeshot, while the two Ramchargers went at it in the second. This time Mozer turned the tables on Thornton and moved on to face Eckstrand in the final. As *Hot Rod* magazine reported, "At the green light, both cars came out of the chute with a bang on a good, even start, but Mozer led the way by only the slightest margin and tripped the beams first with a 12.22 . . . Eckstrand lost with a 12.23!"

The crowd erupted. Super Stock drag racing had truly arrived. Chrysler was at the center of all the hysteria, emotion, and animated media attention.

The West Coast Factor

Detroit is the home of the American automotive industry, but the spiritual home of drag racing is California. In the 1930s, young hot shoes were hopping up 1932 Fords and running them wide open at Harper, Muroc, El Mirage, and Mojave dry lake beds. Thirty years later, Pomona, Lions, Fontana, and others hosted the latest Slingshot Dragsters, Gassers, and Stockers.

While the dragsters were scoring all the headlines and leading magazine features, the Super Stocks were gathering momentum. An increasing number of drivers were gravitating toward them. With the manufacturers all hopping on board, the top quick-draw pilots were being scooped up and absorbed into the factory racing programs. Drivers such as H. L. and Shirley Shahan, Butch Leal, Tom Grove, and Dick Landy were all among the California natives who'd become integral to Chrysler's Stock drag racing program in the 1960s.

The Melrose Missile IV, *now wearing its famous war paint, is pictured at Half Moon Bay in early December 1963. (Photo Courtesy Tom Bettencourt)*

CHAPTER 4

1964

RETURN OF THE HEMI

Following the eccentric, slightly awkward jumble that was the 1962 Chrysler B-Body styling, the company went ultra-conservative with its offerings in 1963 almost in reaction to itself, rather than any directional trend the market was taking. But for 1964, Chrysler got its mojo back.

Its designers penned a striking new two-door hardtop roof profile, available on both its Dodge and Plymouth B-Body models. The hardtop roof offered a total personality transformation to the otherwise understated Chrysler intermediates, resulting in a much more aggressive and sporty theme.

The Fenner Tubbs Co. Hemi Plymouth piloted by Joe Smith makes a pass at Amarillo Dragway in Texas. Fenner Tubbs started the 1964 campaign with a 426 Max Wedge hardtop and would add the Hemi car to the fleet in June 1964.

The hardtop bodywork carried a semi-fastback design with the C-pillars blending down from the roof top to the rear bodywork in a wedge. Yet, the rear glass continued the semi-fastback profile. It looked superb and was unlike anything else on the market. Indeed, the new rear window design was only upstaged, in terms of pure drama, by Chrysler's own crazy new Plymouth Barracuda.

Part of Chrysler's motivation for the slippery hardtop roof shape was, of course, its hostile new approach to the NASCAR Grand National. Ford's facelifted 1963⅓ Galaxie fastback roofline (also fitted to the Mercury Marauder) was created specifically to improve top-end speeds on super speedways, and it was stunningly successful. The big Fords enjoyed a leap in performance of around 10 mph. The amount of horsepower required to achieve a similar improvement was massive.

NASCAR Grand National stock cars and NHRA Super Stock drag cars are totally different animals, requiring quite different approaches to achieve success. Drag cars, despite getting faster every year, weren't achieving close to the speeds seen in NASCAR. So, the fastback roof really didn't offer an advantage.

However, NASCAR Grand National cars were fitted with a massive, extremely robust roll cage that virtually eliminated body flex. Super Stock drag cars, by comparison, had no cage at all. The Chrysler B-Body models were more rigid in two-door sedan form than they were as a hardtop. Furthermore, the sedan was slightly lighter in weight.

1964 Chrysler Super Stock Packages

In October 1963, Chrysler announced the latest variant of its big 426-ci maximum-performance Wedge motor, which benefitted from further improvements. These included new cylinder heads with higher valve ports for improved breathing, wild new exhaust headers, new connecting rods, a new crankshaft, and a larger-capacity oil pan.

Again, two compression ratios were offered: 11:1 (08 code) and 12.5:1 (09 code). The 12.5:1 motor was officially rated at 425 hp but was certainly north of that figure. The latest Wedge was marketed as the 426-III in the Plymouth and as the Ramcharger 426-B in the Dodge.

In addition, a new heavy-duty 4-speed transmission was now available. To date, most of Chrysler's drag cars ran in the Super Stock Automatic class because the beefy TorqueFlite would take virtually any punishment it was subjected to while also offering lightning-fast shifts. But Chrysler didn't have an equivalent 4-speed manual in its arsenal. However, Ramchargers team member Dale

During the pace lap for the 1964 Daytona 500, you have to go right back to the fourth row of the grid to find A. J. Foyt's Galaxie as the first non-Chrysler in the field. Seen in the outside of the front row, Richard Petty went on to dominate the race, leading 184 of the 200 laps. Foyt was the only Ford driver to lead any laps. He led three in total, and Chrysler completely crushed the race. The top Mopar teams were all running the new Hemi motor. (Photo Courtesy Revs Institute/ Bruce R. Craig)

Henry Garcia is aboard the sinister black Burke's Law 1963 Dodge. The car gained its moniker from the popular TV series of the same name that was about Amos Burke, the millionaire captain of the Los Angeles Police homicide unit. Burke would be chauffeured to crime scenes in his Rolls-Royce. Garcia, of Terre Haute, Indiana, was one of the few of the Chrysler contingent to run AA/SA (Stock Automatic), a class created largely to cater to Ford's Galaxie. Note the lack of a hood scoop, which suggests the Dodge ran without the lightweight front end. (Photo Courtesy Geoff Stunkard Collection/Kramer Automotive Archive)

Having run Plymouths since his arrival at Chrysler as a factory driver, Dick Landy switched to Dodge for 1964. He debuted this beautiful Wedge-powered hardtop early in the year. The silver paint was a mainstay for Landy for the next decade. (Photo Courtesy Geoff Stunkard Collection/ Landy Family Archive)

Reeker oversaw development of a new transmission: the A-833.

Chrysler offered the new maximum-performance Wedge motors as part of a full drag racing package. As well as the motor, the bundle included Tri-Y headers, unsilenced air cleaners, a custom oil pan, a heavy-duty radiator, a seven-blade fan, a 3.91:1 rear axle ratio, 5.5-inch-wide wheels wrapped in 7.5x14-inch BSW tires, and a 90-amp battery mounted in the trunk on the passenger's side. Also included

Bud Faubel's old Wedge-powered 1963 Dodge gets set to take on Herb Freels in his new 1964 Wedge-powered hardtop. The track is likely 75-80 Dragway in Monrovia, Maryland. (Photo Courtesy Geoff Stunkard Collection/ Kramer Automotive Archive)

The Melrose Missile V *was one of the latest 1964 two-door hardtop models, pictured at Kingdon Drag Strip in March. Melrose Motors hit the track in early 1964 with this superb Wedge-powered two-door hardtop while waiting on its Hemi-powered sedan. The hardtop scored its share of silverware. (Photo Courtesy Tom Bettencourt)*

Ron Powers's new Wedge-powered 1964 Plymouth Belvedere sedan was fitted with the lightweight front end. (Photo Courtesy Tom Bettencourt)

was a narrower rear axle and rear springs from the 1963 models, which also featured a front main leaf that was 1 inch shorter than stock—thereby shifting the rear axle line forward by 1 inch.

The 11:1-compression 08-code engine package could be ordered for any B-Body model except the police car or taxi and could be equipped with either the TorqueFlite or the new 4-speed transmission. The lightweight body package was not available for this motor.

The 12.5:1-compression 09-code package was available only on the Dodge 330 two-door sedan, 440 two-door hardtop, Plymouth Savoy two-door sedan, and Belvedere two-door hardtop. It came with the lightweight body package that included an aluminum hood with an aluminum air scoop intake, plus aluminum front fenders, front bumper and bumper brackets, radiator air shield and stone deflector, radiator cross bar, and hood-lock support brace.

Weight saving extended to fitting lightweight carpets and the deletion of all sound deadener, undercoat, insulation, and silencer pads. No other options were available. This was indeed a no-frills barnstormer designed and built specifically to be driven a quarter mile at a time as fast as humanly possible.

New Chrysler Recruits

Having worked together for several years running GM products, the team of Dave Strickler and Bill "Grumpy" Jenkins jumped ship and started running Chryslers in 1964 as "the Dodge Boys." Success came quickly with the new partnership.

1964 Drag Racing Highlights

The 1964 national drag racing schedule saw the AHRA show its intent by slotting its opening major event, the Winternationals, on February 9, one week ahead of the annual NHRA Winternationals. The NHRA U.S. Nationals on September 7 retained its position as the most important drag racing competition on the national calendar.

The pair of Milne Brothers Plymouth Belvedere hardtops arrive in style at Kingdon Drag Strip for the 1964 Kingdon Nationals in March. Bob Feuerhelm and Bill Hanyon drove the cars. Shortly after this event, the two Belvederes were put up for sale. Incidentally, the Milne Brothers ran a Belvedere sedan in 1963, which was sold to a buyer in Australia. Feuerhelm traveled to Australia to race the car briefly. It was later converted into a wild road racing car. (Photo Courtesy Tom Bettencourt)

Dick Landy's Wedge-powered hardtop is resplendent in silver paint offset with red lettering and chrome wheels. (Photo Courtesy Geoff Stunkard Collection/Landy Family Archive)

This is the pretty Francis & Parsons Dodge 440 hardtop. Chrysler was still pushing its sedans in drag racing because they were lighter and more rigid but offered the Stage-III Max Wedge and lightweight package on both the sedan and hardtop. (Photo Courtesy Geoff Stunkard Collection/ Kramer Automotive Archive)

The handsome Sutton and Walls Wedge-powered Plymouth hardtop is pictured at Kingdon Drag Strip. (Photo Courtesy Tom Bettencourt)

Here is one of the lavish Dodge Charger S/FX cars that raced briefly from March through July/August 1964. Driven by Jim Nix and Jim Johnson, the 330 sedans were built by Dragmaster and toured the country, appearing at Dodge dealerships and making exhibition passes at racing events. The plan was to power them with the new Hemi motor, but instead, they ran a supercharged Wedge. The cars would ultimately have the rear fenders radiused out to clear the big magnesium wheels and slicks, but this early photo (March 1964) shows the rear fender in near stock form. (Photo Courtesy Geoff Stunkard Collection)

The beautiful Yeakel Plymouth Center 1964 Wedge-powered Plymouth hardtop was prepared and driven by Hayden Proffitt. (Photo Courtesy Tom Bettencourt)

The Yeakel Plymouth Center expanded to two cars in early 1964 with Roger Caster driving the #615 hardtop. Caster finished runner-up to teammate Proffitt at the AHRA Winternationals. (Photo Courtesy Tom Bettencourt)

Hayden Proffitt takes on Tom Grove at Kingdon Drag Strip. Note how low the Proffitt Plymouth sits in the rear. He set up the car to transfer its weight to the rear upon launch and then gradually level out as it ran down the track. Proffitt beat the Missile in this duel. (Photo Courtesy Tom Bettencourt)

Bill "Maverick" Golden poses proudly with the first Little Red Wagon *Dodge A-100 exhibition wheel-stander. (Photo Courtesy James Handy)*

The Melrose Missile V *makes a run. The last year the* Missile *carried this hugely elaborate paint scheme was 1964. (Photo Courtesy Dan Shannon)*

1964 AHRA Winternationals

The first major drag racing event of the 1964 season was the annual AHRA Winternationals in early February at Beeline Dragway in Scottsdale, Arizona. In both Super Stock and Mr. Top Stock, Mopars basked in glory. Dave Strickler won Super Stock Automatic, while new Chrysler recruit, Hayden Proffitt, took out the big one, Mr. Stock Eliminator.

1964 NHRA Winternationals

One week following the AHRA spectacular, the NHRA Winternationals took place on February 15–16. Around 98,000 race fans packed out Pomona Raceway, and the Stocker battles were the biggest drawcards for them making the pilgrimage. The organizers limited car numbers to 500, and of those, 281 were in the Stock divisions.

The Chrysler squad continued to grow in both strength and numbers, and its weaponry included the Ramchargers, the Golden Commandos, Al "Lawman" Eckstrand, Hayden Proffitt, Doug Lovegrove in the Mashak Plymouth, Tom Grove in the *Melrose Missile*, Jim Rodgers, Bill Shirey, "Dandy" Dick Landy, Bill "Maverick"

Golden, and Joe Smith. Lovegrove and Grove were among those to run the sporty new hardtop models, as were the Golden Commandos.

In total, there were 28 Plymouths and 13 Dodges set to wage war on the Ford contingent, which came out fighting in 1964. Ford had Dearborn Steel Tubing build a fleet of 427-ci-powered Fairlanes in enough numbers to qualify them for Super Stock competition. This new potent Ford was aptly named the Thunderbolt. This was truly shaping up to be a battle of the heavyweights.

In the end, it was Gas Ronda aboard one of the new 427 Fairlanes that took top honors in Super Stock, while Super Stock Automatic went to a Chrysler with Jim Rodgers of Scottsdale, Arizona, slaying all the heavy hitters. The 21-year-old Rodgers told the *Los Angeles Times* after the race, "I'm real calm, I don't understand it. I thought I'd be real excited. It's the biggest win of my life."

So, the Fords were the hot ticket in S/S, and the Mopars were the hot ticket in S/SA. Saturday's contests only heightened the suspense for Sunday's action and the much-anticipated Mr. Stock Eliminator.

By the third round, only two Fords survived: those of Dick Brannan and Phil Bonner. But they were put on the trailer by Eckstrand and Mozer. The final four cars were all Mopars: Eckstrand, Lovegrove, Mozer, and Grove. The 28-year-old Grove, a sensation in the *Melrose Missile*, was thumping out impressive times, running an 11.77, 11.71, and 11.64. He was the only Mopar driver sawing a 4-speed.

In the semifinals, the Lawman faced off against the Mashak Plymouth, and it was the reigning champion who was first out of the gates. He held a slender margin, but Lovegrove ran him down and was ahead when it mattered. Then, the youngster Grove scored the upset of the meeting by taking down Mozer with an 11.66.

So, the *Melrose Missile* and the Mashak Plymouth lined up for the final: automatic versus 4-speed. When the Christmas tree flicked through the lights, Lovegrove stormed out of the gates, and led Grove all the way down the track. But his excitement was quickly extinguished. He'd redlit. Grove, smashing out a spectacular 11.63 at 124.13 mph, became Mr. Stock Eliminator, winning himself a new Dodge 440 hardtop for his efforts.

The Exhibitionists

The year 1964 was notable for racing's splintering from pure racing into a form of entertainment. Increasingly, teams were building high-powered vehicles that served no other purpose than to entertain. While the racers still competed with intent, a new breed of exhibition vehicles provided a fascinating and sometimes alarming sideshow to keep punters pumped up between rounds. Very quickly, the manufacturers got on board, recognizing the marketing value to be had from a customized mad-cap vehicle that ran a single pass, drawing everyone's attention.

Return of the Hemi

One week after the NHRA Winternationals, the NASCAR stock car fraternity gathered on the other side of the country for the Daytona 500 in Florida. This was Round 8 of the 1964 Grand National.

Ford Motor Company's fire power was immense. At Daytona, it funded at least 15 Ford Galaxies and Mercury Marauders, run by Holman-Moody, Wood Brothers, Bud Moore Engineering, Bill Stroppe, Bondy Long, and others, and driven by a lengthy list of super stars including A. J. Foyt, "Fireball" Roberts, Fred Lorenzen, Parnelli Jones, Ned Jarrett, Johnny Rutherford, Dan Gurney, Jo Schlesser, Dave MacDonald, Darel Dieringer, and Marvin Panch. Ford was pumping millions into its 1964 racing programs, and it wasn't messing about.

But the much-fancied Ford juggernaut was trumped by a small fleet of Plymouth Belvederes and Dodge Coronets that were capped with the sporty new hardtop roof and powered by an exciting new engine. The Chryslers completely dominated, winning both 100-mile warmup races and claiming the top seven starting positions in the big race.

Paul Goldsmith's Ray Nichols–prepared Plymouth was at the head of the queue, and Richard Petty's similar car was alongside. Such was their speed in qualifying and the two 100-milers, the Chrysler drivers were under instruction to sandbag and not show the true speed of their cars. Come the race, Petty was epic, leading 184 of the 200 laps, heading home for a 1-2-3 finish for Chrysler, as Jimmy Pardue and Goldsmith were chasing him home. Foyt managed to lead just two laps while the Mopars were pitting, and that was as good as it got for Ford.

The new mega-motors powering the Chrysler fleet had been in development since March 1963 and featured a hemispherical combustion chamber cylinder head design fitted to a much-modified and strengthened version of the existing RB block that had underpinned the long-serving Wedge unit. The same 4.25x3.75-inch bore and stroke of the RB was retained, and as such, the new Hemi also measured 426 ci.

Super Stock Hemi Packages

Even at the NHRA Winternationals there was talk of the new 426 Chrysler Hemi being installed in some of the Mopar Super Stocks, but that didn't happen due to various delays in its development. For Chrysler, the Daytona 500 was the priority. Finally, the announcement was made in March that the new A864 426-ci Chrysler Hemi (dubbed the Hemi Charger for the Dodge and Super Commando for the Plymouth) was available to purchase either for circle track or with the Super Stock drag racing package.

The new Hemi drag race motors featured aluminum high-compression pistons, forged connecting rods, and forged crankshaft, made from carbon steel that had been heat treated and chemically hardened using a Tuftride process. Like the Max Wedge, it was fed by two carburetors that were now mounted on an aluminum intake manifold. Initially, Carter carburetors were installed, but further testing found Holley 4160s offered improved performance.

Complex new exhaust headers were crafted. They differed from side to side in their design with the left side being a 4-into-4-into-1 layout, while the right side was 4-into-2-into-1. The dramatic upswept Tri-Y headers that graced the Max Wedge engine bays were sadly no more.

Two versions of the Hemi were available: 11:1 compression and 12.5:1. Advertised horsepower for the 12.5:1 version was 425 hp, but it was generally considered to be north of 550. Torque was listed as 480 ft-lbs.

The new 426 Hemi was not available for order on any street car. It was, however, a pure race motor, and not intended for street use. Indeed, this decision later helped Chrysler come unstuck in the NASCAR Grand National.

As it did with the earlier Wedge cars, Chrysler offered a complete turnkey Hemi Super Stock race car package. Its equipment levels were even more off the scale. The

BILL "MAVERICK" GOLDEN

Bill "Maverick" Golden will forever be linked with the crazy wheel-standing Dodge A100 truck, Little Red Wagon. He first campaigned the exhibition truck in 1965, but prior to that, he was a highly accomplished Super Stock racer, being one of the first factory drivers picked up by Chrysler. Jim Nelson of Dragmasters was involved in getting the Maverick's S/SA Dodges to run hard. The curved top edges of the hood scoop here suggest Golden is still running a Wedge motor, but as soon as the Hemi became available, he made the switch. (Photo Courtesy Geoff Stunkard Collection/Kramer Automotive Archive)

Bill "Maverick" Golden is best known for his crazy antics aboard the Dodge *Little Red Wagon* exhibition truck, but he also enjoyed a significant racing career prior to stepping aboard the famous wheel-stander. Hailing from Shawnee Township, Illinois, Golden gained the nickname "Maverick" by a track announcer because of his decision to race an unconventional Dodge Custom Royal against all the popular Fords and Chevys.

Golden remained a loyal Chrysler racer, even when the company wasn't involved in racing. When he was racing a Dodge Phoenix in 1960, he was offered parts to help his plight. Then, when Chrysler first waded into the sport in 1962, he was quickly scooped up.

Golden's color of choice for his race cars was bright yellow. His boxy Mopar sedans were sometimes likened to taxis. He spearheaded Chrysler's drag racing programs throughout 1963 and 1964 and was always in the fight for race victories. He had Jim Nelson at Dragmaster tune his chassis.

Meanwhile, Dodge Truck Division employees Jim Schaeffer and John Collier had constructed a Dodge A-100 exhibition race truck fitted with a Hemi motor installed in a cradle mounted in the bed. With Chrysler racer Jay Howell at the helm, the *Little Red Wagon* displayed alarming character traits during its early passes, prompting seasoned racers Dick Branstner and Roger Lindamood to get involved in the program and help iron out the bugs.

After performing various chassis and suspension improvements, Howell again pressed the truck into action. This time, he found it picked its front wheels up and could easily hold them in the air. With that, the *Little Red Wagon* went from being a race truck to an exhibition wheel-stander.

For 1965, Bill Golden was brought in to pilot the wild truck, while the mild Hemi Super Stock motor with twin carburetors was replaced by a full race motor running Hilborn fuel injection. Further upgrades were made to the chassis so it could carry a dramatic full-track wheelie with the front wheels several feet off the turf. The *Little Red Wagon* became one of Chrysler's most successful marketing vehicles of all time. Indeed, Maverick was its permanent handler and as integral to the program as the truck itself.

Golden and the *Little Red Wagon* continued their wheel-standing antics well throughout the 1970s, 1980s, and 1990s, before the Maverick retired in 2003. By that time, Dodge's A-100 truck had been out of production for more than three decades. Yet, Chrysler still enjoyed marketing exposure from what was originally intended as an exhibition race truck that had an expected shelf life of probably about 12 months.

There were some spectacular crashes along the way. After a particularly messy wreck in 1975, Golden built a new *Little Red Wagon*, using an existing promotional truck as the basis. Two years later, he set a Guinness world record for performing a wheel-stand that ran for 4,230 feet (1,289 meters), which is more than the length of three quarter-mile drag strips.

Bill Golden died in 2015, but his famed wheel-stander lives on. It was sold by RM Auctions in 2009, and the hammer eventually fell when the bidding hit $550,000. Six years later, it was purchased by stunt driver Mike Mantel, who pilots another famous 1960s Mopar wheel-stander: the Hurst *Hemi Under Glass*. Mantel built a new *Little Red Wagon* for wheel-standing duties, while Bill Golden's original crashed 1964 truck, plus the 1975-built car form part of the display.

A youthful Blue Barnes poses with Snorkasaurus IV, *the Hemi-powered Dodge 330 sedan. Dick Landy's Automotive Research built the motors. (Photo Courtesy Geoff Stunkard Collection/Kramer Automotive Archive)*

Ric Jorgensen stands next to his Hemi Plymouth and its trophy in the foreground. Jorgensen campaigned his car out of Idaho and Washington state. (Photo Courtesy Ric Jorgensen)

Hemi package was listed as the Hemi-Charger for the Dodge and Super Commando for the Plymouth.

Again, the lightweight body package continued. However, it was only available on the two-door sedans. There were around 35 Hemi hardtops built, but these were steel-body cars. Chrysler was clearly placing the emphasis for its Super Stock drag racing successes on the sedans.

The lightweight package included an aluminum hood, hood scoop, front fenders, front bumper, front bumper brackets, and doors. The new hood scoop differed from the Wedge item in that it was wider and featured a flat top. A handful of early Hemi cars were fitted with a twin-hump hood scoop. The hood was held in place with four threaded pins and wing nuts. In addition, the inboard headlights were deleted from the grille on both models.

The lightweight Hemi sedan package extended into the interior, which featured a pair of Dodge A100 thin-line van seats mounted in the front, while the back seat was deleted altogether. In its place, a cardboard panel was installed. Once again, lightweight carpet was fitted, and while the regular interior door mechanisms remained, the factory side glass was replaced with 0.090-inch Plexiglass. The rear window used 0.080-inch tempered glass supplied by Corning Chem-Cor. The only available interior color was red. All other interior accoutrements were deemed unnecessary and were deleted, including sun visors, coat hooks, and a dome light.

The front wheels measured 15x4.5, while the rear had 14-inch steel wheels. They were painted the body color and wrapped in BSW tires.

All 1964 Hemi cars were built during April, May, and June.

1964 Chrysler Altered-Wheelbase Cars

Since their inception in 1962, the new Factory Experimental classes had grown by leaps and bounds in terms of the quality and trickery of the machinery as well as the race fans' reaction to them. The numerous freedoms allowed in FX made for some exciting and spectacular concoctions but wrapped in packages resembling those the fans drove every day on the street.

In the days before massive enclosed race car transporters, teams hauled their cars around the country using much more modest means. Some had open trailers, while others flat towed, including Dick Landy, using a pair of Dodge wagons hooked to an A-frame. Landy's sedan and earlier hardtop are shown with the hardtop now sporting a new coat of white paint on the roof. (Photo Courtesy Geoff Stunkard Collection/Landy Family Archive)

Plug your ears! J. D. Feigelson gets set to make a run in his Hemi Plymouth. His dad had actually ordered a new Sport Fury hardtop with a Stage III 426 Wedge from Sutton Motor Company, but instead, he received the Hemi sedan. When he first set eyes on the black sedan, Feigelson was disappointed. But his string of race victories and countless track invites very quickly changed his mind. (Photo Courtesy J. D. Feigelson)

Blue Barnes ran his 1964 Hemi Dodge Snorkasaurus IV at Fremont Dragstrip. (Photo Courtesy Steve Reyes)

A roadside tire change is being made for the Landy Dodge 330. Note the motorcycle mounted on front of the race car. That'll likely be for getting around the pits and for running errands on the road. The Dodge wagon is rolling on wide chrome wheels. (Photo Courtesy Geoff Stunkard Collection/Landy Family Archive)

THE GOLDEN COMMANDOS

The Golden Commandos was to Plymouth what the Ramchargers was to Dodge. Of course, the members from each team all worked for the same company. First conceived in late 1962, the Golden Commandos helped propel Chrysler's drag racing programs forward as well as provide engineering solutions to products that found their way onto the company's passenger vehicles.

The Golden Commandos, like the Ramchargers, was a team comprised of good friends who not only worked for Chrysler but also shared a passion for drag racing and for seeing the brand achieve racing success. Headed by Ray Kobe, a Chrysler fuel specialist, the Commandos also boasted factory dyno operators Troy Simenson, Steve Baker, Forrest Pitcock, John Dallafior, and others.

There was, of course, a rivalry between the two groups, albeit a healthy one, and one that drove racing forward in the same direction. Like the Ramchargers, the Commandos afforded their racing through sponsorship, predominantly from a Plymouth dealership. Hamilton Motors of Detroit supported the team throughout much of its existence.

From the outset, the Golden Commandos vaulted up to speed on the track and were soon vying for race wins. They finished runner-up at the 1963 NHRA Winternationals. Forrest Pitcock did much of the driving the first two seasons along with Bill Shirey before Al Eckstrand arrived in 1965.

The year 1964 was particularly poignant for the Commandos. The team helped spearhead new Chrysler competition developments, including the Hemi and altered-wheelbase craze. Their cars consistently ran at the pointy end of the field at every event they attended.

Like most of the factory-connected teams, the Commandos moved away from Super Stock racing in 1965 in favor of running an altered-wheelbase Funny Car. It was one of a handful of cars supplied without having been converted to its 110-inch shortened wheelbase, and as such, the team ran the car in stock form at the season-opening AHRA Winternationals, where it finished runner-up to Bud Faubel's 110-inch Dodge. It also competed at the NHRA Winternationals, which didn't allow the new wildly altered machines to compete.

Once they'd completed conversion of their car, the Commandos spent the 1965 season running popular match-bash races, which brought the crowds to the tracks in droves. Indeed, theirs was the first of the Chrysler fleet to race with the new Hilborn fuel injection system.

Much like the Ramchargers, the Golden Commandos underwent various team personnel changes throughout their history. By 1967, while much of the Chrysler contingent returned to Super Stock competition, the Commandos continued to walk on the wild side by building a flopper Funny Car.

By now, the financial support was beginning to dry up. At season's end, the team opted to shut up shop. With that, one of the great 1960s Mopar drag racing teams disbanded, although naturally, various members from within the group continued on within the sport.

Golden Commando #5, the handsome 1964 hardtop, gets the hammer down. Having had their 1964 Hemi sedan maneuvered away and into the clutches of Al Eckstrand, the Commandos were gifted a Hemi motor for fitting into their hardtop along with a set of one-off aluminum hardtop doors. This was to be a successful year for the team, as Commandos pilot Forrest Pitcock made the Super Stock final at the NHRA U.S. Nationals, only to redlight.

Many FX cars had some sort of factory involvement. While Ford had its fleet of Thunderbolts contesting the Super Stock competitions at the 1964 Winternationals, there were also several new 427-powered Mercury Comets gracing A/FX, including a station wagon. It was thought the rearward weight of the wagon would give it an advantage. It was all very exciting, and Chrysler wanted to be part of the show.

Chrysler had intended to have four A/FX cars competing at the Winternationals. Two Dodge and two Plymouth Max Wedge sedans were sent to famed Detroit customizers the Alexander Brothers in February 1964. They were modified to fit the new 426 Hemi motors. In addition, the cars were fitted with aluminum doors.

With the Chrysler Super Stocks having already had their rear axles moved 1 inch, the A/FX cars took the theme much further. The front crossmember in each car was cut and moved forward, while the steering shaft and torsion bars also required treatment.

On the Dodges, the front axle line was moved forward by 4 inches, while on the Plymouths, it was 3 inches. With the Dodges already having a longer wheelbase than the Plymouths, the rear end on these two cars were moved forward 5 inches. The Plymouths, with their stock shorter wheelbase in addition to the 1-inch Super Stock adjustment, were left untouched. The rear fender openings on the Dodges were moved forward with the rear axle, whereas the existing front fender openings on both models were extended forward, rather than cut then moved.

Of the four A/FX cars, the two Dodges were earmarked for the Ramchargers and the Dodge Boys (Dave Strickler), while the two Plymouths were intended to go to the Golden Commandos and Tom Grove (*Melrose Missile*). However, Al Eckstrand did a little clever maneuvering with his high-powered connections within Chrysler and scored the Commandos' car.

Building and testing of the A/FX machines suffered various delays, while the NASCAR program and the Daytona 500 took precedence. Testing had been performed at Irwindale just prior to the Winternationals, but ongoing issues ensured that they never raced, even though they were on display at Pomona.

The first of the four cars to compete was the Ramchargers Dodge, which ran at an NHRA event at Detroit Dragway in April. Although the cars were initially fitted with Carter carburetors, the Ramchargers trialed Holleys and found them to be an improvement, so Holleys were fitted to the production Hemi Super Stocks when they were produced from April through June.

Dick Landy's Altered-Wheelbase Dodge

There was a fifth altered-wheelbase Mopar constructed in late 1964, although this was a self-built effort. Dick Landy campaigned a factory Hemi Dodge Super Stock resplendent in his traditional Mercedes metallic silver. He and his Automotive Research company worked closely with Chrysler engineers.

By the fall of 1964, following the NHRA National Championships, Landy opted to convert the Dodge into an A/FX racer and altered the wheelbase significantly. He moved the back axle forward 8 inches and the front 6 inches. He replaced the entire factory front setup with the beam axle and parallel leaf springs from a Dodge A100 van. The reprofiled racer looked outrageous, and it quickly became a fan favorite. Its wildly altered wheelbase prompted some to credit this as the first Funny Car.

Incidentally, having been stripped of their A/FX Plymouth, the Golden Commandos were gifted one of the very first race Hemi motors to install in their Max Wedge hardtop, which they'd been campaigning since the start of the year. In addition, they received a one-off set of aluminum hardtop doors. The Commandos later received one of the Hemi Super Stock sedans, but the team achieved a lot of success with the hardtop in 1964 and continued racing it throughout the year.

Butch Leal visits Dick Landy's shop. The young Leal became a Ford factory driver at age 19, and by 1964, he was driving one of the latest 427 Fairlane Thunderbolts. But he'd be coaxed across to Chrysler for 1965 to drive a Hemi Plymouth. (Photo Courtesy Geoff Stunkard Collection/Landy Family Archive)

Crew and fans gather around Dick Landy's Hemi-powered Dodge 330 sedan. You just know the kid peering in the driver's window is going to be a race fan for life. (Photo Courtesy Geoff Stunkard Collection/Landy Family Archive)

Tommy Grove lights the bags at Indianapolis Raceway Park in the latest Melrose Missile VI *Hemi sedan. The Hemi lightweight package featured a two-headlight grille, but confusingly, this car carries a Wedge hood scoop with the double humps rather than the flat-top Hemi hood scoop. This was a quirk unique to the very early Hemi cars. (Photo Courtesy Geoff Stunkard Collection/Kramer Automotive Archive)*

1964 NHRA U.S. Nationals

In early September 1964, the NHRA hosted the tenth annual National Championships, the Big Go, the most significant drag racing event on the planet. Taking place over five days, the entry list topped 1,200 cars, while the racers vied for prizes totaling $45,000, the richest prize purse in drag racing to that point.

In addition, and certainly more importantly, they were competing for bragging rights. For the fourth year in succession, Indianapolis Raceway Park hosted the Big Go. More than 100,000 pumped race fans were on hand to witness the biggest and most important drag racing event yet.

While the explosive and spectacular Top Fuel cars remained the headline act, the thundering Super Stocks were now firmly established in the number-two position. With Wednesday being a preparation and tech inspection day, the teams finally got to unleash their monsters on Thursday.

In Super Stock Automatic, if the car wasn't a lightweight 1964 Hemi-powered Dodge or Plymouth, it wasn't in the running. S/SA was a total Chrysler whitewash, with Roger Lindamood of Birmingham, Michigan, setting the early pace in the *Color Me Gone* Dodge. He punched out a best time on Thursday of 11.40 and was followed closely by John Dallafrior's Plymouth at 11.47. Then came Jim Thornton in the Ramchargers Dodge followed by sentimental favorite Hank Taylor of Dickinson, Texas. Taylor was just 15 years old and had only been driving six months! Yet, far from being intimidated by the esteemed company he was keeping, he knocked out a best run of 11.57 in his Hemi Plymouth.

In Friday's running, Thornton moved to the front, thumping out an 11.32, while the positions behind him remained largely unchanged. Such was Chrysler's dominance in S/SA, the first non-Mopar was the Ford of Bill Lawton, mired down in 15th place on an 11.81.

The Super Stock teams spent Saturday tuning their machinery before returning on Sunday to begin eliminations. The large and vocal crowd was primed. In S/SA, every car that made it through to the top eight was a Mopar.

Jim Thornton in the Ramchargers Dodge defeated Jerry Austin in the Nice Guys Dodge with Austin smoking the tires mid-track. Bud Faubel was then taken down by Forrest Pitcock in the Golden Commandos hardtop. In the third heat, Paul Rossi's Plymouth beat Bob Harrop's Dodge, while Dan Smoker, despite breaking traction mid-course, headed John Dallafior

The Ramchargers Dodge gets set to launch during a twilight meeting at Cecil County Dragway. (Photo Courtesy Geoff Stunkard Collection/Kramer Automotive Archive)

"Smoker" Smith's Merrimac Motors S/SA Hemi Plymouth guns the start at the 1964 U.S. Nationals, going up against a 1959 Chevy. (Photo Courtesy Geoff Stunkard Collection/Kramer Automotive Archive)

home, thanks to a big advantage off the line.

In the semifinals, Pitcock defeated Smoker and Thornton beat Russo, laying the foundations for a Chrysler in-house battle in the final. In slaying Russo, Thornton smashed out an impressive 11.26 at 128.93 mph, and perhaps that was playing on Pitcock's mind as the pair rolled to the start line. When the lights went green, the Golden Commandos Plymouth had already left, and Thornton won the race before he even got moving.

The big Stockers all returned for Monday's final day of action, battling for the most coveted prize in Stock car drag racing: Mr. Stock Eliminator. Of the top 16 cars, Butch Leal's was the only non-Mopar to make the show, and he was sent home by Thornton in Round 1. The top eight, therefore, were all Chryslers. The first heat was a repeat of Sunday's S/SA final with Thornton squaring up against Pitcock. And unbelievably, Pitcock redlit again.

In Round 1, the Golden Commandos had barely scraped by Al Eckstrand with a winning 11.59 at 128.02 mph. Thornton, by comparison, ran an 11.39 at 128.93 mph. Pitcock needed to blitz Thornton at the light to have a chance. But redlighting wasn't part of the plan.

In the second heat, Bud Faubel beat John Dallafior and Dick Landy also advanced, fending off Bob Harrop. Roger Lindamood's run was made easy when Jerry Austin jumped the light.

Confusingly, despite being eliminated in Round 2, Dallafior ended up facing Thornton, who beat him on the track before the organizers realized the mistake. Lindamood then took a comfortable victory over Landy and Faubel was given a solo run. With Thornton then beating Faubel in the semi, and Lindamood taking a bye run, it was an all-Dodge final with the famed Ramchargers facing off against the equally celebrated *Color Me Gone*.

The vast crowd was on its feet as the two big Dodges rolled into the starter's blocks. With Thornton having run an 11.31 during eliminations and Lindamood with a best of 11.36, it was too close to call. When the lights flicked to green, it was Lindamood who pulled out a small advantage at the start, which he stretched to a car-length by mid-track. The two Dodges bombed down the strip, and the crowd roared. When they shot through the traps at the end, Lindamood was Champion. As well as winning a giant trophy, Lindamood also got to take home a brand-new Ford Mustang.

The end of 1964 saw a splintering of Stock drag racing competition, with Ford and Chrysler having opted for separate divisions. General Motors had long since exited the sport. As such, the furious inter-brand battles that took place in 1962 and 1963 were largely consigned to history. Dodge and Plymouth products were locking out the headline races at the big events. While that may have detracted somewhat from the original intent of Super Stock drag racing, for Chrysler's marketing team, there were no complaints.

This hotel parking lot hosted a row of Super Stocks, including the pair of Dick Landy Dodges, Bill "Maverick" Golden's Dodge, and a Fairlane Thunderbolt. Landy was running a Hemi-powered sedan by now, and both that and the hardtop were pulled around the country on an A-frame. (Photo Courtesy Geoff Stunkard Collection/Landy Family Archive)

Roger Lindamood races the striking Color Me Gone Hemi Dodge. Lindamood was one of the few to topple the hugely successful Ramchargers team in 1964, including at the all-important U.S. Nationals at Indianapolis. The name Color Me Gone was taken from a line in the popular 1963 song "My Coloring Book." (Photo Courtesy Geoff Stunkard Collection/ Ray Mann Archive)

Dave Strickler in the Dodge Boys Hemi sedan runs a Chevelle at Aquasco Speedway, the first quarter-mile drag strip on the East Coast. As 1964 progressed, the new altered-wheelbase cars began appearing in A/FX competition. These very early altered-wheelbase cars were sowing the seeds for what would ultimately result in the Funny Car division. (Photo Courtesy Geoff Stunkard Collection/Kramer Automotive Archive)

Having opened his 1964 account driving a Ramchargers Dodge, Al "Lawman" Eckstrand worked his way through to the final at the NHRA Winternationals, where he lost to Doug Lovegrove. By the time of the U.S. Nationals in September, he was back aboard his own car(s). He had a busy weekend at the U.S. Nationals, running a pair of Lawman Hemi Plymouths in both Super Stock and A/FX. Note the primered front bodywork on the A/FX machine, following a highway accident that required repairs. (Photos Courtesy Geoff Stunkard Collection/Kramer Automotive Archive)

CHAPTER 5

1965

CHRYSLER STOCKERS GO FUNNY

Although Chrysler's primary target for developing its epic new 426-ci Hemi was the NASCAR Grand National, ultimately, it was the company's drag racing program that benefitted the most—at least initially.

After the slippery new Chrysler hardtops dominated the 1964 Daytona 500, Richard Petty not only claimed his first big Daytona win but also went on to win his first NASCAR Grand National championship. Petty wouldn't get to defend either crown because NASCAR deemed the race Hemi to be ineligible to compete in 1965.

NASCAR's beef with the Hemi was that Chrysler developed and produced it purely as a race motor—and it was right. Chrysler customers couldn't actually order a Hemi for their street car. While the Grand National had progressively evolved away from its original roots as a strictly stock category, NASCAR drew the line at manufacturers developing pure-bred racing engines that were off limits to their regular customers.

Chrysler might have argued that the new Hemi was simply a development of the existing RB motor, itself readily available as an option on several of its road-going models, but NASCAR was having none of it. The Hemi was gone for 1965, and Chrysler opted to withdraw. With that, the Ford teams were left to race each other.

Petty actually scored three race victories in 1965, and David Pearson won two in his Don Nichols–engineered Dodge. But these were Wedge engine cars that really only had any hope of success on short tracks and dirt tracks, where outright horsepower was all but canceled out.

Chrysler spent 1965 building a street version of its Hemi, which could be ordered by customers for their road cars and ultimately won the company a berth in the 1966 Grand National. While its NASCAR ambitions were shelved for now, it focused its 1965 racing operations on drag racing, at which it went all guns blazing.

The new altered-wheelbase craze took 1965 by storm. The NHRA wanted nothing to do with them, but other drag racing governing bodies and event promoters went nuts for them and did whatever it took to shoehorn them into their programs. The crowds loved them, and they were truly spectacular. Here, a crowd at Lions Drag Strip watches in amazement as Butch Leal and Dick Landy go at it. (Photo Courtesy Dan Shannon/Tony Thacker)

This was a sign of things to come. Dick Landy's new altered-wheelbase Dodge is up on the hoist, prior to paint and sign writing. Like many of the Chrysler factory drivers in 1965, the feral new altered-wheelbase cars pulled Landy away from Super Stock competition for the most part. (Photo Courtesy Geoff Stunkard Collection/ Landy Family Archive)

"Wild" Bill Flynn makes a run at Connecticut Dragway in his 1964 Plymouth. Flynn also had a new 1965 Plymouth that he ran briefly at the start of the year in Super Stock competition before he had it converted to an altered-wheelbase car. (Photo Courtesy Charles Milikin Jr.)

Dave Koffel, pictured at York U.S. 30 Drag-O-Way in his Plymouth, ran in C/Factory Experimental. (Photo Courtesy Charles Milikin Jr.)

Joe Otten's 1963 Plymouth is pictured at Vargo Dragstrip in Pennsylvania. (Photo Courtesy Charles Milikin Jr.)

ELTON "AL THE LAWMAN" ECKSTRAND

The Golden Commandos concentrated largely on their altered-wheelbase car in 1965 at the expense of their Super Stock program. Their hardtop was supplied incomplete and required radical wheelbase alterations to be carried out themselves (the Ramchargers and Color Me Gone *cars were supplied likewise). Al "Lawman" Eckstrand piloted the wild Plymouth. (Photo Courtesy Robert A. Carley/Rob Carley Collection)*

The drag racing career of Elton "Al" Eckstrand was relatively short. But as with virtually every other aspect of what appeared to be a charmed and fulfilling life, Al excelled.

Hailing from Detroit, Eckstrand gained a master's degree in social psychology and a doctorate degree in law. In 1955, he began a career in law at Chrysler. Chrysler President E. C. Quinn personally placed him. His nickname "Al" emerged during his time working on drag racing projects with Chrysler Vice President of Sales Byron Nichols. When Chrysler purchased a 30-percent stake in the Rootes Group in 1964, Eckstrand was sent to England to oversee the transition.

Eckstrand was a keen racer, and he engaged in his hobby at the track and, on occasion, on the street. As Chrysler's official drag racing programs began to gain traction, Eckstrand was quick to get involved. He received direct funding from Chrysler and raced a Stanford Dodge 413-ci Max Wedge Dart at the 1962 U.S. Nationals. He made it through to the semifinals only to be put on the trailer by Jim Thorton in the Ramchargers machine in Mr. Stock Eliminator.

For 1963, he drove a second Ramchargers Dodge and swept all before him to win Mr. Stock Eliminator at the NHRA Winternationals. In doing so, he beat Bill Shirey in the Golden Commandos Plymouth.

By the U.S. Nationals at Indy, he was aboard his own car with "Lawman" lettering blazing down the flanks, in reference to his role at Chrysler. Once again, he took down every opponent he faced, including, again, the Golden Commandos Plymouth in the semifinals. In the final, he went head-to-head with Herman Mozer in one of the Ramchargers Dodges, and Eckstrand very narrowly lost on a 12.23 to Mozer's 12.22.

At the 1964 NHRA Winternationals, Eckstrand charged his way to the semifinals, where he lost to Doug Lovegrove in the Mayshak Plymouth. He then secured one of the new altered-wheelbase Hemi cars that he raced throughout the remainder of the year.

For 1965, he joined the Golden Commandos, who were gifted one of the latest Hemi hardtops, which they themselves converted to altered-wheelbase state. Their hardtop was supplied incomplete and requiring the radical wheelbase alterations be carried out themselves. (The Ramchargers and *Color Me Gone* cars were supplied likewise.) However, before doing so, they raced it at the AHRA Winternationals. Eckstrand went right through to the finals, where he faced Bud Faubel's 110-inch-wheelbase car. The much-improved rear weight distribution of the radical altered-wheelbase car told, and Faubel blasted through for the win.

On August 7, Eckstrand raced the Golden Commandos Hemi Plymouth, now rebuilt as a 110 altered-wheelbase car, in the Unlimited Class in the 1965 Super Stock Nationals. Having blitzed all before him, he was pitted against Dick Landy's altered-wheelbase Dodge and blazed down the chute to record a winning 9.77 at 142.40 mph. With that, Eckstrand promptly retired from racing.

Eckstrand left Chrysler in 1965 to establish his own law firm, but he continued performing legal work for Detroit's auto makers. He uprooted to live in England in 1966.

When Eckstrand moved to the "motherland," he took with him the first production Hemi-powered Dodge Charger. The Charger formed part of a new program to train servicemen stationed in Europe on the importance of driver safety, as an increasing number were getting killed in automobile accidents each year after they returned home and acquired the latest powerful muscle cars.

Eckstrand was so passionate about the program, he proposed doing it again a few years later when young Americans were sent to fight in Vietnam. Although Chrysler didn't want to fund the program, Ford stepped up and arranged to send two supercharged Lawman Boss 429 Mustangs to Vietnam. One was destroyed in a shipping bungle, but the other spearheaded a high-performance driving skills tour that largely utilized stock Mustangs and Mavericks. Over the next three years, Eckstrand's professional driving skills tour was demonstrated to nearly a quarter-million returning servicemen, earning him an honorary citation from the Department of Defense.

As a side note, one of his demonstrations was watched by a 5-year-old Vietnamese boy named Hau Thai-Tang. Thai-Tang was so enamored with the Mustang performing the demonstrations that he made it his life goal to become an automotive designer when his family immigrated to the United States. Indeed, he went on to work for Ford and became Mustang chief engineer on the 2005 model that was first to borrow heavily from the classic Mustangs of the 1960s, embracing the new retro look.

Eckstrand returned to England, where he involved himself in restoring castles. He then moved back to the U.S. for good in the late 1990s, settling in Naples, Florida.

Another great passion was photographing birds of prey, and his spectacular photos are displayed in zoos in England and the United States. They are used to promote their preservation as part of conservation programs. They've also been the subject of several exhibitions.

Elton "Al" Eckstrand, the "Lawman," died in 2008.

Drag racing truly benefitted from Chrysler's NASCAR withdrawal. Indeed, it made available turnkey drag cars for two different 1965 categories: a Dodge or Plymouth Super Stock and a Dodge or Plymouth A/Factory Experimental.

1965 Chrysler B-Body Street Cars

Chrysler launched its 1965 mid-sized Dodge and Plymouth models in September 1964. The distinctive, if slightly subdued, styling of the 1964 offerings was altered a little more to produce a slightly cleaner look. The Dodge models were reduced in length from 119 to 117 inches of wheelbase. For the sake of simplifying, they were branded the Coronet, a nameplate Chrysler had put on ice in 1959.

The midsized 1965 Plymouth was called the Belvedere and marketed as the Belvedere I, Belvedere II, or Satellite for the top-of-the-line hardtop and convertible variants. The Fury name was restored to its full-size billing. The B-Body Plymouths retained their 116-inch wheelbase.

Bob Repine's Hemi Thrasher *Hemi-propelled 1965 Belvedere is pictured here at York U.S. 30 Drag-O-Way. (Photo Courtesy Charles Milikin Jr.)*

"Doc" Burgess is in the altered-wheelbase Black Arrow *Plymouth. Bill "Grumpy" Jenkins drove this car later in the year at Indy to beat Charlie Allen's* Atlantic Dodge Flyer Hemi *Coronet. (Photo Courtesy Charles Milikin Jr.)*

Rich Lechner in the ex-Bill Flynn 1964 Plymouth is pictured at Connecticut Dragway. Lechner later fitted the car with fuel injection. (Photo Courtesy Charles Milikin Jr.)

Tommy Grove nails it in the 1964 Melrose Missile VI. By 1965, the sixth Missile had become a "two percent" car with a mildly altered wheelbase, thus making it legal for A/FX competition. (Photo Courtesy Charles Milikin Jr.)

Larry Apocada's 1965 Hemi Plymouth launches in a head-to-head race with a Willys at Fremont Dragstrip. (Photo Courtesy Charles Milikin Jr.)

Likewise, powertrain options for 1965 models were largely unchanged. They ranged from the 225-ci 6-cylinder through to the 426-ci street Wedge, producing 365 hp. V-8 buyers had a choice of either 4-speed manual or TorqueFlite transmissions and gear ratios of either 2.94 or 3.55:1.

1965 Chrysler Super Stock Packages

For 1965, the NHRA tweaked its Super Stock regulations once more, banning the lightweight aluminum bolt-on body parts and demanding the bodies be all steel. In addition, a minimum of 100 cars had to be built to be eligible. To that end, Chrysler set about constructing 101 Dodge Coronet and Plymouth Belvedere I turnkey Super Stock drag cars. The commitment level was impressive and, aided by Chrysler's NASCAR withdrawal, opened up resources that would otherwise have been swallowed by that program.

All of the 1965 Chrysler Super Stocks were based on the two-door sedan body. There were no hardtops. Each car was to have its own Chrysler Vehicle Identification Number (VIN) and sales code (Dodge VINs started with R051, Plymouths with W051), and the company chose to produce turnkey cars to ensure their customers received vehicles that were 100-percent NHRA compliant. All the Chrysler Super Stocks were built at the Lynch Road, Michigan, plant on a regular assembly line, before being sent to a nearby shop where Chrysler engineers completed them.

The Super Stock regulations required all-steel bodywork, but Chrysler still went to remarkable lengths to keep weight to a minimum. It had the front fenders, hood, hood scoop, doors, and radiator support panel all stamped from thin-gauge steel. Some of the components were also acid dipped. The front bumper was made from 0.054-inch-thick steel and mounted on lightweight brackets.

The acid-dipping process involved marinating pieces of metal in a large acid tank for a set period of time, whereby the acid would eat away at the metal, thus reducing its weight. At least one shop in California performed a lot of acid-dipping work for manufacturer-supported race teams, particularly those competing in the NASCAR Grand National.

The factory door glass, quarter-windows, and rear glass were all replaced by 0.080-inch-thick tempered glass made by Corning Chem-Cor. Much like the 1964 Hemi Super Stocks, the interiors were sparce and featured a pair

Bill Rubin makes a charge at Cecil County in his handsome Hemi Plymouth. (Photo Courtesy Charles Milikin Jr.)

This is W. W. "Pee Wee" Wallace's Hemi-powered Plymouth, The Virginian III. *Entered by Mallory's Speed Shop, Wallace ran in both Super Stock and match-bash Funny Car events with an altered-wheelbase variant. (Photo Courtesy Pee Wee Wallace Family Collection)*

Jack Werst is at Cecil County in the famous Mr. 5 And 50 *Hemi Plymouth, tuned by Bill Jenkins. (Photo Courtesy Charles Milikin Jr.)*

of Bostrom Companion bucket seats similar to those fitted to the Dodge A100 van, while the back seat was removed entirely and replaced with a cardboard panel. The lightweight carpet was finished in tan. The seats, door trims, and cardboard panel were metallic tan. The visors, dome light, and coat hooks were deleted. The battery was mounted in the passenger-side trunk floor on a sturdy steel plate and plastic tray.

The mighty A990 426-ci full race Hemi was much the same as it had been in 1964, but the solid-lifter camshaft was redesigned. With the new NHRA restrictions, Chrysler engineers looked to make frontal weight savings in other areas, including the motor. The heads were cast in aluminum, while aluminum and magnesium were used in other parts of the engine to shed further ounces where possible. The big dual 4-barrel intake manifold was cast in magnesium, rather than aluminum, and topped with a pair of Holley 4160 carburetors, which were shrouded in unsilenced chrome air cleaners.

Other than the hood scoop, the 1965 Chrysler Super Stocks looked like regular low-line B-Body models. Although the Dodges had their inner headlights removed, they were replaced by an additional grille section riveted in place.

Buyers had only two transmission options. They could choose from the A833 4-speed manual or the A727B TorqueFlite automatic. The 4-speed wore an aluminum case and housing, and racers would bash through the gears via a Hurst DP-4-65 Competition Plus shifter. The TorqueFlite sported a high-speed stall converter, was modified for manual shifting, and had a reverse pattern.

Once again, the rear springs had the 20-inch front leaf section, which shortened the wheelbase on both cars by 1 inch. But the Dodge also featured the shorter Plymouth rear spring hangers, which reduced wheelbase by an extra inch, making it the same as the Belvedere. The big 8.75-inch Chrysler rear end carried 4.56:1 gears and Sure-Grip limited-slip differential.

The retail price was $4,717 for the Dodge and $4,671 for the Plymouth. That was certainly an eye-watering price for a baseline B-Body Chrysler in 1965 (an entry-level Belvedere started at $2,198), but these were very specific cars, partially hand-built and designed for a single purpose. Even the greenest of racers should expect to punch out low-11-second quarter-mile times with little effort. The professional teams, of course, stripped the cars down and rebuilt them, honing every detail in search of the magical fractions that separate winners from the also-rans.

1965 Chrysler Altered-Wheelbase Cars

Meanwhile, Chrysler also committed to producing a small number (11 plus a mule car) of altered-wheelbase A/FX race cars based on the two-door hardtop body.

Following the 1964 racing season, Ford switched its attention to the A/Factory Experimental class. It already ran a fleet of 427-ci Mercury Comets in A/FX in 1964, while its 427-powered Fairlanes ran in Super Stock. Neither the Comet nor the Fairlane street cars were offered with a big-block engine.

The conversions were outsourced to Dearborn Steel Tubing. Ford could potentially have produced the minimum 100 required 427-powered Fairlanes or Comets (or both) but opted instead to concentrate on the exciting A/FX category, which was quickly becoming a fan favorite. For 1965, aside from a lone 427 Fairlane Thunderbolt for Darrell Droke, Ford focused its attentions on the new Mustang pony car with its short 108-inch wheelbase and dramatic fastback roofline.

For any car manufacturer, there are multiple reasons for entering racing competition, including promoting the sporting, performance, and endurance qualities of its products. In addition, there is the pure egotistical drive to tackle and beat rival manufacturers in a public arena.

In late 1964, Ford's massive Total Performance program was on a global scale. Its vice president, Lee Iacocca, announced, "We will stay in open competition as long as we feel it contributes to better automobiles for the public. It's estimated that 43 million people a year now go to motorsport events. We may be old fashioned, but with that many people in the stands, we figure it's a pretty good place to show how well our products can perform in direct competition with the products of other manufacturers."

Dick Landy's wild new altered-wheelbase Dodge is pictured in the Fremont pits in March 1965. With Landy being one of the very first to build an altered-wheelbase car in late 1964, it seems natural he fully embraced this new breed of machine when they exploded in popularity in 1965. (Photo Courtesy Tom Bettencourt)

Stuffed with a 427 single overhead camshaft (SOHC) featuring hemispherical combustion chambers, the slinky little Mustangs were deemed 100-percent legal for NHRA A/FX. The NHRA allowed wheelbase movement of up to 2 percent from the stock arrangement, and even with the Mustang having its back axle moved forward 2 inches, it still fell comfortably within the regulation requirements.

On hearing of Ford's decision to run the Mustang, Chrysler's logical step was surely to counter by introducing a Hemi-powered variant of its compact Dodge Dart and Plymouth Barracuda, both of which were its Mustang rivals in new car showrooms. Instead, it stuck with the B-Body platform, and simply went savage in its wheelbase alterations. The end results were not subtle at all. Ultimately, the A/FX Chrysler hardtops arrived at an impossibly stubby 110-inch wheelbase, despite being around 23 inches longer in overall length than a stock Mustang.

The altered-wheelbase Mopars had their rear axle line moved forward by 15 inches and the front by 10 inches. Resting at a standstill, they appeared to be teetering on the back wheels with the front tires barely making contact with the ground. The rear end modifications were achieved by removing a 15-inch section out of the floor and chassis directly ahead of the front of the spring mounting, cutting the rear floor pan carrying the back axle and springs, and shifting the whole section forward into the vacant space. A new 15-inch section of flat sheet was then added in at the rear to fill the void. The rear wheel openings were also moved forward.

Up front, the crossmember and upper control arm supports were all moved forward 10 inches, and new front side members were fabricated. Longer and thicker torsion bars were installed, plus a longer steering shaft and rear torsion bar mountings were lowered. The Hemi motor was held in place via mounts added to the side members rather than the crossmember.

Of course, the big B-Body Chryslers were put on a strict weight loss program, which included having the entire body shell acid dipped. Likewise, new bolt-on body panels, including the front fenders, hood, taller A/FX hood scoop, doors, and decklid were all produced in fiberglass, while the front bumper was also lightened.

Being factory-produced cars, the intention was that the A/FX racers carried a Chrysler VIN, but in most cases, this didn't actually happen.

Unlike Chrysler's 1965 Super Stocks, the altered-wheelbase cars were fitted with a roll cage, which is a half-body construction positioned behind the single driver's seat. Part of the reason for the cage, aside from its safety features, was to help the massively compromised acid-dipped hardtop body shells withstand the violent twisting forces being transmitted through them. Certainly, the bodies had become structurally weak, and teams had to perform various fixes to keep them from completely tearing apart. It was common for back windows to pop out. Likewise, the general quality of the workmanship was relatively poor.

Much of the fabrication work was performed by Amblewagon, a Troy, Michigan, company that normally produced ambulances. However, a few teams were sent an unaltered acid-dipped body, a donor Super Stock, plus the requisite parts so they could carry out their own conversions. The Ramchargers, Golden Commandos, and *Color Me Gone* A/FX altered-wheelbase Mopars were all converted by their respective teams.

Chrysler hadn't informed the NHRA of its intentions to build the altered-wheelbase cars, and naturally, when NHRA officials first laid eyes on the whacky looking creations, they didn't know what to make of them. Certainly, they couldn't accept them into A/FX. At best, they could run B/Altered or exhibition. That they didn't qualify wasn't really a problem. Increasingly, match races and exhibition races, as well as events run by rival sanctioning bodies, offered outlets to campaign outlaw cars. Their outlandish looks and fiendish performance ensured that event promoters would concoct creative ways to accommodate them.

Increasingly, drag racing was evolving into a form of entertainment rather than pure head-to-head competition. Manufacturers were assisting in the construction of vehicles that served no other purpose than to wow the crowds. Indeed, the crazy *Hemi Under Glass* wheel-standing Plymouth Barracuda and Bill "Maverick" Golden's even more bizarre *Little Red Wagon* Dodge A100 truck were prime examples. The crowds lapped it up, and naturally, the promoters were highly motivated to include them in their programs.

New Chrysler Recruits

In addition to its ever-evolving race car fleet, Chrysler continued to grow its team of factory-supported drivers. It coaxed Butch Leal across

Dave Strickler launches hard at York U.S. 30 Drag-O-Way in his 1965 Dodge Coronet altered-wheelbase hardtop. Strickler received one of the six official altered-wheelbase Dodges that were completed prior to delivery. (Photo Courtesy Charles Milikin Jr.)

The super side profile of Dave Strickler's altered-wheelbase Dodge Coronet shows just how dramatic the 1965 Mopar alterations were. (Photo Courtesy Charles Milikin Jr.)

Dick Landy lets it rip in his altered-wheelbase Dodge Coronet at Bakersfield. This was one of the six Dodge factory altered-wheelbase cars. Like many of the Chrysler factory teams, Landy spent much of 1965 campaigning this car in whatever competition it was accepted at the expense of his Super Stock commitments. But by 1965, this new breed of wild machinery had really captured the public's attention, and event promoters were keen to shoehorn them into their programs. The cigar clenched between his teeth is clearly visible here. His friend Andy Andrews got him into the cigars. Although Landy never smoked, and the cigars were never lit, Andrews would hand him one for luck. Very soon, "Dandy" Dick couldn't be without them. (Photo Courtesy Charles Milikin Jr.)

Ronnie Sox cruises up the return road at Cecil County in his altered-wheelbase Plymouth Belvedere. It was rare that the Sox & Martin team ran the car without the hood. In addition to the altered-wheelbase hardtop, the Sox & Martin team built its own altered-wheelbase sedan. (Photo Courtesy Charles Milikin Jr.)

In addition to his regular Plymouth Super Stock, new Chrysler recruit Butch Leal was supplied one of the wild new altered-wheelbase cars. Note the air dam beneath the front bumper. The factory altered-wheelbase cars weren't supplied with these fitted. They were a preference for some teams. (Photo Courtesy Dan Shannon/Tony Thacker)

Butch Leal wows the crowd (some of which stood on the hood of their Chevys) at Cecil County. (Photo Courtesy Charles Milikin Jr.)

Bill Flynn launches the Yankee Peddler Dodge at Connecticut Dragway. The bold gold and candy red sedan started the 1965 racing season as a stock-bodied Super Stock car before Flynn had Dick Branstner convert it to an altered-wheelbase variant early in the year. Initially, it ran carburetors, but it soon sported Hilborn fuel injection. (Photo Courtesy Charles Milikin Jr.)

from Ford, and it brought the racing partnership of Ronnie Sox and Buddy Martin from Mercury to campaign its cars in 1965.

The six Dodge altered-wheelbase cars were assigned to the Ramchargers, Roger Lindamood (*Color Me Gone*), Dick Landy, Bob Harrop (*The Flying Carpet*), Dave Strickler, and longtime Chrysler campaigner Bud Faubel (*Hemi Honker*). The Plymouths went to Tom Grove (*Melrose Missile*), Lee Smith, Forrest Pitcock, and Al Eckstrand (Golden Commandos), plus new signings Butch Leal (*The California Flash*) and Sox & Martin (*Paper Tiger*). One of the two cars that went to the Golden Commandos was the prototype mule.

Meanwhile, a further altered-wheelbase Chrysler was constructed at Dick Branstner's shop in Michigan for its owner Bill Flynn. Flynn was due to receive an altered-wheelbase hardtop but following delays decided to convert his Hemi Dodge Super Stock sedan, the *Yankee Peddler*. Flynn had raced the Dodge at the 1965 Winternationals in its original guise before it was sent to Branstner for altered-wheelbase and lightweight-body-panel conversion.

ROGER LINDAMOOD

Roger Lindamood was a late bloomer in the world of drag racing. He didn't enter the sport until he was 35. Prior to that, he cut his teeth in the rough and tumble world of speedway racing, competing on the dirt and asphalt short tracks in and around Michigan. He achieved his success not just through his driving but also through his mechanical expertise. He worked for Chrysler in its transmission department.

Lindamood was instrumental in the Ramchargers drag racing team switching from manual to automatic transmissions, and it was through this relationship that he first met race car fabricator Dick Branstner. It was Branstner who, in 1963, convinced Lindamood to give drag racing a punt. He really wasn't interested. He thought it looked boring.

During his drag racing career, Lindamood's cars were traditionally painted white and blue and carried the name *Color Me Gone* down the flanks. Inspired by a line in the popular 1963 song "My Coloring Book," Lindamood's team was said to have written in shoe polish "I'm A Plymouth . . . Color Me Gone" on the car at one event, and a track announcer picked up on it. As every drag car had to have a name, *Color Me Gone* was a keeper.

As well as racing, Lindamood was regularly recruited for testing duties. The list of famed whacky racers he piloted includes the *Little Red Wagon* Dodge A100 wheel-stander and Branstner's rear-engined Dodge station wagon *The Cotton Picker*.

Throughout his 15 years in drag racing, Lindamood remained loyal to the Chrysler brand. He only ran Super Stocks for a short time in 1964 and 1965 before switching to one of the exciting new altered-wheelbase cars. He opened his 1965 account at the AHRA Winternationals and NHRA Winternationals by running one of a handful of acid-dipped Hemi hardtops that had yet to have the 110-inch altered-wheelbase treatment. As such, he still qualified to compete in Super Stock, where he reached the final in Top Stock Eliminator. He also went to the semifinal in Mr. Stock Eliminator as the last stock-wheelbase Chrysler driver still standing. From there, he converted the car to 110-inch altered wheelbase and dove headfirst into Funny Car competition and never looked back.

Despite his long list of racing achievements, most of which were in Funny Car competition, it was his victory at the 1964 U.S. Nationals that he was most proud of. It was here where he faced and beat the dominant Ramchargers team that had been tearing through the Super Stock division all year.

Roger Lindamood died in 2018 at age 91.

*Roger Lindamood launches hard in the **Color Me Gone** Hemi-powered Plymouth hardtop at the 1965 AHRA Winternationals at Beeline Dragway. Note the car's stock wheelbase. Although this would become an altered-wheelbase car, its initial outings were in stock form. (Photo Courtesy Paul Hutchins)*

This is a stunning close-up of Bill Flynn's beautifully painted Yankee Peddler. (Photo Courtesy Charles Milikin Jr.)

Raphael Shields throttles up on the McCroan Autos Sales Hemi A Go Go Dodge Coronet. The Garland, Texas–based Coronet was flat-towed to the track, which is evident by the matching ball hitches on the front of the race car. (Photo Courtesy Jack Ravenna)

1965 Drag Racing Highlights

The 1965 national drag racing season dawned, as was now a tradition, with the AHRA Winternationals kicking things off, followed quickly by the NHRA Winternationals. But with the arrival of the new altered-wheelbase cars, the NHRA in particular struggled to accept them, and its 1965 events suffered as a result of their absence at many of these meetings. However, the rapid rise in popularity that drag racing was enjoying prompted the creation of a new event: the NHRA Springnationals. It was in early June at the spectacular new Bristol International Dragway. Despite the best efforts of the NHRA, the Funny Cars were invited to the party.

1965 AHRA Winternationals

The first big event on the 1965 calendar was the AHRA Winternationals, which took place from January 29 to 31, at Beeline Dragway in Scottsdale, Arizona.

Unlike the NHRA, the AHRA was more willing to accommodate the weird-looking Chrysler altered-wheelbase cars. Its Stock car rules were formatted as follows:

- S/S-1: up to 3,200 pounds with a stock wheelbase
- S/S: up to 3,200 pounds with an altered wheelbase up to 2 percent
- U/S (Ultra Stock): up to 3,000 pounds with an altered wheelbase up to 12 percent

The S/S and U/S cars could also be fitted with lightweight body panels and any tire size the team could get its hands on.

Eight 110-inch altered-wheelbase Chryslers were completed and running at the Winternationals, including those of Landy, Sox & Martin, Leal, Smith, Faubel, Pitcock, and Harrop. In addition were the Ramchargers, *Melrose Missile*, Eckstrand's Golden Commando, and *Color Me Gone* hardtops, which had been acid dipped and wore the fiberglass body panels but hadn't yet gone under the knife to receive the 110-inch altered-wheelbase modifications due to time limitations. As such, they'd run in S/S and S/SA.

The outlandish altered-wheelbase cars drew enormous attention from fans and racers alike. Ford factory

Shirley "the Drag-On Lady" Shahan switched to racing Chryslers in 1965 even though it meant ditching her favored 4-speed manual to run an automatic. She took it to the boys too! The Shahans teamed up with another new Chrysler recruit, Butch Leal, a longtime friend of H. L. Shahan. (Photo Courtesy Geoff Stunkard Collection/Ray Mann Archive)

Unlike the Ramchargers, Golden Commandos, and Color Me Gone hardtops, the Sox & Martin Plymouth was one of those supplied to the team with its wheelbase already altered. This was Sox & Martin's first major event as a Chrysler factory team, having been coaxed across from Ford. (Photo Courtesy Paul Hutchins)

Also running its stock wheelbase at the AHRA Winternationals was the new 1965 Ramchargers Dodge hardtop. Like the Color Me Gone and Golden Commandos Plymouths, this car was supplied by Chrysler with an acid-dipped body, which the team would themselves convert to a 110-inch altered-wheelbase car. But here at Beeline Dragway, the team hadn't yet had the chance to perform the radical conversion. (Photo Courtesy Paul Hutchins)

Not all the 1965 altered-wheelbase Mopars were factory-supplied cars. Some teams simply built their own, including Al "Flying Dutchman" Vanderwoude, who converted a 1964 Belvedere sedan. (Photo Courtesy Dan Shannon/Tony Thacker)

driver Phil Bonner arrived with both a 427 SOHC Falcon and a Mustang, but Ford wouldn't allow him to run the Mustang in the U/S class against the Mopars. The company would stand its ground throughout 1965 for all AHRA events.

Wacky though they might have been, the altered-wheelbase cars were getting down the track in a hurry! Some looked like a handful. The manual transmission variants were giving trouble. Landy's 4-speed was like a wild horse, kicking its tail out sideways with each gear change and seemingly trying to spit its rider into the audience. But very soon, the top cars were dipping into the 10s.

It was at this event that track announcer Jon Lundberg reportedly referred to the odd-looking altered-wheelbase Chryslers as "Funny Cars." The term quickly caught on.

Mr. Stock Eliminator fielded the fastest 16 qualifiers with several runs pitting the 110-inch-wheelbase cars against the 2-percent cars. The final had Eckstrand going up against Faubel's 110-inch-wheelbase car. Although both were lightweight hardtops, the advantages enjoyed by the radical altered-wheelbase creation was evident as soon as they launched. Faubel immediately put a car length on Eckstrand and held it to the end. He ran a 10.96 at 129.31 mph.

Chryslers continued their winning performances in the other Stock categories. Mike Buckel, aboard the Ramchargers Dodge, won Top Stock Eliminator, while Joe Smith, driving Fenner Tubbs's Plymouth took out S/S-1. S/S was won by Dave Strickler's Dodge.

Dick Housey (far lane) and Bill "Grumpy" Jenkins await the tree in the finals at the 1965 NHRA Winternationals as the crowd watches in suspense. (Photo Courtesy Clinton Wright)

1965 NHRA Winternationals

One week after the Winter Championships came the NHRA Winternationals at Pomona, California. What was traditionally a three-day event had to be condensed into a single day due to rain and fog on the Friday and Saturday. Somehow, despite the challenges, every scheduled contest took place.

The Winternationals perhaps highlighted a growing problem with the NHRA Super Stock regulations. Chrysler was the only manufacturer building cars to the new rules, and as such, its products spent the weekend racing each other. Top Stock Eliminator consisted of a dozen 1965 Hemi Plymouths. Bill Andress was the lone 4-speed campaigner. He was gone in the first round, beaten by Paul Rossi. When the field was whittled down to two contestants, it was Dick Housey up against Bill "Grumpy" Jenkins. The Grump took the win on an 11.39 at 126.05 mph.

By 1965, Jenkins and Strickler had parted company, and Grumpy was driving Doc Burgess's Hemi-powered *Black Arrow* Plymouth.

The four 115-inch wheelbase lightweight Chrysler Hemi hardtops that contested the AHRA event the week prior (the Ramchargers Dodge, *Color Me Gone* Dodge, *Melrose Missile* Plymouth, and Golden Commandos Plymouth) were entered in Factory Stock Eliminator (A/FX). They'd face four SOHC 427 Comets and five SOHC 427 Mustangs in the 13-car field.

Of the Chrysler contingent, the only pilot that progressed as far as the semifinals was Tom Grove in the *Melrose Missile*, but he failed to reach the final. This was the only 1965 NHRA event in which the Chryslers were eligible to contest A/FX. Shortly afterward, all four cars were completed to full 110-inch altered-wheelbase state, and were thus deemed ineligible from thereon forward.

1965 NHRA Springnationals

Among the new high-profile events established in 1965 was the NHRA Springnationals on June 6 at the magnificent new Bristol International Dragway facility in Tennessee. The track, pit area, and accompanying buildings had effectively been carved into a pair of hilltops. The four-story timing tower was plumbed with air-conditioning, an unprecedented luxury.

The significance of the event and its location ensured all the top teams were present. It was here the NHRA ran its exciting new Funny Car Match Bash, which included the altered-wheelbase Mopars. The NHRA was adamant the outlaw Chryslers wouldn't be competing at its event, but track owner Larry Carrier was adamant they would. He recognized the crowd-pulling attraction of these spectacular rigs and ultimately won the stare down.

The Springnationals attracted the altered-wheelbase cars of Lee Smith, Sox & Martin, the Golden Commandos, Bob Harrop, Dave Strickler, and Bud Faubel. Ford's big guns included "Dyno" Don Nicholson's Mercury

The glorious Hemi-propelled 1965 Melrose Missile Plymouth hardtop wouldn't look like this for long. It was destined to become an altered-wheelbase projectile. (Photo Courtesy Dan Shannon/Tony Thacker)

Tom Atanasoff of Lansing, Michigan, runs hard at Indianapolis Raceway Park in his Hemi Plymouth Belvedere Super Stock. (Photo Courtesy Charles Milikin Jr.)

HILBORN FUEL INJECTION

Bill Flynn romps down the chute at Cecil County. Note how the hood is lifting in the front center, as it lacks support due to the giant hole cut out of the top for the tall injectors. (Photo Courtesy Charles Milikin Jr.)

In June 1964, approval was given to begin development of a Hilborn mechanical fuel-injection system for the altered-wheelbase Mopars. It took several months of trial and error before the complex setup could be tested in a racing environment.

Pitcock's Golden Commandos Plymouth ran injection at the AHRA Winter Championships, and very soon thereafter, Chrysler engineers had the system working nearly faultlessly. With fuel injection installed, Ronnie Sox ran a 10.04 in a grudge match against Arnie Beswick's berserk altered-wheelbase Pontiac GTO in mid-April. With further refining, it busted out a run of 9.98 at York U.S. 30 Drag-O-Way, again while facing Beswick.

This achievement, assisted by a nitromethane fuel mix, marked the first time that an unblown, stock-bodied car dipped into the 9s. Very soon after, the other altered-wheelbase Chryslers were also equipped with the Hilborn setup.

Dick Landy is shown here at Numidia Dragway. At various times throughout 1965, Landy ran the Dodge with fuel injection. Like most of the teams running the altered-wheelbase cars, he experimented with its ride height as a way of transferring weight to the rear tires. Certainly, this car sat a lot taller than most in 1965. The rear leaf springs look impossibly stretched! (Photo Courtesy Charles Milikin Jr.)

Jim Thornton in the Ramchargers Dodge smokes the bags at Cecil County. Although a factory altered-wheelbase car, this particular version was supplied to the Ramchargers as an incomplete acid-dipped body in white, and the team completed its construction. (Photo Courtesy Charles Milikin Jr.)

DAWN OF THE FUNNY CARS

Al "Flying Dutchman" Vanderwoude spent a lot of time in 1965 with his front wheels in the air. He went on to embrace the new Funny Car craze with gusto with a series of mad-cap machines that captured the public's imagination. This early shot of his 1964 Plymouth was taken prior to the car being fitted with Hilborn fuel injection. Because these cars weren't accepted into any NHRA recognized class, they were forced to be shoehorned into whatever division would accept them. In this case, the Flying Dutchman was running C/Altered. (Photo Courtesy Charles Milikin Jr.)

Although not an official term in any sense, the Funny Car name was quickly adopted by anyone attempting to describe the crazy altered-wheelbase monsters in 1965. A variety of exciting races were concocted by track promoters just to have these cars perform in front of the fans. The United Drag Racers Association (UDRA) held several meetings headlined by a mix of NHRA A/FX and AHRA Super Stock-1 cars.

The UDRA held an event in early March at Famosa Drag Strip that attracted the altered-wheelbase cars of Landy, Leal, H. L. Shahan, and Cecil Yother, who'd now taken the helm of the *Melrose Missile* in place of Tom Grove.

The ETs these cars were producing underlined the terrific progress they were making. In the first heat, Landy faced Leal's *California Flash* and laid down a winning 10.43 at 135.13 mph. Leal lost with a 10.73. At the AHRA Winternationals just six weeks earlier, the altered-wheelbase cars were barely dipping into the 10s. Now, they were running half a second faster. Landy faced Yother in the finals, and he again romped down the strip with a winning 10.45 at 136.12 mph.

While Chrysler built the radical altered-wheelbase cars to run A/FX, they weren't eligible, which was a loss both to Chrysler and Ford. Without genuine competition, Ford and Mercury victories were somewhat meaningless,

Taylor Clark's Competition Body Shop 1965 Hemi Belvedere altered-wheelbase sedan was another car that was built outside of the factory cars. (Photo Courtesy Charles Milikin Jr.)

Ronnie Sox guns it at Cecil County in the Sox & Martin Plymouth. The team is running fuel injection here. Notable also is the start of the team's Cragar sponsorship and the fitment of the Keystone wheels that would become a Sox & Martin mainstay for years to come. (Photo Courtesy Charles Milikin Jr.)

so following the NHRA Winternationals, representatives from both manufacturers gathered to discuss options going forward. A middle ground of sorts was achieved by agreeing that the 110-inch-wheelbase Mopars would run at a minimum weight of 3,200 pounds and Ford's A/FX cars would run against them.

Launching hard out the box at Gainesville is Ronnie Sox and Don Nicholson. Nicholson's stock-wheelbase 427 Comet spent a chunk of 1965 competing in A/Factory Experimental before it went under the knife, emerging as an altered-wheelbase car. (Photo Courtesy Doug Boyce)

Al Graber's wild fuel-injected Tickle Me Pink Dodge sedan is shown. This was another of the self-built altered-wheelbase cars that appeared in 1965. (Photo Courtesy Charles Milikin Jr.)

Comet and Dick Brannan's Mustang, running SOHC 427s. In the end, however, the finals featured the Mopars of Harrop and Strickler with the latter taking home the trophy on a 10.64 at 131.57 mph.

Other Mopars of interest at this event included Richard Petty's altered-wheelbase fuel-injected Hemi-powered Plymouth Barracuda, with which the NASCAR ace went on to win B/Altered. NASCAR car builder Cotton Owens, who like Petty was having a relatively quiet year in the wake of Chrysler's NASCAR snub, brought along his crazy rear-engined Dodge Dart station wagon, *the Cotton Picker*.

In addition, Bristol marked the first public appearance of the wheel-standing Hurst *Hemi Under Glass*, the rear-engined Plymouth Barracuda driven by "Wild" Bill Shrewsbury.

Following the Winternationals in February, the NHRA adopted a new system for Top Stock Eliminator (formerly Mr. Stock Eliminator). The various cars and classes had fragmented notably, resulting in smaller fields throughout. Top Stock Eliminator featured the top 40 cars from A/FX, S/S, S/SA, AA/S, and AA/SA. The class-winning cars and the next seven-fastest qualifiers were eligible. No more than eight cars from any one class could qualify.

The Grassi Motors 1963 Plymouth Super Stock, pictured at Bakersfield, was driven here either by Gene Shindle or Dave Grassi. As the big factory teams moved away from Super Stock in 1965, the smaller independents had a better shot at the prizes. (Photo Courtesy Charles Milikin Jr.)

When NASCAR banned the Chrysler Hemi engine for the 1965 Grand National, reigning champion and Daytona 500 winner Richard Petty went drag racing instead. Petty Enterprises built this stout little altered-wheelbase Hemi-powered Plymouth Barracuda that he used for match racing and would run in any class that took him. The "Outlawed" lettering on the door refers to NASCAR's Hemi ban. Petty debuted the car in November 1964. But tragedy struck in February 1965, when the car crashed at Southeast International Dragway in Dallas, slewing off course and into the crowd. An eight-year-old boy was killed and at least eight others were injured. Petty was devastated, and he took the wreckage home and buried it. He did build another Barracuda drag car, but following the accident, his heart was never really in it. He returned to NASCAR when the Hemi became legal in 1966. (Photo Courtesy Revs Institute/Pete Biro)

The concept of exhibition cars exploded in drag racing in 1965 with many varied creations born in quick succession. Certainly, one of the most notable was the Hurst Hemi Under Glass, the Plymouth Barracuda wheelstander. George Hurst hired "Wild" Bill Shrewsbury to take care of driving duties for the 1965 season. (Photo Courtesy Charles Milikin Jr.)

The altered-wheelbase cars of Dave Strickler in his Dodge and Lee Smith in his Plymouth (far lane) scurry toward the traps at Bristol International Dragway in the 1965 Springnationals. Funny Cars were booming, and Strickler capitalized on their popularity by winning the "Funny Car Bash." (Photo Courtesy Bristol International Dragway)

With there now being a sizable speed difference between the classes, a new starting procedure was introduced. Beginning at the Springnationals, a handicap system based on the existing record for each class was used. The slower car started farther down the track than the faster car, with both being sent away at the same time. First to the finish was the winner, regardless of top speed. Ultimately, all the big-name factory machines were eliminated, leaving Mike Schmitt of California as Top Stock Eliminator champion in his 1964 Ford Galaxie.

1965 Super Stock Magazine Nationals

Another new event was launched in 1965. The Super Stock Magazine Nationals was held at York U.S. 30 Drag-O-Way on August 7, and it underlined the mass-popularity of Stock car drag racing. Sponsored by *Super Stock & Drag Illustrated* magazine, this was effectively an outlaw event, but thanks to grand prizes and quality management, the event drew instant credibility.

With the NHRA continuing to repel the altered-wheelbase cars, events like the Super Stock Magazine Nationals seized the opportunity to milk the enormous popularity of these machines for all their worth. An Unlimited Class was created specifically for the wildest and most feral creations, and it included the altered-wheelbase Chryslers of Landy, Eckstrand, Harrop, Faubel, as well as the Mr. Norm entry driven by Gary Dyer. In addition was Pete Seaton's *Shaker* Chevrolet Chevelle, and Dick Jesse's *Mr. Unswitchable* Pontiac GTO. Many of the teams were running nitromethane fuel mixtures.

After Landy beat Dyer in the semifinals, he faced Eck-

George Weiler aboard Bud Faubel's Hemi Honker *1964 Dodge battles Ken Montgomery's* Triple Nickel *1965 Plymouth in a Super Stock contest at Cecil County. Faubel himself was at this event, racing his own altered-wheelbase Dodge hardtop. (Photo Courtesy Charles Milikin Jr.)*

strand in the finals. Eckstrand had beaten Harrop. Eckstrand, the Golden Commandos pilot, went on to win with a blazing 9.67 at 142.40 mph.

Other matches were based on vehicle weight and included a 2,700-pound class that featured several more altered-wheelbase Mopars running on gasoline. These included Lee Smith, Ronnie Sox, Butch Leal, and Dave Strickler. Strickler and Sox were due to meet in the final, but it had to be canceled due to the event running late, and the prize purse was split.

The 3,000-pound class featured more altered-wheelbase Mopars, including those for Bill Jenkins (*Black Arrow*), the Sox & Martin sedan, and Cecil Yother's *Melrose Missile*. Sox took the win, beating Billy McDuell's Mercury Comet with a 10.37 at 131.96 mph.

The 3,200-pound class included Shirl Greer's *Tension* Dodge, Charlie Doyle's *Outlaw* Plymouth, and the Plymouth of Melvin Yow. Yow advanced through to the finals but lost to John Healey's Tasca Ford Mustang.

Finally, the 3,400-pound class required a minimum 110-inch wheelbase and carburetors, so it was effectively a Super Stock contest. Mopar entrants included Arlen Vanke's Plymouth, Jack Werst's *Mr. 5 & 50*, Tom "Smoker" Smith, Dave Koffel, Bill Rubin, and George Weiler aboard Bud Faubel's 1964 Dodge. The result of the final had to be canceled and re-run, with one driver redlighting and the

It was glorious looking at the pit area at U.S. 30 Drag-O-Way during the 1965 Super Stock Magazine Nationals. In the foreground was the Sox & Martin Plymouth Super Stock sedan and the altered-wheelbase Melrose Missile *Plymouth hardtop. Sox & Martin also campaigned an altered-wheelbase hardtop at this event. (Photo Courtesy Bob Mace/Jack Ferris Collection)*

This is another of the Hemi Super Stockers. Charlie Allen's Atlantic Dodge Flyer *competes at Indianapolis. (Photo Courtesy Charles Milikin Jr.)*

Here is Super Stock action at the 1965 U.S. Nationals with Bill Andress's 1965 Hemi Plymouth gapping David Landers. (Photo Courtesy Charles Milikin Jr.)

Joe Aed is pictured at Indianapolis Raceway Park, where he won the C/A contest in his altered-wheelbase Plymouth. This is very likely the car driven by Al "Lawman" Eckstrand in 1964. (Photo Courtesy Charles Milikin Jr.)

Wes Koogle runs hard in his Hemi-powered 1965 Dodge Super Stock sedan at Indianapolis Raceway Park. (Photo Courtesy Charles Milikin Jr.)

Dave Strickler in his Super Stock Hemi Dodge battles Bud Shellenberger in Bill Nicely's 1964 Ford Galaxie at Indy. Despite the NHRA's awkward handicapping system, Shellenberger won the ultimate prize in Super Stock drag racing: the Super Stock Eliminator at the U.S. Nationals. (Photo Courtesy Charles Milikin Jr.)

Pictured at the U.S. Nationals at Indy is Bob Harrop in the famous Flying Carpet Hemi Dodge. (Photo Courtesy Charles Milikin Jr.)

Butch "the California Flash" Leal joined Chrysler for the 1965 season, moving across from Ford. As well as his 110-inch altered-wheelbase Plymouth hardtop, Leal also raced, on occasion, this Super Stock sedan. Like many of the Mopar factory racers in 1965, Super Stock racing took a step back, unless, as here at the U.S. Nationals, the altered-wheelbase cars weren't welcome. (Photo Courtesy Geoff Stunkard Collection/Ray Mann Archive)

Don Peluso is pictured at Indy in his 1965 Plymouth Super Stock. (Photo Courtesy Charles Milikin Jr.)

other found to be 150 pounds underweight. Ultimately, Smith emerged to beat Rubin in an all-Mopar final.

1965 NHRA U.S. Nationals

Early September signaled the biggest and most significant event in all of drag racing: the annual National Championships at Indianapolis Raceway Park. The Labor Day weekend spectacular attracted 130,000 race fans and boasted $135,000 in prizes. More than 1,100 entries were received.

The NHRA wasn't backing down on its stance regarding the altered-wheelbase Mopars. As such, these machines were forced to run in Fuel Dragster, Altered, and any other catch-all category that would have them.

Funny Cars were grabbing a lot of attention in 1965, taking some of the focus away from the big Stockers. But the NHRA Nationals restored the natural order.

Super Stock competition was well represented, and not surprisingly, it was dominated by Mopars. With many of the Chrysler regulars focusing on altered-wheelbase cars throughout much of 1965, the Nationals offered a chance for them to dust off their Super Stocks once more, as the Nationals placed greater importance on this class.

Strickler, Leal, and Harrop were all running cars effectively bolted back together just for the Nationals. Lack of seat time didn't seem to affect Strickler and Leal, however, as they met in the Super Stock finals. Leal busted out of the gates with an epic 0.01-second margin, and while Strickler had the top-end speed, he couldn't reel in the *California Flash* pilot.

Meanwhile, in Super Stock Automatic, the pace setters were the Mopars of Bob Harrop in the *Flying Carpet*, Jack Werst in *Mr. 5 & 50*, and Wes Koogle, all running 11.30s and 11.40s. The impressive Koogle had been involved in

a vicious accident the year prior and lost a leg as a result. He was told by medical experts he wouldn't walk again for at least a year, but within a few months, he was both walking and racing with a prosthetic limb.

Koogle faced Harrop in the semifinals and narrowly lost. Harrop faced Werst in the final and won with an 11.39 at 126.05 mph.

Top Stock Eliminator provided enormous entertainment, as the highly fancied factory cars were all knocked out, leaving the independent 1964 Ford Galaxies of Bud Shellenburger and Bob Coble to scrap in the finals. In the end, Shellenburger claimed the biggest and most important victory in Stock drag racing, scoring himself a new Plymouth Barracuda in the process.

1965 NHRA World Championship Finals

The last big NHRA event of 1965, in a year already bursting at the seams with big events, was the newly introduced World Championship Finals at Tulsa Southwest Raceway.

The World Finals followed a new format for the NHRA, in that only invited cars could compete. To be invited, cars had to finish either first or second in the season-long points championship in their home division. The NHRA was split into eight divisions, seven of which were geographical, and another comprised as a travelers' division. From those eight divisions, six recognized Eliminator categories vied for points (Top Fuel, Top Gas, Top Stock, Junior Stock, Competition Eliminator, and Street Eliminator). It was, in essence, a best-of-the-best competition.

Top Stock Eliminator was comprised of 10 cars from 5 Stock-based divisions (S/S, S/SA, AA/S, A/FX, and AA/SA), including those for Ray Christian (AA/SA Dodge), Dick Charbonneau (AA/SA Plymouth), Joe Smith (S/SA Plymouth), Don Grotheer (AA/S Plymouth), Arlen Vanke (S/S Plymouth), Gas Ronda (A/FX Ford), Bill Lawton (A/FX Ford), Bob Spears (AA/S Ford), Mike Schmitt (AA/SA Ford), and Les Ritchey (A/FX Ford). Due to the wildly varying speeds, races were conducted using a handicapping system.

Spears, Christian, Smith, Vanke, and Lawton all progressed beyond the first round. Mustang A/FX pilots Ritchey and Ronda were favorites heading into the competition, but Ritchey missed a shift in his run against Spears, while Ronda's motor went sour when he met

Jack Thomas's Chicagoland Dodge Dealers Association 1965 Hemi Coronet is making a run at the U.S. Nationals at Indy. (Photo Courtesy Charles Milikin Jr.)

Christian. Ronda ran a 10.90 to Christian's 12.12 but couldn't overcome the handicap.

In Round 2, Spears beat Vanke with a winning 12.06 versus 11.84, while Smith also progressed, taking down Christian. Lawton lucked-out and got the bye. He then faced and beat Spears in an all-Ford semifinal, running a 10.65 ET in the process. Smith was assured a berth in the finals when he got the bye.

So, Smith lined up in the Fenner Tubbs S/SA Hemi Dodge against Lawton's faster A/FX 427 Mustang to duke it out in the final. Despite Lawton knocking out a 10.56 in his quest to hunt down the Mopar, he was still behind at the finish. Smith was crowned 1965 NHRA Top Stock Eliminator World Champion.

In many respects, 1965 was the best and most successful year in Stock drag racing to date. Increasingly, event promoters were falling over themselves to accommodate the Stock classes, and entirely new events were established specifically for these cars. But the key ingredient that thrust Stock car drag racing into the limelight, making it one of the most prominent of all drag racing categories, was largely lost by 1965. With General Motors having withdrawn from racing, and with Ford and Chrysler essentially competing in different classes, these contests had evolved into single-make competitions, and that took some of the shine off the racing.

Chrysler went to a lot of effort to design and build its fleet of Hemi drag cars, but such was the evolution of racing and the rules they were constrained by, its teams traveled the length and breadth the country to race each other. Thus, the very essence of competition— one manufacturer testing its products against those of its rivals—was missing.

In the name of all that was right and fair, the fastest car was no longer winning the grand prize in Stock drag racing—not that Bud Shellenburger and Joe Smith minded.

The 1965 Stock-based drag racing season witnessed an even greater chasm develop, as Chrysler and Ford moved further still away from Super Stock in its purest form. As drag racing evolved further into a form of entertainment as opposed to a strict outlet for competition, the manufacturers saw fit to demonstrate their capabilities by building more and more outlandish cars. This was, after all, a marketing exercise to them, and they won, either way.

The race fans didn't seem to mind too much, and ultimately, the crazy new altered-wheelbase cars formed the basis of a completely new racing division. But for now, it would seem, the new Funny Car match-bash contests would take center stage, albeit, at a cost to Super Stock racing.

When you're a drag racing fan and you pull in behind the Sox & Martin altered-wheelbase Plymouth, you snap a photo! Alan Lewis captured this image of the Paper Tiger. *(Photo Courtesy Alan Lewis)*

SUPER STOCK SNUB

Chrysler opted not to release a new Stock drag race package for the 1966 season, which was not really surprising. The high-profile Stock divisions had become fragmented by 1965, and the limited manufacturer participation was affected as a result. The key ingredient that launched Stock drag racing from the "hot dog and fries" class to the headline act was the drama and intensity of factory produced and supported big-block heavyweights slugging it out to showcase who truly built the fastest car. That had all but dissolved by 1965.

With General Motors having withdrawn from racing in 1963, Chrysler and Ford were thus pitched against one another in a two-horse race. But by 1965, Ford shifted its efforts to the NHRA A/Factory Experimental division, while Chrysler split its focus between Super Stock and its madcap altered-wheelbase cars for which there was no official class.

Although intended for A/Factory Experimental, the NHRA was having none of it, and in drag racing, the NHRA was the biggest game in town. Instead, the whacky altered-wheelbase Mopars spawned the beginnings of the new unofficial Funny Car division. However, in 1965, this wasn't yet a recognized class and nor was its title. It was simply a loose-fitting catchphrase adopted by track announcers to describe this strange new breed of ill-proportioned, outrageously spectacular creations.

Lack of official recognition didn't matter when the Funny Cars were quickly becoming one of the most popular spectacles in all of drag racing. Event promoters were clamoring to shoehorn them into their programs. Indeed, Bristol track owner Larry Carrier actually overrode the NHRA's wishes that Funny Cars not be included at the 1965 Springnationals.

The rising popularity of the weird and feral Funny Cars was having an impact on the top-ranking Super Stock divisions. Most of the factory-affiliated Chrysler teams, for example, mothballed their Super Stocks in favor of their altered-wheelbase cars. Sox & Martin, the Ramchargers, the Golden Commandos, Butch Leal, Dick Landy, Roger Lindamood, and the *Melrose Missile* gravitated away from Super Stock competition to focus almost exclusively on Funny Car and match-bash contests.

By 1965, Chryslers were racing each other for victories in Super Stock competition, and as such, there was little incentive for Chrysler to invest in developing a new and faster package for 1966. Likewise, the Stock Eliminator competitions that amalgamated the best and fastest Stock machines throughout the various divisions, and which had evolved into one of the highlights at most events, were now being fought as handicap contests with the slower car given a head start. Invariably, the fastest cars weren't the winners. So, why would Chrysler commit money and energy into building a faster Super Stock machine?

This handsome 1966 Hemi Plymouth sedan ran in UDRA Super Stock by Jim Evans, Tom Evans, and Willy Cleve. (Photo Courtesy Jim Brooks/Jim Schild)

It didn't look too fearsome, but Jere Stahl's little white Plymouth sedan smoked 'em in 1966, winning the Top Stock Eliminator at the NHRA Springnationals, U.S. Nationals, and World Championship Finals. He flew the Chrysler flag in Super Stock when many of the big guns were running altered-wheelbase cars. (Photo Courtesy Geoff Stunkard Collection/Ray Mann Archive)

The Professor was a former 1965 Plymouth Belvedere Hemi Super Stock that was now sporting Hilborn fuel injection and running in A/FX competition. This was typical for many cars once their Super Stock careers had ended. (Photo Courtesy Charlie Suggs)

Gas Ronda and Tom "the Mongoose" McEwen go at it. Funny Car racing was all the rage by 1966, and the cars were wild. The Mongoose ran a 1965 Plymouth Barracuda powered by an injected Hemi mounted in the rear. (Photo Courtesy Charles Milikin Jr.)

Two Mopar legends, Jere Stahl and Bill "Maverick" Golden, drive back up the return road at Cecil County. (Photo Courtesy Alan Lewis)

Herb McCandless, "Mr. 4-Speed," unloads his Hemi Belvedere. His open trailer was basic, but by contrast, many racers hauled their cars to the track on an A-frame. (Photo Courtesy Geoff Stunkard Collection/McCandless Family Archive)

The Chrysler Street Hemi

Chrysler was happy to loosen its grip on its drag racing programs because it was making a much-heralded return to the NASCAR Grand National, and that required commitment. Submitting to NASCAR's demands, Chrysler spent a chunk of 1965 developing and producing a street variant of its 426-ci race Hemi, which customers could then request when ordering their new road car. By doing so, Chrysler qualified the Hemi for the Grand National, the theatre for which it was originally intended.

It was common for a manufacturer to produce an improved version of a street motor for competition, but Chrysler was breaking new ground by going the other way. It detuned a race motor for use on the street. Exactly how successful that transition was is debatable.

As motoring journalist Joe Oldham once wrote, "The Chrysler hemispherical combustion chamber engine was conceived as a racing engine. Its sewer-sized ports and manhole-cover sized valves were designed to provide massive amounts of air and fuel while running at wide-open throttle down a drag strip or on a superspeedway. It was never meant to provide a street car with low-end torque or good throttle response. And it couldn't."

That said, Chrysler's ambition and determination should be applauded. Naturally, the Hemi was an impractical street engine. But NASCAR only mandated that the engines powering the Grand National cars be production items that were available to anyone who wanted one installed in his or her new road car. The goal here was to homologate the Hemi for racing by offering it in street cars. Practicality didn't come into it.

For all intents and purposes, the Street Hemi was a moderately detuned race Hemi. It featured lower 10.25:1 compression so it could run on premium pump gas. It was decked with cast-iron heads with slightly larger 2.25-inch intake valves because they didn't necessitate the steel seats fitted to the aluminum race heads. Whereas the race Hemi used a 312-degree camshaft with 88 degrees of overlap, the street variant was equipped with a 276-degree unit with 52 degrees of overlap. In addition, the street Hemi was topped with an aluminum intake manifold carrying a pair of Carter AFB carburetors line astern with the back carburetor using an automatic choke. To make it more user-friendly for everyday living, hot air from the exhaust manifold heated the intake manifold to aid in cold-weather starting and driving.

Dyno testing of the street Hemi had it punching out 463 hp at 6,000 rpm and 405 ft-lbs of torque. Although, Chrysler naturally listed its official figure at a more conservative 425 hp at 5,000 rpm and 490 ft-lbs of torque.

Not surprisingly, there weren't many takers for the Street Hemi option in 1966. It was an expensive proposition at around $900. But that figure covered more than just a simple motor installation. The Hemi required its own unique crossmember while heavy-duty rear springs were attached via reinforced front spring mounts. In addition, a pair of steel plates were welded to the chassis for added strength.

Being a sporty motor, most street Hemis were ordered with the Dodge or Plymouth two-door hardtop: 627 for the Coronet and 1,348 for the Belvedere II and Satellite. In addition, 86 Coronet and 136 Belvedere two-door sedans were ordered. What was a little more surprising was that there were orders for 26 Coronet convertibles, 37 Belvedere II and Satellite convertibles, a handful of (at least 4) Coronets, and a rumored single Belvedere four-door sedan. These were surely the ultimate sleepers.

1966 Chrysler B-Body Street Cars

Chrysler's 1966 B-Body intermediates were based on those of 1965 but underwent wholesale styling changes. In almost every respect, the 1966 offerings were truly striking and dramatic, featuring crisp, sharp lines. The sedans had notably svelte C-pillars that provided an airiness and were fleet of foot. There was no hint of stodge.

The two-door hardtops in both the Dodge and Plymouth range were sensational-looking cars. The fastback roofline was extended and stretched at the C-pillars to appear much more aggressive even though the tapering of previous years was carried through. The distinctive Chrysler intermediate DNA was not lost, but the 1966 models looked faster and sportier in every way than their predecessors. Chrysler stylists knocked it out of the park.

The wheelbase remained unchanged from 1965, but the updated styling produced a newfound sleekness over previous models. Naturally, with Dodge being more upmarket than Plymouth, the Coronets still retained a 117-inch wheelbase (Plymouths remained at 116 inches) with four headlamps. They carried extra girth—notably additional front and rear overhang.

Chrysler didn't make a song and dance about its Hemi-powered street cars. Externally, there was little to distinguish a Dodge or a Plymouth packing a Hemi other than some subtle metal badges on the front fenders. Within a few years, the Chrysler marketing team would set the world ablaze with an explosion of color, noise, and trippy advertising campaigns that sent Mopar performance into a league of its own. But in 1966, the company still operated with a modicum of decorum.

Chrysler's B-Body Dodge and Plymouth were particularly handsome and dramatic in two-door hardtop form, and this model came equipped with a street Hemi. For the most part, however, drag racing teams opted for the two-door sedan body, as it was more rigid and a little lighter. (Photos Courtesy Geoff Stunkard Collection)

MELROSE MISSILE

Melrose Motors, a Plymouth dealer from Oakland, California, entered a series of cars in drag racing from 1962 through 1967. The cars enjoyed their greatest successes when driven and tuned by Tom Grove, who was a mechanic at Melrose Motors.

Carrying the simple but wildly effective name of *Melrose Missile*, the cars were numbered I through VII, although two more cars came a little later.

Charlie Di Bari was the driving force behind the *Melrose Missile* cars. His father owned Melrose Motors, and Di Bari was a big drag racing fan. While Grove prepared the cars and also drove, Di Bari also did a little racing himself.

The Melrose Motors team ran a few Plymouth Belvederes in 1962, although they carried "Melrose Motors" and "Power Tuned by Tom Grove" signage predominantly with *Melrose Missile I* and *II* in small letters on the rear quarters. In 1963, the famous flaming missile decorations with "Melrose Missile" in great big letters began to be featured.

In 1963, the *Melrose Missile* really began to perform on the national stage (there were also two 1963 cars, *Melrose Missile III* and *IV*), as Grove won the Super Stock division at the NHRA Winternationals.

There were two Hemi-powered *Melrose Missile* cars for 1964: a hardtop and a sedan. The hardtop was *Melrose Missile V*. The season highlight was Grove winning Mr. Stock Eliminator at the big NHRA Winternationals in the *Melrose Missile V I* sedan.

Melrose Missile VII was the team's new 1965 car. Starting out as a stock-wheelbase hardtop, it was converted into an altered-wheelbase car early in the year as the burgeoning Funny Car phenomenon began to gather momentum.

When Grove went to race an A/FX Mustang in 1966, Melrose Motors's involvement in racing was cut back. Cecil Yother bought the 1965 car along with the *Melrose Missile* name and evolved it massively from its original foundation as a stock-wheelbase hardtop to an altered-wheelbase hardtop and finally in 1966 to a feral altered-wheelbase roadster. Briefly, Melrose Motors ran a 1967 RO23 Belvedere, but this was short-lived.

The last *Melrose Missile* was a flip-top fuel-injected Barracuda Funny Car that Yother campaigned briefly from early 1967. When it became apparent that he wouldn't be competitive without installing a blower, Yother, like several others of his era who didn't fancy the prospect of having a bomb nestled between his legs, opted instead to retire the Barracuda and quit racing.

The 1965 Melrose Missile underwent an astonishing transformation through to 1966. It began as an acid-dipped hardtop with a stock wheelbase in early 1965 races. Then, it went under the knife, emerging in 110-inch altered-wheelbase guise within a few months. By 1966, the top had been lopped off, and the wild Mopar raced as a roadster complete with a rear deck spoiler and driver canopy. (Photo Courtesy Tom West/ Lou Hart)

1966 Chrysler B-Body Drag Cars

Although Chrysler didn't produce a turnkey Super Stock drag racer for 1966, teams were now well adept at building their own. Invariably, the two-door sedan was favored over the sporty two-door hardtop because it was lighter and more rigid. It looked less racy, but winning races was all that mattered. The customer would order the base package without the radio and delete the heater option for which a $70.32 credit was given. Naturally, teams built brand-new cars for 1966, but perhaps even more so, many simply continued campaigning their 1965 machinery.

Butch Leal continued to run his 1965 Hemi Plymouth Super Stock through 1966 and also competed in Factory Experimental. (Photo Courtesy Steve Reyes)

Chrysler's decision to opt out of Stock drag car construction for 1966 proved to be on the money. The rapidly rising popularity of the new Funny Car Match Bash races was syphoning the top teams from both Super Stock and Factory Experimental. Drag racing is purely a form of entertainment, and event promoters will always favor the most entertaining classes because they attract the most punters. In 1966, few classes in drag racing could top the pure theatre and entertainment value of the altered-wheelbase oddities in the Funny Car ranks. Where the money goes, the big teams soon follow.

The NHRA finally softened its stance on the Funny Cars and introduced its new Experimental Stock (XS) class for 1966 as a sort of catch-all, including Factory Experimental cars that fell outside the current-year-only rule. Most A/FX cars racing in 1966 were updated 1965 Mustangs, and even those broke out of the maximum 2-percent wheelbase-adjustment requirement with their new altered-wheelbase modifications.

Of course, none of the altered-wheelbase Mopars qualified. Factory Experimental stumbled along with sparce fields until it was finally put to sleep at the end of the year.

1966 Drag Racing Highlights

This was to be a strange year for Chrysler Super Stock drag racing because most of the factory-supported teams had made the shift across to Funny Cars. In addition, there was Chrysler's decision not to produce a new factory Super Stock car. It should have been a hollow year— one without any highlights at all of which to speak. Yet,

Larry Griffith's sinister-looking 1966 Dodge Coronet ran a Hemi and a 4-speed in a two-door hardtop. With Chrysler opting not to produce a factory Super Stock package in 1966, many racers, Griffith included, simply built their own. (Photo Courtesy Jim Brooks/Jim Schild)

Perhaps the most alarming looking of all the altered-wheelbase cars, and certainly one of the most extreme, was the White Tornado 1964 Dodge, pictured here at Halfmoon Bay. No doubt, it would have lifted the front wheels with ease. (Photo Courtesy Tony Bettencourt)

An open trailer and the open road made the life of a drag racer in the 1960s an adventure. Race for money, pay a few bills, and hope to go professional one day. "Mr. 4-Speed" Herb McCandless gets set for a road trip. (Photo Courtesy Geoff Stunkard Collection/McCandless Family Archive)

it celebrated several highlights, including an NHRA victory for Shirley Shahan.

There was also a new inter-brand rivalry between the ever-growing presence of Bill "Grumpy" Jenkins and his former partner Jere Stahl. The pair rose to fame together racing Chryslers in the Super Stock ranks before Jenkins was effectively let go and he became a Chevy racer—and a highly competitive one at that.

1966 AHRA Winternationals

As always, the first top-flight event to kick-start the season was the AHRA Winternationals, which moved from Beeline Dragway in Arizona to Irwindale Raceway, California, in 1966. The Chrysler contingent included Roger Lindamood's new 1966 Dodge and the 1965-model Plymouths of Ronnie Sox, Butch Leal, and Shirley Shahan's aptly named *Drag-On-Lady*. But Irwindale would not be a fruitful event for the Chrysler contingent.

1966 NHRA Winternationals

The big NHRA Winternationals at Pomona was up next, and it was here that Shirley "the Drag-On-Lady" Shahan slayed the best and fastest Super Stock driv-

Shirley "the Drag-On-Lady" Shahan whooped all the guys in Top Stock Eliminator competition at the 1966 Winternationals to become the first female to score an NHRA Eliminator crown. (Photo Courtesy David McWilliams)

By 1966, having raced Super Stocks before switching across to an altered-wheelbase car in 1965, "Wild" Bill Flynn dove headfirst into the crazy new Funny Car division in 1966 with his latest Yankee Peddler, an injected Hemi-propelled Plymouth Barracuda. (Photo Courtesy Charles Milikin Jr.)

A pair of Mopars commence battle at Capitol Raceway, including the Bounty Hunters' 1965 Hemi Coronet in the far lane, driven by Tom Sneden and sponsored by Bob Banning Dodge. (Photo Courtesy Alan Lewis)

ers in the country to win Top Stock Eliminator. In doing so she became the first female driver to win an NHRA-sanctioned event final.

Shahan drove the 1965 Plymouth prepared by her husband H. L. Shahan and beat Roger Lindamood, Butch Leal, Mike Schmitt, Don Grotheer, and 1965 Winternationals Stock winner Bill Jenkins to reach the final. She faced off against Ken Heinemann's 1966 Plymouth in the final, winning with an 11.26 at 125.75 mph against Heinemann's losing 12.01 at 121.78 mph.

1966 NHRA Springnationals

Bristol International Dragway hosted the second annual NHRA Springnationals in early June. The latest and craziest of the Funny Car fleet

Ed Miller gets set for a fast run in his 1965 Hemi Plymouth during the 1966 NHRA U.S. Nationals at Indy. (Photo Courtesy Geoff Stunkard Collection/Ray Mann Archive)

were split into CC/FD for blown cars or the new NHRA A/XS class for unblown. Ronnie Sox made it all the way to the final of A/XS, where he faced Tom Grove's SOHC Mustang but lost to the Ford driver.

It was at this event the Factory Experimental division suffered its worst performance yet. Only one car was entered in C/FX and none in A/FX.

Jere Stahl, driving his 1966 Hemi Plymouth, came out on top of the 13-car field in A/Stock. He faced off against Arlen Vanke's 1965 Plymouth in the finals, which he won.

Stahl also excelled in the big Top Stock Eliminator contest. He beat the S/SA Plymouth of Mary Ann Foss in Round 1 and Alvert Olster in Round 2. He had the bye in Round 3 and then beat Joe Smith's Plymouth the next time out to face Mike Schmitt's Desert Motors Ford B/FX SOHC Galaxie in the final. Schmitt had already won Street Eliminator, beating Al Joniec's Mustang in the handicap-start feature. The Ford versus Plymouth final had the big crowd whipped up with anticipation, but it was Stahl all the way. He thumped home a powerful 11.80 at 119.20 mph to Schmitt's disappointing 12.15, which fell way short of his own 11.66 record.

Jere "Total Tuned Headers" Stahl had built a reputation as the go-to guy for power-packing exhaust headers. Teams from drag racing, stock car racing, and road racing beat a steady trail to his shop. His Top Stock victory was the first of a three-peat that ultimately included the 1966 NHRA U.S. Nationals and the World Championship Finals.

1966 NHRA U.S. Nationals

The annual NHRA U.S. Nationals at Indianapolis Raceway Park was still the biggest drag racing event on the planet in 1966. The five-day epic attracted 112,000 race fans with 50,000 alone showing up for Sunday's action. The line of cars trying to enter the facility stretched 8.5 miles back to

The Jere Stahl and Bill Stiles Hemi Plymouth 4-speed was a thorn in the side of Grumpy Jenkins throughout the 1966 racing season. (Photo Courtesy Clinton Wright)

Indianapolis. More than 1,300 cars were entered for competition by Friday, and at least another 200 were turned away simply because there wasn't space for them in the pits. It was the largest entry yet for an NHRA event.

For the fans, there was almost too much to see. Three of the mad new flip-top Mercury Comets attended and duked it out in S/XS category. "Dyno" Don Nicholson, "Fast" Eddie Schartman, and Ron Leslie piloted the Comets, which featured a full chrome-moly tube-frame chassis crafted by Logghe Stamping Company, Autolite coilover shocks, and a beam front axle with no front brakes. The SOHC Ford motor was set 25 percent back in the frame with the driver mounted where the rear seat would be if these were actual stock cars, which they very much weren't. The bodies were made from fiberglass, lifted up at the front, and were attached by hinges at the rear.

The A/XS division pitted Ford against Chrysler. The Sox & Martin team arrived with its 1966 Plymouth

SOX & MARTIN

Having developed a taste for the new Funny Car match-bash competitions in 1965 with their altered-wheelbase Belvedere, Ronnie Sox and Buddy Martin prepared a purpose-built, altered-wheelbase, fuel-injected, Hemi-powered Barracuda for 1966. (Photo Courtesy Buddy Martin)

Ronnie Sox began racing in 1957 with Buddy Martin starting a year later. Both drivers hailed from North Carolina, and in 1962, they teamed up at the behest of Martin. He, apparently, was tired of being beaten by Sox but could also see the pair forming a formidable partnership.

When Sox & Martin joined forces, they were both campaigning 409 Chevys, so they pooled their money to acquire the latest 427-ci Z11 Impala. While Sox became the designated driver, Martin focused his attention on car preparation, unearthing new tricks and tweaks.

The Sox & Martin pairing quickly found success, and by the end of 1963, they signed a deal to race a factory 427 Mercury Comet in NHRA A/FX the following year. With that, they went on a rampage. Sox beat Don Nicholson's factory Comet A/FX at the 1964 NHRA Winternationals and beat Richard Petty's Barracuda in a match race at Piedmont Dragway later in the year. The team racked up a long list of racing successes.

All of that success got Chrysler's attention, and Sox & Martin were coaxed across to race a factory Plymouth Super Stock and altered-wheelbase car in 1965 that they named the *Paper Tiger*. The race wins kept on coming.

For 1966, Sox & Martin largely ignored Super Stock

Barracuda and worked through a myriad of Fords. It reached the final, where Ronnie Sox faced Bill Lawton's Mustang. A redlight for Sox decided the outcome before the race even started.

Meanwhile, in the real Stock cars, Arlen Vanke emerged at the top of the pile in C/S, taking an easy victory in the final when his opponent, Howard Colby, redlit. Both drivers were aboard 1966 Plymouths. Other notables included Jere Stahl and Bill Jenkins.

Having been dropped from the Chrysler fold at the end of 1965, despite winning that year's Winternationals at the wheel of Doc Burgess's *Black Arrow* Hemi Plymouth, Jenkins switched to a 327-ci small-block-powered Chevy II for 1966. It was the first *Grumpy's Toy*. The high-spinning small-block ensured that Jenkins could run a significantly lighter weight than the big Chryslers, saving around 760 pounds.

This was perhaps the first Stocker built to exploit the competition in favor of Funny Car match-bash racing. Their mega new fuel-injected, Hemi-powered altered-wheelbase Plymouth Barracuda scored a spate of victories.

The Sox & Martin partnership proved to be formidable. Sox gained notoriety for being both lightning fast and supremely accurate with a manual transmission. The team really hit its stride with the introduction of the new LO23/BO29 Mopar Super Stocks in 1968. Ronnie Sox blasted to multiple national victories, including the 1968 AHRA Springnationals and NHRA Springnationals, the 1969 AHRA Winternationals and U.S. Open, and the NHRA Springnationals, U.S. Nationals, and World Finals.

But that was just the warmup.

For 1970, and with the latest Plymouth 'Cuda, the Sox & Martin squad effectively owned the new NHRA Pro Stock division for the next two years. After Bill "Grumpy" Jenkins claimed the silverware at the Winternationals and Gatornationals, the Sox & Martin team took control with Sox winning the Springnationals, World Finals, and Supernationals.

In addition, they also fielded a new Plymouth Duster that "Mr. 4-Speed" Herb McCandless stepped aboard early in the year. McCandless raced the Duster to victory at the U.S. Nationals. Meanwhile, more success was achieved over in AHRA competition, including race wins at the Winternationals, Pro Am Nationals, and U.S. Open, plus further AHRA Super Stock wins at Frontier International Raceway, Detroit Dragway, Bristol International Dragway, New York National Speedway, Beeline Dragway, and others.

Incredibly, 1971 was even better! Sox won the NHRA Winternationals, Gatornationals, Springnationals, Le Grandnational, U.S. Nationals, and Supernationals. In addition were IHRA victories in the Pro-Am Nationals, Spring Nationals, Southern Invitational Drag Championship, and All-American Nationals, and those were just the national competitions. It was immense.

When the curtain lowered on the 1971 NHRA Super Season, Ronnie Sox had notched up 15 national race wins. To date, the NHRA had held 49 national events, so Sox had won nearly a third. More than that, his first NHRA national event was the 1964 Winternationals. Therefore, he'd actually taken part in just 37 events. At the time, Sox was far and away the most successful driver in all NHRA competitions. Top Fuel driver Don Garlits was second with seven national race wins.

As 1971 drew to a close, it seemed like nothing could halt the Sox & Martin juggernaut. But the NHRA had other ideas. Wanting to inject more variety into its Pro Stock race results, it introduced a new weight-break system for 1972 that completely toppled the Chrysler domination. Indeed, it wasn't just the Sox & Martin team that was affected. All the Mopar teams now found themselves scrambling to keep pace with tiny small-block-powered Chevy Vegas and other pint-sized compacts that had been offered a sizeable handicap. Things were never the same again for Ronnie Sox and Buddy Martin.

Sox's victory at the 1971 season-ending Supernationals at Ontario Motor Speedway was his last-ever NHRA national event win.

The Sox & Martin team continued its successful car-building enterprise along with its Chrysler performance clinics. Their cars still enjoyed success in IHRA and AHRA competition, where the weight breaks imposed by the NHRA weren't nearly as drastic. Eventually, the pair went their separate ways, and although "The Boss" Ronnie Sox continued as a driver well into the 1980s, the high watermark he set with Buddy Martin in the late 1960s and throughout the first two years of Pro Stock was never repeated. The pair were celebrated as drag racing royalty throughout their lives.

Ronnie Sox died in 2006 at the age of 67.

Don Grotheer, pictured at the 1966 U.S. Nationals in his Hemi Plymouth, had a good year, scoring big wins in both A/Stock and AA/Stock. (Photo Courtesy Geoff Stunkard Collection/Ray Mann Archive)

advantages gained by running a smaller motor and bucking the trend of dropping in the biggest and most powerful engine between the frame rails. Jenkins bolted out of the gate and built an advantage with the Hemis trying to run him down at the top end. *Hot Rod* magazine referred to Grumpy's red and white Chevy II as a "science car."

For the big one, Top Stock Eliminator, Ed Miller was the fastest qualifier of the 25-car field with an 11.28. Miller was aboard the S/S Plymouth raced by Arlen Vanke in 1965. But when the contests had all been run and only two drivers were left to wrestle over the silverware, it was Stahl and Jenkins who emerged from all the smoke and dust. Jenkins knew he had to nail the start but was a little too trigger-happy, and he gifted Stahl the victory before the big Plymouth even cracked its tires. Stahl took the win with an 11.73 at 119.68 mph to Jenkins's redlighting 11.76 at 118.11 mph.

1966 NHRA World Championship Finals

The 1966 NHRA season concluded with the second running of the grandly titled World Championship Finals in late October. It was here in Tulsa, Oklahoma, that Jere Stahl rounded out his trifecta of Top Stock Eliminator victories that began at the Springnationals in June. Quizzed on his chances to score his third straight victory prior to the event, Stahl confidently responded, "The car is right, I feel my attitude is right, and I'm relatively confident I can make the tree work for me."

The media had been busy whipping up a storm over a make-believe rivalry between Stahl and Bill Jenkins.

In fact, the pair were good friends and held each other in high regard. Despite being very different personalities, they were both quite similar when it came to their approach to racing.

Following the Nationals at Indy, Jenkins's Chevy II was wrecked and went over an embankment when the driver of his hauler fell asleep on his way back to the shop in Pennsylvania. With precious little time available, Jenkins sourced a replacement from local dealership Penske Chevrolet (owned by Roger Penske) and transferred all the salvageable running gear from the wreck across to the new unit. The replacement Chevy II was painted factory white and kick-started a theme for predominantly white cars that continued throughout Jenkins's racing career.

Naturally, when all the eliminations had been fought and only two cars remained, it was Stahl and Jenkins. The big Plymouth took a narrow victory with an 11.65 at 122.44 mph to Jenkins's losing 11.73 at 119.04 mph.

So, 1966 had most of the big-name Chrysler factory teams missing in the Super Stock ranks, but it still proved to be a highly entertaining year. More so, it was hugely successful. But Chrysler was done with the fun and games of altered-wheelbase Funny Car racing, and it shifted focus back to its roots in Super Stock.

The year 1967 saw the launch of a new factory Super Stock drag package as well as a return to the ranks for many of its high-profile teams, as it sought to get back to basics in the category that had been so good for the Mopar brand.

CHAPTER 7

1967

GETTING BACK TO BASICS

The good news was that Chrysler returned to building turnkey drag cars in 1967. Chrysler's marketing team finally realized the sportiest of its sporty engines should only be fitted to the sportiest of its sporty cars. As such, in 1967, customers could only order the street Hemi to be installed in the Dodge Coronet R/T two-door hardtop, Dodge Charger R/T, or Plymouth Belvedere GTX two-door hardtop. The R/T (Road and Track) and GTX packages were new for 1967. That was it!

Chrysler wanted to showcase its most stylish and athletic models on the racetrack, and not its bare-bones low-line sedans. Yes, the top-line models provided increased profit margin for the company, but really, racing is a sport, and campaigning a manufacturer's sportiest models was a practice Chrysler's showroom rivals had been perfecting for years.

The final year for the current generation Coronet and Belvedere was 1967. Styling changes were minimal and mostly focused on trim pieces as well as the introduction of the R/T and GTX packages.

New NHRA Super Stock Rule Changes

For 1967, the NHRA gave its Stock divisions another shake-up, and what fell out were 10 different Super Stock classes based on a factory-rated horsepower-to-weight ratio. They were split into either stick shift or automatic: stick SS/A to SS/E, and automatic SS/AA to SS/EA. The

Parading for the crowd prior to the start of the 1967 Daytona 500 (which unfortunately for Chrysler was won by Mario Andretti in a Holman-Moody Fairlane), the Sox & Martin team shows off the new Plymouth Belvedere RO23 Hemi Super Stock drag racing weapons to the stock car fraternity. (Photo Courtesy Buddy Martin)

weight-versus-horsepower system was as follows:

- SS/A: 0.00 to 6.99 pounds per hp
- SS/B: 7.00 to 7.69 pounds per hp
- SS/C: 7.70 to 8.69 pounds per hp
- SS/D: 8.70 to 9.49 pounds per hp
- SS/E: 9.50 pounds per hp and above

The automatic classes were the same as above.

1967 Chrysler Super Stock Packages

The dazzling 1967 Plymouth Belvedere RO23 of Ferris Motors is pictured at Great Lakes Dragaway. (Photo Courtesy Jim Brooks/Jim Schild)

The Chrysler drag packages were built to comply with Super Stock/B class regulations: 7.00 to 7.69 pounds per rated horsepower. Continuing with the company's positive new marketing approach, the cars were all high-line two-door hardtop Dodge Coronets or Plymouth Belvederes.

NHRA Super Stock regulations for 1967 required that just 50 units be produced to qualify. Any flat-tappet camshaft, intake manifold, ignition, and exhaust headers could be used. Tires were free, although they had to fit inside the stock fenders. Also, roller cams weren't allowed, and the factory-supplied carburetors couldn't be replaced with aftermarket items.

The first batch of Chrysler Super Stocks underwent initial construction in February 1967. Compared to the increasingly ballistic creations the company was unleashing by 1965, the 1967 drag packages were surprisingly modest. Chrysler wanted to get its drag racing program back to basics to have its factory drivers campaigning cars that were closely related to those its dealers were selling across the country. That's what attracted the company to racing in the first place.

RO23 and WO23

The cars were assigned a special VIN and body identification number, including RO23 for the Plymouth and WO23 for the Dodge. The bodies remained stock, although they were ordered without sound deadener, insulation, or undercoating. In addition, there was was a heater and radio delete. As per the regulations, the bodies were all steel, although metal body components had been acid dipped. Chrysler continued its tradition of adding a ram-air hood scoop to feed gobs of air to the carburetors, which in this case was punched from thin-gauge steel.

Up front nestled the big 426-ci Hemi, which was just a mildly warmed variant of the street unit, including cast-iron block and heads and 10.25:1 compression. Piston rings were high-strength cast iron, while the lifters carried an extra 0.0005-inch diametrical clearance.

Don Grotheer launches hard at LaPlace Dragway in his Hemi Plymouth. Cable Chrysler-Plymouth of Oklahoma City came on board as a sponsor, eventually prompting the Cable car name, which would adorn several more Grotheer Plymouths.

Jack Thomas's beautiful Dodge Boys 1967 WO23 Coronet was sponsored by Oak Park Dodge in Forest Park, Illinois. (Photo Courtesy Jim Brooks/Jim Schild)

After two years running the wild altered-wheelbase cars in 1965 and 1966, Ronnie Sox and Buddy Martin returned to Super Stock competition in 1967, running this handsome RO23 Belvedere. Even the factory cars traveled modestly in 1967. (Photo Courtesy Charlie Suggs)

Dick Landy beats a Buick Gran Sport at Riverside. The popular road course track featured a massive main straight that doubled as a drag strip. (Photo Courtesy Steve Reyes)

Where the RO/WO Stockers differed most to regular street Hemi cars was the intake manifold. Although outwardly the same as the stock aluminum street manifold, the Super Stock variant had been heavily breathed on by Arlen Vanke and Bill Stiles. Whereas the standard intake featured four cut-out holes to correspond with each carburetor bore, the Super Stock variant had the front bores cut out to reveal a single large chasm, while the rear was almost the same aside from a partial divider at the back.

A Carter AFB model 4139 carburetor was mounted in front and a 4140 in the back. They featured different primary clusters, needle and seat, and accelerator pump clusters and jets. Although resulting in a loss of torque below 3,000 rpm, both torque and horsepower benefitted enormously.

The Hemi was supplied with the standard cast-iron Street Hemi headers and 2.25-inch-diameter exhaust while a set of Hooker Headers were stored in a Hooker Headers box in the trunk where the battery was relocated. In addition, there was a shroud that helped seal the carburetors to better increase the ram-air effect. This too was placed in the trunk for shipping.

Bill Nugent's glorious Ramsmoke II 1966 Dodge Coronet had a beam front axle and blocked-out headlights, signifying this car didn't run in Super Stock. The Coronet was a big car by 1967 drag racing standards, but even still, it nearly got the front wheels off the deck. (Photo Courtesy Jim Brooks/Jim Schild)

For a period in 1967, Sox & Martin, Jere Stahl, and Bill Jenkins formed a match-race tour to sell to event promoters. The three racers would take turns running against each other. This was during their visit to Aquasco Speedway, after which they packed up and headed to Cecil County for a night race. (Photo Courtesy Alan Lewis)

Ronnie Sox leans forward at speed as he gets ready to grab another gear. (Photo Courtesy Alan Lewis)

The Sox & Martin GTX puts a fender on Bill "Grumpy" Jenkins at Aquasco Speedway as the crowd looks on in suspense. Note the staging lanes in front of the grandstands. (Photo Courtesy Alan Lewis)

The Hemi Plymouths of Jere Stahl (near lane) and Ronnie Sox leave in tandem at Aquasco Speedway. Note the race Hemi scoop on Stahl's Plymouth, while the Sox & Martin GTX runs the regular production hood. (Photo Courtesy Alan Lewis)

Like the Sox & Martin team, Dick Landy also returned to Super Stock racing in 1967. He campaigned a pair of beautiful Dodge Coronets. The silver car at the rear was built in late 1966 and fitted with a 440 and TorqueFlite. It would ultimately be repainted blue with a white top (like the car in front) to promote Dodge's White Hat Special package. At the same time, it was fitted with a Hemi. (Photo Courtesy Tom West/Lou Hart)

Dick Landy launches his Coronet at Riverside. (Photo Courtesy Steve Reyes)

Customers had a choice of either the A727 Torque-Flite or A833 4-speed transmission. The TorqueFlite carried a 2.45:1 low gear and reverse-pattern modification, so it had to be shifted manually via the standard column shift. The 4-speed manual had a 2.66:1 low gear and had the synchronizers removed along with every second tooth on the engagement gears. This modification allowed for ultra-slick gear shifts at full power. The 4-speed was fitted with a short-handle Hurst Competition Plus shifter.

The big thumping Hemi fed its power to the back axles via Chrysler's Sure-Grip differential (8¾ inches on the TorqueFlite cars and the Dana and 9¾ inches on the 4-speed cars), packing 4.86:1 gears on the TorqueFlite-equipped cars and 4.88:1 on the 4-speed cars. Heavy-duty leaf springs were employed with drum brakes front and rear. Standard Street Hemi cars were equipped with 11-inch-diameter drum brakes front and rear, but the Super Stock drag cars featured smaller 10-inch drums up front to help reduce rolling resistance.

The enhanced Prestolite transistor ignition (Chrysler's formative electronic ignition system) was mounted on the inside of the firewall. A special distributor and coil and racing plug wires were also incorporated.

An RO/WO Super Stock could be ordered in any color, as long as it was WW1 white with black interior. Whereas previous Chrysler Super Stock cars sported a pair of bucket seats up front, the RO/WO cars were fitted with a bench seat while lighter weight carpet lined the floor. Wheels were steel 15x6-inch items painted white and wrapped in 7.75x15 tires.

For those not associated with Chrysler or a Chrysler dealership, the suggested retail price for an RO/WO Super Stock was $3,831 for the Plymouth, and $3,875 for the Dodge.

Although the NHRA minimum production requirement was for 50 of each model, the exact number of RO/WO cars actually built is a little murky. It's almost certainly less than 50. Regardless, the classy new Mopars were cleared to race, although they missed early season

Don Grotheer launches his beautiful RO23 Belvedere at Tulsa Raceway Park in early 1967. Grotheer had a successful year, winning AA/Stock at the Winternationals and NHRA Division 4 points championship. (Photos Courtesy Chuck Conway)

The Ramchargers helped spearhead Super Stock racing in the early 1960s from a "hot dog and fries" category to a main event. Likewise, they were pioneers in the new altered-wheelbase and Funny Car phenomenon. (Photo Courtesy Revs Institute/Tom Burnside)

competitions, including the NHRA Winternationals, as they were still to be constructed.

1967 Drag Racing Highlights

The 1967 national drag racing schedule opened with the AHRA Winternationals on January 29, having returned to Beeline Dragway. The new RO/WO cars missed this event and the NHRA Winternationals that followed a week later before finally making their debut at the NHRA Springnationals. With the return of a Chrysler factory Super Stock in 1967 and its army of factory teams, the category elevated itself to new heights.

1967 AHRA Winternationals

At the AHRA Winternationals, Bill Jenkins took the victory in his updated Chevy II, *Grumpy's Toy*. He took full advantage of the new tire rule (and a lack of genuine Chrysler competition with the new RO/WO cars still in production) by fitting the Chevy with Oldsmobile station wagon wheels in the back. The offset allowed him to squeeze 9-inch-wide tires inside the stock fenders.

1967 NHRA Winternationals

The first of the NHRA's major events for 1967 was the Winternationals in Pomona in early February. It was noteworthy that Chrysler's on-track rivals were all shrinking in size. In 1967, there was an influx of teams running Chevrolet's new pony car, the Camaro, which had launched in September 1966 and could be ordered with either a small-block or one of two 396-ci big-block engine options. Jenkins soon switched to a big-block Camaro, but at the Winternationals, he campaigned his 1966 Chevy II once more.

The Chrysler Super Stock fleet at the 1967 Winternationals included those of Arlen Vanke, Don Grotheer, Joe

Smith, Ed Miller, Richard Charbonneau, and "Dandy" Dick Landy, among others. Dandy Dick, however, was the only one of the contingent to show up with a new 1967 model. It wasn't a WO23 Dodge, of course, but a converted GTX street car.

The 1966 serial winner Jere Stahl opted not to make the long trip from the East Coast. After winning a spree of events in 1966, the relationship between Chrysler and Stahl had soured. Chrysler stopped its support of Stahl after a disagreement over transmissions, and he struggled to get his Mopar to perform on wider 9-inch tires in early 1967 contests.

As usual, Mopars dominated most of the Super Stock classes they entered. Ed Miller won SS/A, and Don Grotheer won SS/B. In the automatic divisions, there were more Chryslers enjoying the spoils. Joe Smith took top honors in SS/AA, Richard Carbonneau in SS/BA, Arlen Vanke in SS/CA, and Dave Kempton in SS/DA all driving Plymouths.

The biggest and most important contest for the Stockers, Super Stock Eliminator, highlighted the NHRA's clumsy handicapping system, which drivers were increasingly exploiting. With the new 1967 weight breaks introduced, SS/A and SS/B were the only two divisions to have an established class record set prior to the event.

Meanwhile, Eddie Vasquez, driving an SS/C Chevy II, set a new class record during the event at a conservative 12.72. Vasquez ran a Bill Jenkins motor and was capable of slicing a 12.1 if he needed to. But he just rumbled on down the track, and with each run, he clicked off times near the SS/C class record. It was called "sandbagging," and it had become a common theme in Super Stock Eliminator.

Jenkins was considered a hot favorite to win the event but managed to eliminate himself when he redlit in the first round. That was supposed to leave the door

BUTCH "THE CALIFORNIA FLASH" LEAL

"He's not a Larry; he's a Butch." Those were apparently the words Larry Leal's grandmother said when she first set eyes on him—and the name stuck.

Leal grew up in a farming community in Tulare, California. When he was 14, he built his first hot rod, a 1931 Model A, using abandoned parts from neighboring farms. When he was 16, Butch made a deal with his father who ran a trucking company that if he worked all summer loading hay for the family business with no pay, his dad would buy him a new car. He chose a 1960 Chevy El Camino.

Pretty soon, Leal was stopping off at his local track, Famoso Drag Strip in Bakersfield. He won a trophy in his first attempt. Through racing, he met H. L. Shahan, and a long friendship developed. Leal and Shahan rebuilt the El Camino as a dedicated race car, and the trophies kept coming.

Leal then purchased a new 1962 409 Chevy Biscayne, and even though he was still a teenager, he had become a serious racer. There followed a 1963 Z11 Impala. When Leal learned General Motors was bowing out of all racing, through Mickey Thompson, he became a Ford factory driver with a new lightweight Galaxie.

For 1964, Leal was aboard one of the new 427-ci A/FX Fairlane Thunderbolts. He was just 19 years old. During dinner with track promoter Ben Christ, Christ suggested Leal needed a name because all the racers had names. Christ's wife said, "You're a clean-cut, kind of flashy person. Why not 'California Flash,' since you were born and raised in California?" With that, the California Flash was born.

Following a string of successes, Leal was approached by Bob Cahill, who coaxed him across to Chrysler to race a Hemi Plymouth Super Stock in 1965. From there, he embraced the burgeoning altered-wheelbase and early Funny Car contests. Having been inspired by the new fiberglass bodied flip-top Mercury Comets, he contracted Logghe Bros. to build him a chassis. On top of which was draped a stretched fiberglass Plymouth Barracuda body with power coming from a fuel-injected Hemi.

Although Leal's attention had turned to the altered-wheelbase and Funny Car contests, 1967 saw him make a brief return to the Super Stock ranks, albeit while still campaigning the Barracuda Funny Car. He ordered a WO23 Plymouth Coronet, which was painted in his traditional orange and white. He campaigned it in a handful of events, but his heart now was with Funny Cars.

Leal was near completion of a second flip-top Barracuda in 1968 and was planning to power it with a

Butch Leal campaigned this WO23 Dodge Coronet in 1967, but he was really just keeping his hand in while completing a new flip-top Barracuda Funny Car. (Photo Courtesy Steve Reyes)

blown Hemi on nitro. But after witnessing two vicious blower explosions on his friend Jack Chrisman's car, he began second-guessing his choices. When Don Schumacher phoned and asked if he was interested in selling the car, he was happy to let it go. With that, he returned to Super Stock competition in a new Hemi Coronet, but when Mickey Thompson came calling with an offer to race an SOHC Mustang, Leal returned to the Ford squad.

For 1970, Leal built a Camaro to run in the new Pro Stock division, which brought limited success. He returned to racing Mopars in 1971, building a Plymouth Duster from a donor supplied by Chrysler. Ron Butler built the chassis while Joe Allread built the motor with Leal's help.

Despite a late start, Leal quickly got up to speed and was one of the few to challenge the Sox & Martin squad for pure speed. Indeed, Leal faced Sox in the semifinals at the Super Nationals in Ontario and beat the 'Cuda to the finish. However, Buddy Martin protested, and Leal's Duster was found to have a 57.2 rear weight distribution when the rules only allowed 55 percent, and the California Flash was promptly disqualified.

Like the rest of the Chrysler contingent, Leal found Pro Stock wins hard to come by in 1972. But he notched up success at the NHRA All Pro Championship Series in January and also enjoyed victories in AHRA competition.

Leal had Ron Butler build him a tube-frame Duster in 1973, and he won NHRA Le Grandnational at Sanair Super Speedway. For 1974, he switched to running a 4-speed classic 1965 Plymouth in Super Stock.

By 1977, the California Flash was racing a Plymouth Arrow. At season's end, he decided to retire from racing and focus his energies on his other passion: golf.

In 2022, Butch completed his authorized bio, *Butch "The California Flash" Leal* with CarTech.

open for one of the Mopar contingent to knock home the win. But no one had accounted for the NHRA handicapping system. No one, that is, except Vasquez. He clicked win after win, running right at the SS/C record, until he met Rochester, New York's Ed Miller and his 1965 A990 in the final.

Miller had been running strong all day with an 11.66, 11.43, and 11.69, but he wasn't getting near the SS/A class record of 11.18. When he was set away 1.5 seconds after Vasquez, he didn't have a hope of catching the Elko, Nevada, driver, who produced an almost perfect 12.74 (relative to his class record) to be crowned 1967 NHRA Winternationals Super Stock Eliminator champion.

1967 NHRA Springnationals

The new RO/WO Mopars got their first run in a major event at the third-annual NHRA Springnationals at Bristol, Tennessee. Bristol was set upon by all the heavy hitters and the latest 1967 drag racing machinery, including Bill Jenkins with his new 396-ci big-block SS/C Camaro plus a fleet of 427-ci SS/C Ford Fairlanes.

The squadron of Fords, which tallied around eight factory-backed cars and another six independents, looked impressive sitting in the pits, but they were a disappointment on the track. The Ford teams were blaming a lack

It doesn't get bigger than victory circle at Indianapolis for the NHRA U.S. Nationals. Jack Thomas (with trophy) celebrates with his wife as well as Jim Brooks (right rear) and crewmembers Jim Kavanaugh and Rex Hanief. (Photo Courtesy Jim Brooks/Jim Schild)

Gene Snow and his wild Dodge Dart Funny Car Rambunctious. Although the new Funny Car breed wasn't yet officially recognized by the NHRA, many teams invariably found somewhere to race their creations within the NHRA system. Snow and Rambunctious won C/Fuel Dragster at the 1966 NHRA U.S. Nationals at Indy, and they repeated the feat in 1967. (Photo Courtesy Geoff Stunkard Collection/Ray Mann Archive)

Bob Brown celebrates with his team in victory circle at the NHRA U.S. Nationals. (Photo Courtesy Geoff Stunkard Collection/Ray Mann Archive)

JERE STAHL

Jere Stahl's RO23 Plymouth is adorned in his favored white and rolling on Cragar mags. Although a keen drag racer, Stahl's Total Tuned Headers business also built headers for speedway and road race cars, including SCCA Trans-Am cars. He built the headers for the hugely successful Penske Racing Camaros, among others. (Photo Courtesy Geoff Stunkard Collection/Ray Mann Archive)

Born in 1935, Jere Stahl was a hot rodder who in the mid-1950s took his self-built 1939 Chevy coupe with its much modified and bored 253-ci inline-6 truck motor drag racing.

Stahl worked in a few Chevrolet dealerships in upstate New York before joining the service where he fully embraced the auto mechanics program. While stationed in Frankfurt, Germany, Stahl made use of the base library when a dense fog prevented flying, and it was there he stumbled upon a book called *The Sports Car* by Colin Campbell. He became enamored by the section on intake and exhaust tuning, and upon returning home in 1957, he enrolled in an automobile technical training school.

While attending the Daytona 500 race in 1962, Stahl and a friend took a jaunt to the drag races at Spruce Creek. While talking to Corvette racer Don Gist, Stahl was asked to build a set of better-flowing headers for Gist's 327 motor. Stahl designed the headers but had someone in Florida build them. When asked his recommendation for who to build the engine (Bill Jenkins or Don Nicholson), Stahl suggested Jenkins.

With the rebuilt engine and Stahl headers fitted, Gist set a new national record and then beat Jenkins's *Old Reliable* 1962 Chevy driven by Dave Strickler in Street Eliminator. In 1962, aftermarket header options were limited Tri-Ys built by Jerry Jardine, Frank Saunders, Doug Thorley, and Bob Hedman.

Stahl then built a set of headers to fit the 409 Chevy and asked Strickler to run them. He agreed, and although Jenkins wasn't impressed by the way they looked, when the times showed how well they performed, suddenly, Stahl found himself in the performance header business.

Pretty soon, Stahl received orders from Don Nicholson, Eddie Shartman, Sox & Martin, and Malcolm Durham. To escape the harsh Michigan winters, Stahl moved to Pennsylvania, where he briefly shared a shop with Jenkins before moving to his own facility.

Stahl's Total Tuned Headers was soon branching into other areas of the sport, including road racing and stock car racing. Furthermore, he decided to become a testbed for his own products and ran a fleet of Chryslers in drag racing from 1964 through 1967. In 1966, Stahl won Top Stock Eliminator at the NHRA Springnationals, U.S. Nationals, and World Championship Finals. After the relationship between he and Chrysler soured in 1967, he stepped away from driving to concentrate on his header business.

Although he made a brief comeback in 1971 racing in Pro Stock, Stahl was kept busy with business. He was happy to remain on the sidelines.

The great header guru, Jere Stahl, died in 2016.

SHIRLEY "THE DRAG-ON LADY" SHAHAN

Shirley Shahan switched to one of the latest WO23 Dodge Coronet Super Stocks in 1967. (Photo Courtesy Steve Reyes)

After having been contracted to Plymouth the last two years, for 1967 Shirley Shahan switched to Dodge. As well as campaigning her new Coronet, Shahan also ran this makeshift Hemi Dodge sedan in NHRA's orphan C/XS class. Note that this is actually a 1965 Plymouth with Dodge nose and lettering. (Photo Courtesy Steve Reyes)

Drag racing is notable among all forms of motorsport for the number of female drivers who have excelled. Shirley "the Drag-On Lady" Shahan was one of the true pioneers.

Born and raised in California, Shirley Bridges came from a racing family and learned to drive by the time she was 10. At age 17, she married racer and mechanic H. L. Shahan, and the pair went racing together. Initially, the Shahans raced Chevys, and pretty soon H. L. found himself doing less driving, as his wife was proving to be a genuine hot shoe. Furthermore, she was a demon with a stick shift. In the first March Meet at Famoso Drag Strip in 1959 and independently run by the Smokers Car Club, Shahan sliced and diced a big field of Stockers in her 1958 Chevy to take the win.

Shirley and H. L. both raced, while H. L. proved to be a master tuner. But by the early 1960s, he was preparing cars for Butch Leal and Ronnie Broadhead, among others.

Bob Cahill and Dick Maxwell at Chrysler approached the Shahans about switching brands for 1965, and the pair started campaigning a Hemi Plymouth Belvedere as part of a program paired with Leal. The switch meant Shirley had to switch from her beloved stick shift to an automatic, which she wasn't too happy about. She quickly adapted and soon started taking names. She reached the final at the 1965 Hot Rod Championship at Riverside before winning the event the following year.

Meanwhile, she reached the Super Stock final at the 1966 AHRA Winternationals, but her most historic win came one week later at the NHRA Winternationals, where she met Ken Heinemann's Hemi Plymouth in the Super Stock Eliminator final and went on to take the victory.

Carol Cox was the first female driver to win an NHRA national event when she took an S/SA victory at the 1961 Winternationals with her Pontiac Ventura, but Shahan was the first female to win an Eliminator crown.

Chrysler never actually paid the Shahans to race its products; instead, it supplied the cars and parts for free. Regardless, in 1966, she quit her day job at SoCal Gas Company and went racing full-time. She and H. L. had three children, but her fame exploded, and she made the transition to follow her passion.

Throughout 1966, H. L. evolved the Belvedere into a fuel-injected altered-wheelbase car running on nitro.

The Shahans was one of the few teams to stick to racing Super Stock in 1966 when most of the Chrysler fleet jumped ship for the growing Funny Car craze. Naturally, with the announcement of the new factory RO/WO Mopar Super Stocks for 1967, the Drag-On Lady was soon equipped with one of the big swoopy coupes. However, having raced for Plymouth since their arrival at Chrysler, Dodge managed to coax the Shahans across to its fold, and as such, Shirley raced a new WO Coronet in 1967.

With Chrysler packing a lot more heat with the 1968-introduced LO23/BO29 Mopar pairing, the Drag-On Lady switched to one of the rapid little Darts. For 1969, the Shahans received a better offer from American Motors Corporation, and they switched to racing AMC products both in Super Stock and the new Pro Stock division.

Life was tough for the pioneering women of drag racing. In the early days, they were banned from competing

Shirley Shahan is in her office doing what she does best. (Photo Courtesy Patrick Foster)

at NHRA national events. When they were finally granted permission, a lot of the guys didn't take too kindly to getting beat. Protests were common. If one of the guys got put on the trailer by one of the girls, she must surely be cheating, right?

But the likes of Cox, Shahan, Shirley Muldowney, Roberta Leighton, Barbara Hamilton, Paula Murphy, and others, stood their ground and won. They battled the system and chauvinism as much as they battled the car in the next lane.

In 2022, Shirley completed her authorized bio, *Shirley Shahan: The Drag-On Lady* with CarTech.

Pictured at Tulsa Raceway Park for the 1967 NHRA World Championship Finals is Jere Stahl's RO23 Plymouth. Stahl stepped away from racing at season's end to concentrate on his successful header business. (Photo Courtesy Chuck Conway)

of horsepower on cylinder-head and intake-manifold design that showed all the right numbers on the dyno but came up short on the track. For what it was worth, Harold Dutton's Fairlane fared the best, but it too was soon on the trailer.

By contrast, the Chrysler contingent was actually having the opposite problem. The new Super Stock haulers were running too quick, and drivers had to back off early to avoid blowing the doors off the existing class records, the punishment for which was instant disqualification.

In Super Stock Eliminator, Dutton went out in Round 2 after succumbing to the flying Ronnie Sox, who was simply immense. Sox had already beaten Arlen Vanke, and when he got done with Stahl, went on to nail Bill Stiles, and then Ron Mancini before he met Jenkins in the final. The Grump became another casualty of

The Sox & Martin Plymouth is resting in the Tulsa paddock during the NHRA World Championship Finals. It had been a successful year for the team, which took home plenty of silverware, but the years that followed would be better still. (Photo Courtesy Chuck Conway)

Flanked by the enemy. Hubert Platt's Fairlane is surrounded by fast Mopars. (Photo Courtesy Chuck Conway)

the beautiful red, white, and blue Plymouth GTX. Sox romped home to victory with an 11.34 at 123.45 mph.

1967 NHRA U.S. Nationals

Indianapolis Raceway Park hosted the annual NHRA U.S. Nationals in early September. This event saw the advent of AA Fuel Dragsters and the top Funny Cars running ultra-low tire pressures. The baggy boots were the topic of much discussion, and magazines ran catchy headliners such as "Flying on Flat Tires." Combined with slipping clutches, the fastest AA Fuel Dragsters were running sub-7-second times. The Ramchargers rail popped a jaw-dropping 6.76 ET.

Mopar drivers collected plenty of silverware in the Super Stock divisions with Bob Brown winning SS/A in his 1965 Plymouth, punching out an impressive 11.01 at 123 mph along the way. Ray Christian won SS/AA in his 1967 Dodge while Ronnie Sox won SS/B, beating the similar 1967 Plymouth of Gary Ostrich in the final. Tom Myl won SS/BA in his 1967 Plymouth, and Gene Takash won SS/EA in his 1967 Dodge.

Bill Jenkins faced off against Bob Brown in Super Stock Eliminator. Brown, the faster of the two, couldn't catch the little white Camaro in the handicapping system, and a curious system it was. With both drivers nailing the start, neither redlighting, and both making strong runs, the slowest car won. But those were the rules! Racing has historically shown that those who play the game smartest usually come out on top.

1967 NHRA World Championship Finals

The 1967 NHRA World Finals were in late November. Despite dropping an engine during his last timed run prior to Eliminations, Ed Miller busted his way through the 16-car field to meet Dick Arons in a Bill Jenkins–prepared SS/EA Camaro in the final.

The NHRA had made attempts to prevent the sandbagging that helped Eddie Vasquez win the Winternationals at the start of the year. It also reduced the field

from 30 to 16 cars, and drivers had to qualify to ensure a berth. Those who missed the cut included reigning World Finals champion Jere Stahl and Arlen Vanke. Miller, incidentally, was driving Vanke's old 1965 SS/A Plymouth. This would be the final outing for Stahl. He'd hang up his helmet when he returned home to concentrate on building headers for his customers.

Jenkins redlit early in the proceedings, and the Chrysler representatives were no doubt happy to see Miller outrun Arons in the final with an 11.19 at 114.35 mph to Arons's losing 12.32 at 120.80 mph. Miller was no doubt happy to take home the $10,000 winner's check offered up by Hurst Performance.

And so it was, 1968 saw Chrysler return to Super Stock racing with a vengeance, and its drivers scored some major wins. But this was a season beset with controversy, as the NHRA handicapping system tended to overshadow the achievements on the track. Things would only get worse.

Dick Landy's Dodge Coronet rests in the paddock at Indianapolis for the 1967 NHRA U.S. Nationals. Next to the Coronet can be seen a brand-new 1968 Dodge Charger, which itself became part of Landy's racing fleet. (Photo Courtesy David McWilliams)

CHAPTER 8

1968

CHRYSLER GOES BIG IN ITS SMALLEST PACKAGE YET

For those ordering a new 1968 Dodge Dart Super Stock (or Plymouth Barracuda), this was how their car looked when the owner took delivery. Although it didn't look like it, this was a turnkey car, complete with exhaust system and mufflers. Chrysler rightly reckoned each team would apply its own war paint, and as such, supplied its Super Stocks painted in primer grey with the black gel-coat nose panels. Likewise, each team fit its own wheels and tires. Those fitted here are merely to make it mobile. This particular car was for Jack Thomas. (Photo Courtesy Jim Brooks/Jim Schild)

Chrysler launched its latest generation B-Body intermediate Dodge and Plymouth models in late 1967. The new Coronet and Belvedere incorporated the popular Coke-bottle styling trend that manufacturers were wholeheartedly embracing during the late 1960s. The hard edges and straight lines of the previous generation offerings were replaced by soft curves, pumped rear hips, and a far more organic shape.

The wheelbase remained the same at 117 inches for the Dodge, and the marginally stubbier Plymouth at 116 inches. Bodystyles included the four-door sedan, four-door station wagon, two-door convertible, two-door post, and two-door hardtop. Engine options ranged from the 225-ci slant-6 through the 440-ci Wedge, and 426-ci Hemi.

By 1968, the pony car and muscle car/super car phenomenon was in full swing, and customers were increasingly overwhelmed by a plethora of mad street machines boasting audacious exterior architecture and catchy brand names. For its new-generation intermediates, Chrysler launched the Dodge Super Bee and Plymouth Road Runner. Both were basic trim models sporting ballistic engines, which were the very ingredients from which the company's drag racing models were brewed.

Neither the Coronet nor the Belvedere was part of Chrysler's grand plans for its 1968 Super Stock drag

Chrysler's new Plymouth Road Runner became a popular choice among racers in 1968. This is the beautiful Cooper Motors example launching at Fremont. (Photo Courtesy Steve Reyes)

Bob Lambeck, aboard Dick Landy's glorious new Dodge Coronet R/T, faces off against a classic 1964 Belvedere at Half Moon Bay. (Photo Courtesy Steve Reyes)

Lee Smith guns his handsome new Hemi-powered 1968 Road Runner. Smith had made the switch from campaigning an altered-wheelbase 1965 Belvedere. (Photo Courtesy Jim Brooks/Jim Schild)

Ronnie Sox in the Road Runner squares off against an AMC Rambler at Riverside. (Photo Courtesy Steve Reyes)

For 1968, the Sox & Martin team built this new Plymouth Road Runner, which ran alongside its new Barracuda. Here, Ronnie Sox battles Dave Strickler's Corvette at Lions Drag Strip. (Photo Courtesy Steve Reyes)

"AKRON" ARLEN VANKE

Arlen Vanke from Akron, Ohio, began racing in the early 1950s in a 1940 Ford sedan hot rod with a hopped-up flathead V-8. Vanke's parents were both supportive of his racing, helping fund uprated speed equipment parts for the little Ford before purchasing a new Chevy in 1956. From there, his racing successes quickly multiplied, winning 36 regional events in succession.

In 1961, when a buddy of Arlen's began campaigning a new 409 Chevy, Vanke could see Super Stock competition as an opportunity to propel his career forward. Very quickly, Vanke found himself owning a new 1962-model Pontiac with the optional 421-ci Super Duty motor.

Arlen Vanke invariably presented his cars among the best and most vibrant of the era, and his BO29 Barracuda was no exception. (Photo Courtesy Wes Eisenschenk)

With the new steed came a small amount of sponsorship from Bill Knafel Pontiac.

Throughout 1962, Vanke went on a winning spree with the big Pontiac and carved out a reasonable income as a semiprofessional driver through the NHRA's new points program. His momentum continued into early 1963, before General Motors suddenly withdrew from racing and cut off all support to its racers.

When that happened, Vanke switched to Chrysler. In 1964, he purchased not one but two Belvederes: a Wedge and a Hemi. Vanke then chocked up a stack of success over the next two years, particularly with the Hemi. Despite it all, Vanke was disappointed not to receive any support from Chrysler. He returned to Pontiac and teamed up once more with Bill Knafel, who campaigned a dealer-funded program of GTOs dubbed *Tin Indians*.

Despite struggling with parts failures, Vanke and the Pontiacs were quick. He now had the attention of Chrysler, which came to him with an assist to get him back into a Mopar. With that, "Akron" Arlen became a staunch Chrysler supporter.

Over the next few years, he emerged as a leading contender in Super Stock competition in the NHRA and the AHRA. Aboard a BO29 Barracuda, he won the most coveted prize of all, the 1968 NHRA U.S. Nationals, as well as the AHRA Winternationals in 1969. He narrowly lost to Ronnie Sox in the AHRA U.S. Open later that same year.

When the NHRA switched to its Pro Stock format for 1970, Vanke prepared a new Plymouth Duster, and it was mighty. He reached the final on three occasions: at the U.S. Nationals, World Finals, and Supernationals. Each time, he faced a Sox & Martin car (Herb McCandless at Indy, Ronnie Sox at Dallas and Ontario), and each time he just missed out on the big prize. But certainly, he'd made a statement and became hugely successful in regional events.

For 1971, Vanke built a new Plymouth 'Cuda but didn't enjoy quite the level of success in NHRA Pro Stock as he'd accomplished in the Duster. He reached the semifinals twice, only to be beaten by Sox. He did, however, win the 1971 AHRA Winternationals, beating Bob Lambeck's Dodge Dart in the final.

Vanke was a victim of the NHRA's new weight breaks in 1972 and had a tough year. Although he was sometimes the go-to man for developing Chrysler racing components, Vanke never received full factory support, and as such, he was forced to fund his own racing. In 1973, he decided to wind down his career, bowing out as a highly successful independent racer who could genuinely foot it with the factory squads.

He'd carved an excellent reputation for building tough race motors. In 1995, he built a replica of his 1968 U.S. Nationals–winning BO29 Barracuda and began campaigning it on the nostalgia circuit while adding to his fleet a few years later with a 1965 Belvedere.

Arlen Vanke died in 2017 at age 80.

In addition to the rest of his fleet, Dick Landy also built this neat little Dodge Dart for Super Stock/EA competition. The Dart, when running the stock bodywork without the radiused rear wheel openings of the factory-built Super Stock examples, looks modest by comparison. The SS/EA Dart ran a 440 motor. (Photo Courtesy Steve Reyes)

Lee Cameron's P.D.Q. Dodge is pictured at Riverside. (Photo Courtesy Steve Reyes)

Dick Landy again had a busy schedule in 1968, including running his 1967 Coronet in SS/B competition. (Photo Courtesy Steve Reyes)

Lee Cameron, pictured at Fremont Dragstrip, makes a run against a Ford Fairlane in his 1967 Coronet. (Photo Courtesy Steve Reyes)

The Appaloosa WO23 Dodge Coronet of Mike Schmitt launches at Fremont Dragstrip. This is thought to be the car raced previously by Butch "the California Flash" Leal. (Photo Courtesy Steve Reyes)

The short-lived RO23 Melrose Missile Super Stock was campaigned in 1967 and briefly in 1968. (Photo Courtesy Steve Reyes)

The Jenkins Satellite 1965 Coronet is pictured at Fremont. The smaller independent teams kept the older Mopars running strong as the factory teams moved to the latest equipment. (Photo Courtesy Steve Reyes)

The Count Down Jr. 1964 Plymouth gets a head start over the Hyper Bus 1968 LO23 Hemi Dart at Half Moon Bay. Dial-in time for the Plymouth is 11.47 compared to 10.73 for the Dart. (Photo Courtesy Steve Reyes)

The Miller and Guenther 1965 Plymouth launches at Fremont. The hood scoop suggests the classic Belvedere is running a Hemi. (Photo Courtesy Steve Reyes)

The Rettig Brothers were longtime campaigners of Mopar products. (Photo Courtesy Steve Reyes)

racing initiatives. Indeed, the company was injecting some much-missed crazy back into its program, the likes of which hadn't been seen since the feral Super Stock and altered-wheelbase monsters of 1965.

1968 Chrysler Super Stock Packages

For 1967, Chrysler launched its latest sporty compacts: the Dodge Dart and Plymouth Barracuda. These were Chrysler's answer to Ford's game-changer: the Mustang. Well, sort of. Upon launch, the Mustang exceeded all sales expectations, selling more than 100,000 units within four months of its April 17, 1964, unveiling. Sales were more than 680,000 by the end of 1965 and topped 1.3 million by the end of 1966. The Mustang's massive success prompted a new market segment named in its honor: the pony car market.

Interestingly, Chrysler launched its third-generation Dodge Dart and first-generation Plymouth Barracuda a matter of weeks before the Mustang arrived. Both models shared a similar theme, size, and layout to the Ford pony car, but neither captured anywhere near the public and media attention and adoration.

The Mustang's success ensured the pony car market fast became a busy place. By late 1966, Chevrolet arrived with its new Camaro and Mercury with its Cougar. In early 1967, the Camaro's sibling, the Pontiac Firebird, was also born. Even American Motors Corporation (AMC) got in on the act, unveiling its new Javelin in late 1967. Increasingly, manufacturers were funding racing programs for these models because they were new and fresh, and the public were buying them in vast quantities.

The Sports Car Club of America (SCCA) established a road racing series in 1966 called the Trans-American

Sedan Championship that was specifically based around the dimensions and engine size of the Mustang. It did this knowing full well that other manufacturers would jump on board as their own pony cars came to market. The ploy worked, and the SCCA Trans-Am series exploded.

Manufacturers were increasingly switching their drag racing programs away from the larger models and downsizing to their pony cars, most of which offered both small-block and big-block engine options by 1968. Chrysler was also about to embrace this bold new world.

The 1968 A-Body Dart and Barracuda were significantly smaller and lighter than the Coronet and Belvedere. The Dart had a wheelbase of 111 inches; the Barracuda was an even more compact 108 inches. Indeed, the Barracuda shared the same wheelbase as the Mustang

Jack Thomas's new Dart Super Stock is partially stripped to begin preparation for paint work, wheels, and a racing exhaust system. The as-supplied exhaust and muffler can be seen on the floor. They were going straight into the bin. (Photo Courtesy Jack Thomas/Jim Schild)

and Camaro. In 1967, both models could be ordered with a 383-ci big-block as the largest and most powerful offering.

For 1968, however, Chrysler designed and produced a small batch of specific Super Stock cars with the mighty 426-ci Hemi squeezed between the front wheels.

LO23 and BO29

Both the 1968 Dart and Barracuda Super Stock models carried a Chrysler VIN that included an "O," denoting their intention as Super Stock drag cars. The VIN began with either LO23M8B for the Dodge and BO29M8B for the Plymouth. Both models used the two-door hardtop body. The standard Barracuda was available in two different two-door hardtop bodystyles, including a fastback and a notchback. Only the fastback was used for the Super Stock program.

The new Mopar Super Stocks were assembled at Chrysler's Hamtramck plant as regular 383 cars but with specific additions and deletions pertaining to their intent. Each model was built in two batches: the first in February and the second in May. The partially completed cars were then sent to Hurst Performance, where final assembly took place, including installation of the Hemi engines.

Chrysler intended that its customers and racers would add their own paint schemes and wheels, and as such, produced its Super Stocks finished in special-order light grey primer. They were rolling on black-painted steel wheels that were 14 inches in diameter in the front and 15 in the back. The cars were ordered without sound deadener, underseal, and a heater. The passenger-side mirror was also deleted.

The steel doors and front bumper were acid dipped, while the front fenders, hood, and hood scoop were all molded in fiberglass and finished in black gelcoat. The hood wasn't physically attached to the body, so it could be lifted off completely as required. It was held in place via four chrome-plated pins and clips. The hood scoop was immense! It towered above any previous Mopar Super Stock hood scoop. The inner fenders and engine compartment were finished in gloss black as were the doorjambs because most teams would leave these areas untouched when applying their own war paint.

To squeeze the monstrous Hemi into the engine compartment, the right-side inner fender panel and upper control-arm bracket had to be massaged for clearance. The modification looked for all the world like it'd been performed with a large hammer. Dearborn Steel Tubing carried out similar remodeling of Ford's 1964 Super Stock factory Fairlane firewalls to make space for dropping the big 427 motors into them. Haste of work was paramount—aesthetics less so. The brake master cylinder was offset for more clearance.

Although essentially built on the same platform (except for the Dodge's longer wheelbase), the Dart and Barracuda sported quite different bodywork. The Darts in particular looked like shrunken 1967 Coronets and

Harold Dutton raced for Bob Maddox Chrysler-Plymouth of Forrest Park, Georgia, campaigning this 4-speed BO29 Barracuda. (Photo Courtesy Marvin T Smith)

Another Georgia racer, Robert Nance ("Mister Plymouth"), received his BO29 Barracuda equipped with automatic transmission in March 1968, and he competed in local events. (Photo Courtesy Marvin T. Smith)

Larry Griffith's beautiful LO23 Hemi Dart Super Stock gleams in its custom blue lace paint and rolls on Cragar SS mag wheels. (Jack Thomas Photo, Courtesy Jim Schild)

The Hyper Bus *Hemi Dart launches at Fremont during a night race. (Photo Courtesy Steve Reyes)*

Ruel Nichol in the beautiful Denny's Dyno LO23 Hemi Dart is pictured at Half Moon Bay. (Photo Courtesy Steve Reyes)

featured similar partially enclosed rear fender wheel openings. The 1968 Dart Super Stocks, therefore, had the rear openings radiused out to allow fitment of fat racing wheels and tires. The recontoured openings loosely followed those of the stock front wheel openings. No such modifications were required on the Barracudas.

Transmissions

Customers had a choice of either the A727 TorqueFlite transmission modified for manual shifts or the A833 4-speed manual. Both units used floor shifters made by Hurst. The 4-speed manual was mated to a heavy-duty 10.5-inch clutch disc and

Now resplendent in its war paint, the Super Stock Dart of Jack Thomas is rolling on American Racing Wheels. (Photo Courtesy Jack Thomas/Jim Schild)

flywheel. The TorqueFlite used a high-stall torque converter. The rear axle was a narrowed 8.75-inch Chrysler unit with 4.86:1 gears for TorqueFlite-equipped cars and a narrowed 9.75-inch Dana-Spicer 60 unit with 4.88:1 gear ratio for the 4-speed cars.

Interiors

Interiors for the 1968 Super Stocks featured a pair of Bostrom Companion bucket seats up front with the rear seat deleted and replaced by a cardboard panel. The front buckets were mounted on lightweight aluminum brackets, and the passenger seat had no seat belt. There were no armrests and no window cranks, and everything was swathed in black vinyl.

The windows in the doors featured 0.080-inch-thick glass, as did the rear quarter windows, which were fixed in place. The door glass could be slid up or down by pulling on a woven strap. Both the Dart and Barracuda carried stock instrument panels with block-off plates covering the heater and radio openings. The battery was mounted on a steel plate on the passenger-side trunk floor.

Engine

The 426-ci Hemi was similar to the Street Hemi but ran an increased 12.5:1 compression. It carried an aluminum cross-ram intake manifold like that fitted to the 1964 drag cars and was topped with a pair of 4-barrel Holley 4150 carburetors and unsilenced air cleaners. The camshaft was a 1968 street Hemi unit with 0.484/0.475-inch lift and 284 degrees of duration. Spent gases made their

way through Hooker Headers connected to straight pipes that dumped down beneath the car ahead of the rear wheels. The ignition system used a Hemi dual-point distributor and Prestolite Transignitor.

Midyear Offering

A mule Barracuda Super Stock was ready for testing by early January 1968. The program ran under the direction of Tom Hoover in Chrysler Special Vehicle Engineering. Bob Tarozzi and Larry Knowlton oversaw design and development. Initial tests at Irwindale Raceway in California uncovered a variety of issues that had to be worked through. Eventually, the car ran fast and straight, dipping into the mid- to high-10-second bracket.

From there, the fleet of Dodge and Plymouth Super Stock racers were constructed. Eighty-three Darts and 72 Barracudas were built.

The manufacturer's suggested retail price (MSRP) for the Dart was $5,146, and the Barracuda was $5,214. To the uninitiated, that might appear to be a lot of money for a car with no paint and no warranty, but the uninitiated would have been blissfully unaware that these Super Stock specials even existed. Chrysler didn't advertise them, and only participating dealers and specific race teams would have been alerted to them. They were very special cars, and in fact, a bargain at the price. They quickly found new homes.

Super Stock Darts wound up with Dick Landy, Jack Thomas, Larry Griffith, Shirley Shahan, Bill Bagshaw, Dick Oldfield, Larry Cooper, Bill Flynn, Chick Brignolo, Preston Honea, Charlie Castaldo, Rich Thomas, Melvin Yow, Ron Mancini, and countless others.

The Barracudas went to Sox & Martin, Arlen Vanke, Ed Miller, Don Grotheer, Russell Funk, Bill Stiles, Claude Bradshaw, Ken Montgomery, Gary Ostrich, Judy Lilly, Jack Werst, etc. The list went on and on.

The NHRA shuffled its Super Stock power-to-weight ratios once more for 1968 and introduced Super Stock/F:

- SS/A: 0.00 to 5.99 pounds per hp
- SS/B: 6.00 to 6.99 pounds per hp
- SS/C: 7.00 to 7.69 pounds per hp
- SS/D: 7.70 to 8.69 pounds per hp
- SS/E: 8.70 to 9.49 pounds per hp
- SS/F: 9.50 pounds per hp and above

The Chrysler Super Stocks naturally fell into SS/B and SS/BA (for automatics), which, in 1968, became the fastest division in Super Stock drag racing. Of course, under the handicapping/sandbagging system, that didn't guarantee race wins.

The beating heart is shown nestled in the front of the Jack Thomas Dart. (Photo Courtesy Jack Thomas/Jim Schild)

Ruel Nichol in the gold-colored Denny's Dyno Dart chases the Rettig Bros. 1965 Hemi Belvedere. (Photo Courtesy Steve Reyes)

Two Super Stock Mopars leap in unison with Bill Stiles in the Barracuda and Shirley Shahan in the Dart at Cecil County Drag-O-Way. (Photo Courtesy Clinton Wright)

It's a Hemi Super Stock showdown at Riverside. (Photo Courtesy Steve Reyes)

The Liberty Dodge LO23 Hemi Dart of JC South is shown here. (Photo Courtesy Marvin T. Smith)

With testing and developing of the Barracuda mule still ongoing when the 1968 racing season kicked off, many Chrysler teams simply carried on with their existing machinery. Although, the cigar-chomping Dick Landy had a beautiful new Dodge Charger R/T and Coronet R/T prepared. His brother Mike drove the Coronet. Likewise, the Sox & Martin team also built a new Plymouth Road Runner.

1968 Drag Racing Highlights

The NHRA continued its somewhat despised (by those racing the faster cars) handicapping and time-break system in 1968, whereas the AHRA instead went for a simple heads-up contest at its events. This being the purest form of racing, it seemed quite logical, but Super Stock drag racing had evolved almost beyond recognition. The NHRA was simply trying to ensure that its paying spectators were treated to a show with unexpected results.

The wild new Chrysler LO23/BO29 Super Stock cars weren't ready for either the AHRA Winternationals on January 28 or the NHRA Winternationals on February 4. However, at the NHRA Springnationals on June 16, spectators and media alike watched in awe as these epic factory monsters strutted their stuff—at least in qualifying, if not the race.

1968 AHRA Winternationals

Competition for the Chrysler contingent in 1968 included Bill Jenkins's Camaro, of course. But in addition, Ford released a fleet of 428-ci Cobra Jet Mustangs, which lined up in a variety of Super Stock classes. Hubert Platt debuted one of the new Cobra Jet Mustangs at the AHRA Winter Championship at Lions Drag Strip on January 28, but he redlit in Round 1.

The AHRA had ditched the handicap start system in favor of heads-up racing for 1968, and both Landy and Sox went right through to the final of Super Stock Eliminator. Landy stormed to an easy victory when Sox jumped the gun.

1968 NHRA Winternationals

One week later at the NHRA Winternationals, six of the gleaming white Mustangs arrived. They were driven by Hubert Platt, Gas Ronda, Jerry Harvey, "Dyno" Don Nicholson, and Al Joniec. The Mustangs ran in C/Stock Automatic, Super Stock/A, Super Stock/E, and Super Stock/EA. Platt performed double duty, driving one Cobra Jet in C/SA and another in SS/E, Harvey ran SS/E as did Joniec, and Nicholson ran SS/EA.

With no Hemi Barracudas yet in the Sox & Martin stable, it was up to the 1-year-old 1967 GTX to battle Ford's latest attempt at reclaiming the crown of Super Stock. Hubert Platt wasn't having any of it, and he laid down an impressive 11.09 to Ronnie Sox's 11.74. (Photo Courtesy georgiashaker.com)

Butch Leal in a Landy's Dodge hits the gas as Buster Coach watches from between the two race cars. Note the number of photographers in the background, as the Winternationals was seen as one of drag racing's premier events. (Photo Courtesy Butch Leal's Scrapbook)

The Chrysler big guns ran in multiple classes. Landy brought several Dodges, including one piloted by Butch Leal and the Coronet for his brother Mike. Leal faced off against Joniec in the SS/E final and lost.

Ed Miller won SS/B in his elderly but still highly potent 1965 Hemi Plymouth, beating Johnathon Livingston's similar car in the final, and blitzing an 11.08 in the process. Tom Crutchfield won SS/BA in his 1965 Dodge while Dave Wren took the spoils in SS/DA in his positively vintage 1963 Plymouth. Landy won SS/EA and SS/FA.

The big one, of course, was Super Stock Eliminator. The field narrowed down to Joniec and Wren. In the end, Wren gifted Joniec the win by triggering the red light.

Dick "Barney" Oldfield is in The Good Guys *LO23 Hemi Dart at Indy for the 1968 NHRA U.S. Nationals. (Photo Courtesy Geoff Stunkard Collection/Ray Mann Archive)*

1968 NHRA Springnationals

The next major NHRA event was the Springnationals at Bristol, and the Super Stock division was packed to the gunnels with quality machinery. The new 1968 Chrysler factory LO23/BO29 Super Stock cars were out in force. Landy, Sox & Martin, Mancini, Grotheer, and several others were all equipped with the latest Hemi Mopar arsenal. Facing them were Jenkins, Arons, Joniec, Platt, and every other top dog running a Ford or a Chevy.

In qualifying, the Chrysler teams were letting it rip and punching out elapsed times of more than half of a second under the existing SS/B and SS/BA records. It was phenomenal!

Ronnie Sox continued his power runs throughout the SS/B contest. He faced Vanke's Hemi Barracuda in the final and busted out a 10.52 at 131.19 mph. In SS/BA, Larry Cooper's Hemi Dart beat the similar machine of Mary Ann Foss, running 11.05 at 128.02 mph.

All the excitement surrounding the Super Stock class competitions only heightened anticipation for the coveted Super Stock Eliminator on the final day of the event, but the show couldn't have been more disappointing. While the drivers could run flat out in their class contests, the NHRA applied an automatic disqualification for running under the existing record in Super Stock Eliminator. As such, the massive crowd was treated to the sight of almost every car jumping on the brakes before the finish line to avoid breaking out.

Hot Rod magazine scribe Lee Kelley pulled no punches. He wrote, "Super Stock Eliminator was a joke. After showing the crowd how quick they could run on Saturday, the Super Stockers came back Sunday with the old foot-on-the-brake routine to disappoint the capacity crowd. The show was more boring than it was exciting as car after car stormed off the line only to go slipping and sliding through the lights with the brakes on to keep from going under the NHRA records. The announcer kept calling it 'strategy drag racing,' but a much better term would be 'bush league.'"

In the end, Sox met Grotheer in the final. Sox switched to his 1967 Plymouth GTX, running SS/D after his Barracuda suffered damage when the tire spun itself on the rim. In the end, both drivers broke out. Sox actually had the brakes locked up as he went through the traps; smoke poured from the tires as he slid across the line. Grotheer managed to control his braking a little better but still had the brakes on. Officials declared Sox the winner, as he broke out less. Go figure.

1968 NHRA U.S. Nationals

The sandbagging situation worsened at Indianapolis Raceway Park in October. To qualify for the 32-car field in Super Stock Eliminator, a driver must either a) win his or her class or b) be among those to run closest to the existing class record.

At Indianapolis, company politics reared its ugly head with some unsavory results. Chrysler personnel in attendance instructed Ronnie Sox to throw the race in the SS/B final to allow Wylie Cossey driving a BO29 Barracuda to qualify for Super Stock Eliminator. Sox jumped so early he launched when the first yellow light came on. The stunt was obvious to all attending the event, and no one had anything positive to say.

"Akron" Arlen Vanke, in his beautiful 1968 BO29 Hemi Barracuda, makes a run at the NHRA U.S. Nationals. (Photo Courtesy Geoff Stunkard Collection/Ray Mann Archive)

The Drag-On Lady Shirley Shahan is pictured in her Hemi Dart at the 1968 NHRA U.S. Nationals. This was one of her last races aboard a Mopar before switching across to an AMC AMX after she and husband H. L. scored an American Motors Corporation contract. (Photo Courtesy Geoff Stunkard Collection/ Ray Mann Archive)

Sox won SS/D with his 1967 Plymouth GTX, so he still qualified for Super Stock Eliminator, as did Ostrich, who won SS/BA with his 1968 Barracuda. Rudy Schings won SS/CA in his 1967 Plymouth.

In Super Stock Eliminator, Arlen Vanke met Wally Booth's big-block SS/E Camaro in the finals, which the affable Mopar pilot duly won.

1968 NHRA World Finals

At the NHRA World Finals, the 16-car Super Stock Eliminator field boasted 11 Mopars, including the LO23/BO29 monsters of Jim Hale, Larry Cooper, John Hagen, Gary Ostrich, Joe Smith, Judy Lilly, Paul Richardson, Bob Lambeck, and Don Grotheer.

By the semifinals, Grotheer was the only one still standing. When he redlit against Bill Jenkins, an all-Chevy final was ensured. Such was the handicapping system used in Super Stock Eliminator. It had been a strange year.

The Casler Racing Tires-sponsored Wiley Cossey-owned/driven RO23 Plymouth is pictured at the 1968 NHRA World Championship Finals. Cossey was a longtime Southern California Super Stock racer. (Photo Courtesy Chuck Conway)

NO NEW CHRYSLER SUPER STOCKS

As it did in 1966, Chrysler opted out of designing and building a turnkey Super Stock for the 1969 season. The decision made sense on several levels. Its 1969 A-Body compacts were largely unchanged from those of 1968—bar a few minor details. Its teams, therefore, could continue racing their 1968 cars, extracting another year from their investments while the cars themselves remained current.

The 1968 Mopar Super Stocks had little class competition in 1968 aside from other Mopars. So, the time and cost for Chrysler to do it all again, either with a clean sheet or even as an evolution of the 1968 racers, made little sense. The awkward NHRA handicapping system for the all-important Super Stock Eliminator competitions at the biggest events certainly didn't guarantee that a Chrysler would stand in victory lane. Indeed, sometimes their sheer speed actually worked against them.

Focus on NASCAR

More importantly, at least for Chrysler, was the need to invest financial and engineering emphasis on its massively upscaled NASCAR Grand National program. While the Grand National continued its chaotic calendar that featured a race somewhere in the United States almost every weekend, there were still only a handful of events that really mattered. They were all held on superspeedways. Bill France, the high-flying NASCAR president, was about to add the immense new Talladega Superspeedway to his arsenal in 1969. France's goal for Talladega was that it be longer and faster than Daytona International Speedway.

With an emphasis for the high-profile Grand National races being on the biggest and fastest tracks, the focus for automotive manufacturers naturally turned to designing, constructing, and homologating cars that performed at their best around these colossal temples of speed. In

This Super Stock/EA battle was between the handsome Mopars of Jack Davis and Dick Landy. As ever, Landy compiled a new fleet of cars for the new year, including this beautiful Charger R/T. (Photo Courtesy Tom West/Lou Hart)

The BO29 Hemi Barracuda of the Sox & Martin team rests in the Gainesville pits during the 1969 NHRA Gatornationals. (Photo Courtesy Charlie Suggs)

Sox & Martin scored a contract with Keystone wheels, and their race cars sported Keystones for years to come. (Photo Courtesy Charlie Suggs)

It was a monstrous little car, and the Sox & Martin squad was at the top of its game by 1969. But NHRA handicapping rules during Super Stock Elimination competitions meant being fastest wasn't always best. (Photo Courtesy Charlie Suggs)

The Sox & Martin BO29 Barracuda faces off against the Lenox Dodge LO23 Dart at the 1969 Gatornationals. (Photo Courtesy Charlie Suggs)

1968, Ford did a better job than Chrysler in producing a car that was best suited to the ultra-fast superspeedways with its slinky new fastback Torino and Mercury Comet siblings, which were as slippery as eels. Naturally, they won all the important races, including Daytona, Darlington, and Charlotte. The new Dodge Charger and Plymouth Road Runner, in contrast to the sweeping Fords, featured deep-set grilles and jutty C-pillar roof sections that greatly hindered their top speeds.

Indeed, so heavily were the odds stacked in Ford's favor and such was Ford's performance advantage over Chrysler in 1968 that longtime Mopar stalwart Richard Petty did the unthinkable and jumped ship, ditching his Road Runner in favor of a Torino in November 1968. As if Chrysler wasn't already motivated enough to turn the tables on Ford, this single act truly made headlines for all the wrong reasons.

The outcome of Chrysler's Grand National revenge was perhaps the most uncompromising, unorthodox, and eccentric production car ever produced: the berserk Dodge Charger Daytona.

The Charger Daytona sported a long, pointed "beak" and tall (23 inches above the rear deck) stabilizer wing, along with a flush rear window, and other performance-enhancing features, all in the name of pure, unadulterated top speed. The Daytona made its competition debut at the 1969 Talladega 500 in mid-September, and while this escalated into a largely farcical event with countless drivers boycotting the race due to tire safety issues, Bobby Isaac demonstrated the impact the Daytona would have in the sport by firing off a pole position lap at over 196 mph. The race was won by the Ray Nichols–prepared Daytona of Richard Brickhouse. This was the only Grand National victory for Brickhouse.

The research and development needed to usher the Daytona from concept to fruition was monumental. The commitment to then produce the minimum required 500 street cars to homologate the model for racing was even greater still. Few people wanted to own a Daytona street car, and they were a tough sell. Even in the crazy, hazy muscle car era of the late 1960s, they looked outrageous.

Riding on 14-inch-diameter wheels and stretching to nearly 19 feet in length (the Daytona was longer than a Cadillac Coupe De Ville), even Bob McCurry, Dodge's general manager, was reportedly quoted as stating this was the ugliest car he'd ever seen while giving it the green light for production in February 1969. But that didn't matter to Chrysler. The only requirement was that a minimum 500 units be produced to make the model eligible to contest the Grand National. It achieved that. Here was the result of total devotion by Chrysler—all in a quest for another 5 mph!

Danny Byrd's My 'Cuda *1968 Barracuda is pictured at Fiesta of Five Flags Speedway in Pensacola, Florida. (Photo Courtesy C. Mike Cook)*

Bill Tanner's Lenox Dodge *Dart, JC South's* Liberty Dodge Dart, *and Robert Nance's* Mister Plymouth *Barracuda rest in the pits at Fiesta of Five Flags Speedway. (Photo Courtesy C. Mike Cook)*

Georgia's Robert Nance's Mister Plymouth *1968 BO29 Barracuda is pictured at Phenix Dragway in Phenix City, Alabama. (Photo Courtesy C. Mike Cook)*

Tom Smith's Hemi Power 1968 Barracuda is pictured at Fiesta of Five Flags Speedway in Pensacola, Florida. (Photo Courtesy C. Mike Cook)

Arlen Vanke's vintage Plymouth Belvedere is sporting a beautiful lace green paint scheme. (Photo Courtesy Geoff Stunkard Collection)

Arlen Vanke continued running his BO29 Hemi Barracuda during the 1969 season in Super Stock competition. (Photo Courtesy Geoff Stunkard Collection)

Everyone wants their photo taken with a Hemi Mopar. (Photo Courtesy Geoff Stunkard Collection)

Much like the Sox & Martin squad, Landy also opted out of running his Dart in Super Stock Eliminator competition at some NHRA events and instead he raced the Charger in B/Modified Production. (Photo Courtesy Geoff Stunkard Collection/Phillip Smith Archive)

The Super Stock drag racing program paled into insignificance. As such, the Chrysler Super Stock drag racing teams either updated their existing 1968 machinery with 1969 trim or simply left them as they were. Either way, they looked like current models for onlookers and were certainly up to the task at hand.

1969 Drag Racing Highlights

The 1969 NHRA season would, in some ways, be a repeat of that from 1968. The epic Chrysler LO23/BO29 cars were still strangled by handicapping and breakouts in the all-important Super Stock Eliminator competitions, forcing drivers to run to a set time rather than truly open them up, which is what the fans and media wanted to see.

While the frustrations continued, from it all came a spark of hope that something could be done for the future. Indeed, 1969 proved to be a crucial year because from this, a new heads-up professional Stock-based drag racing division would be given life. Sometimes, things have to get worse before they get better.

1969 AHRA Winternationals

The weekend of January 25 and 26 featured the 1969 AHRA Winternationals at Beeline Dragway. Without the much-despised handicapping system still employed by the NHRA, Mopar drivers fully unleashed their Hemi Super Stockers in Eliminations.

Ronnie Sox used his Road Runner to beat Dick Hallahan's Mustang in Top Stock Eliminator, and Arlene Vanke blazed his Barracuda to victory in Super Stock Eliminator, defeating the Mustang of Ed Terry.

1969 NHRA Winternationals

The 1969 NHRA national season launched, as always, at Pomona for the annual Winternationals and was the weekend following the AHRA event. Already controversy abounded, as the Sox & Martin and Dick Landy teams voiced their disapproval of the bungled Super Stock Eliminator handicapping system by boycotting the competition.

Both teams still competed at Pomona with Sox running the Road Runner in A/Modified Production and Landy in the Charger in B/Modified Production. Both drivers were eligible for Street Eliminator, which wasn't hobbled with the handicapping system, and they threatened to remain there, as one team spokesperson suggested, "until the NHRA sees the light and comes up with a sensible solution to heads-up racing."

Super Stock Eliminator

So, two of the Mopar superstars would be missing from Super Stock Eliminator, the most prestigious of all the Stock division competitions. Not to worry. The Super Stock divisions were still well bolstered, and 32 cars qualified from the various classes. Among them were 12 Fords, 7 Plymouths, 7 Chevys, and 6 Dodges.

American Motors Corporation (AMC) had entered Super Stock drag racing competition, just as it had done in other racing contests, such as the Trans-Am road racing series. None of the AMC squad made the cut at Pomona.

As predicted, several drivers fell victim to the handicapping breakout system. They included Dick Arons (Camaro) and Larry Cooper (Dart).

Don Grotheer is pictured in his beautiful BO29 Hemi Barracuda during the 1969 Super Stock Nationals. (Photo Courtesy Alan Lewis)

But much more bazaar was the account of several drivers failing to even reach the staging areas on time due to Pomona's heavily congested pit area. Camaro drivers Wally Booth and Jim Hayter had their day cut short as a result.

Meanwhile, Bill Jenkins redlit in Round 1 against Jerry Harvey's Mustang, Shirley "the Drag-On Lady" Shahan, was put on the trailer by Arlene Vanke.

With all the drama and controversy out of the way, it was Don Grotheer in the *Cable Car* Plymouth Barracuda who faced Harvey's blue and gold Mustang in the final. Grotheer ran a 10.79 at 119.68 mph to take the win, jumping on the brakes just before he crossed the finish line, so as not to break out.

Street Eliminator

The Street Eliminator competition was suddenly thrust into the limelight with the last-minute additions of the Sox & Martin and Landy Mopars. In the end, it was the two Chrysler superstars who lined up in the final. Landy gifted Sox the win, however, by redlighting.

In other competitions, Joe Fisher was at the helm of the Sox & Martin Plymouth GTX in B/Modified Production. But he was taken down by Herb McCandless in the Landy Dodge.

That the Sox & Martin squad even had any cars at the Winternationals was a small miracle in itself. The team's transporter was involved in a road accident following the AHRA Winternationals the weekend prior, and both race cars were severely damaged. The Road Runner was thrown off the trailer and flipped. A massive rebuild took place at Hooker's Ontario plant, and they arrived at Pomona looking like nothing had ever happened.

1969 Super Stock Nationals

York U.S. 30 Drag-O-Way hosted its annual Super Stock Nationals,

Charlie Castaldo's beautiful LO23 Hemi Dart is shown at speed during the 1969 Super Stock Nationals. (Photo Courtesy Alan Lewis)

The little AMC AMX pops a wheelie in its quest to beat Dick Landy's Charger out of the hole at the Super Stock Nationals. (Photo Courtesy Alan Lewis)

Everyone stops and takes notice when the Funny Cars make their run, including Ronnie Sox, who is seen standing on the deck of the transporter in the background. (Photo Courtesy Alan Lewis)

DON GROTHEER

Don Grotheer of Cushing, Oklahoma, was a longtime Mopar racer who campaigned some of the best-looking and fastest cars anywhere.

Grotheer, a sheet-metal worker, began racing on the street and on the track as a teenager aboard a 1950 Ford before switching to a fleet of 1957 Chevys, each one better and faster than the last. He won his first race in 1958. He was a self-taught racer and wrenched on his own cars.

After running Ford Starliners and a 406-powered 300 from 1960 through 1963, Grotheer then began a relationship with Chrysler products that lasted almost to the end of his racing career. He purchased a Stage I 426 Max Wedge Plymouth Belvedere provided by his good friend Tom Sparks of Sparks Motors. Sparks had sourced two cars: an automatic and a 3-speed manual. Grotheer took the latter.

At the AHRA Nationals at Green Valley in Texas, Grotheer set top speed for Plymouths and won a Stage I Max Wedge motor for his troubles. The car was gifted by Chrysler.

Don Grotheer's 1969 Plymouth Road Runner served multiple purposes as both a clinic car and, on rare occasions, a race car. On this occasion, Grotheer entered the bird at the 15th-annual U.S. Nationals, competing in SS/EA. (Photo Courtesy MotorTrend and Petersen Automotive Museum Archive)

For 1964, he upgraded the Belvedere with a Stage II motor and won the AHRA Top Stock World Championship and the NHRA South Central Division Top Stock points championship. Indeed, he was one of just a handful of Mopar campaigners wielding a stick shift.

By late 1965, having set an NHRA AA/Stock national record, Bob Cahill at Chrysler put Grotheer in touch with Dick Maxwell, who was keen to help the young Oklahoma racer with his program. Maxwell suggested that if Grotheer purchased a new 1966 Belvedere street Hemi, Chrysler would supply all the parts free of charge. With Edmonds Chrysler of Edmonds, Oklahoma, onboard as sponsor, Grotheer won the AA/Stock class at the 1966 NHRA Winternationals, beating Bill Jenkins's Chevy II in the final. He also won the 1966 NHRA Division 4 points and the Tulsa Gold Cup.

For 1967, he switched to a new Hemi Belvedere that he campaigned in regional and national events with backing from Cable Chrysler-Plymouth of Oklahoma City (gaining the "Cable Car" name that adorned several Grotheer cars). He won AA/Stock at the Winternationals for the second year in succession and again won NHRA Division 4 points.

In 1968, Grotheer was gifted one of the latest BO29 Barracuda Super Stocks, which truly thrust him to national prominence. For the most part, he ran it as a 4-speed, but on occasion would switch across to an automatic given the class records at specific events and the clunky NHRA handicapping system. With the Barracuda, he set a new NHRA SS/BA national record at the 1969 Winternationals and won the 1970 SS/B class at the same event.

It was in 1969 when Grotheer became the western region performance advisor for Chrysler's massively popular Plymouth Supercar Clinics. Ronnie Sox and

Buddy Martin were running the clinics nationwide but couldn't keep up with demand from Chrysler-Plymouth dealers, so Grotheer was brought in to help carry the load, and he quickly found himself running three to four clinics a week.

For 1970, Grotheer stepped up to the new NHRA Pro Stock division with a self-built Plymouth 'Cuda built from an acid-dipped body. With this car, he reached the final at the AHRA U.S. Open, where he was beaten by Ronnie Sox. Meanwhile, he continued to campaign his beloved 1968 Barracuda Super Stock.

For 1971, he had a new 'Cuda professionally built by Don Hardy Race Cars, which set top speed on its debut event at the NHRA Gatornationals. In addition, he raced a new 1971 Plymouth Road Runner in B/MP, which enjoyed a lot of success. Butch Leal guest-drove the Road Runner at the AHRA Winternationals and NHRA Winternationals and won his class in both encounters. Grotheer went on to gain multiple victories with the big Plymouth.

Despite the NHRA inflicting its new weight breaks for 1972, Grotheer actually had his best year in Pro Stock to date. He made the finals at the Winternationals and Springnationals, losing both times to Bill Jenkins's new small-block tube-frame Vega, which dominated the class. He also reached the semifinals at the Summernationals and won the AHRA Pro Stock race at Tulsa in June.

Feeling cornered by the NHRA weight system, Grotheer switched to a new Ford Pinto for 1973. On debut at the U.S. Nationals at Indy, he out-qualified all the Mopar teams and reached the semifinals. It was an immensely fast little car. But without sponsorship, he sold it at season's end and retired from racing to focus on his sheet-metal business.

Like many of his era, however, Grotheer got involved in nostalgia drag racing. He built a replica of his 1968 Barracuda Super Stock in the late 2000s featuring countless parts from the original car. Although, without having a roll cage, it's purely used for display purposes.

Calling the schedule "demanding" was an understatement for Don Groth-eer, as he scheduled 50 Supercar Clinic appearances with his 1969 Road Runner and 1968 Barracuda. Add that to competing full-time in the South Central Super Stock Circuit and appearing nationally at the biggest payout tracks, and it's a wonder how he found time to keep his cars so dominant.

HERB MCCANDLESS "MR. 4-SPEED"

Herb McCandless of Memphis, Tennessee, was perhaps the ultimate hired gun of Super Stock and Pro Stock drag racing. He drove his own cars, but he was just as comfortable and formidable, peddling another owners' steeds.

Like many, his formative years in drag racing were aboard Chevy products. But in early 1965, through Chrysler Assistant Regional Manager John Moore, he was offered the chance to purchase one of the latest Hemi-powered Plymouth Super Stocks. The car wasn't a gift; the 21-year-old had to stump up $3,500 to own it, and to do so, he financed it through Chrysler Commercial Credit. McCandless was supplied 1 of 10 4-speed cars, and he quickly became a demon manual shifter.

It was Moore who came up with the name "Mr. 4-Speed," which adorned the sides of McCandless's Hemi Plymouth and others that followed. With most Chrysler drivers going the automatic-transmission route, McCandless's speed, finesse, and accuracy sawing through a manual transmission made him a standout. Manual transmissions weren't to everyone's liking, and many racers struggled with them.

Over the next two seasons, McCandless racked up the trophies and prize money before switching to a new 4-speed Plymouth Belvedere RO23 in 1967. He didn't warm to the big Belvedere and was pleased to get his hands on one of the latest LO23 Hemi Dodge Darts when they became available in 1968. Again, he opted for a 4-speed and had "Mr. 4-Speed" lettering emblazoned down the flanks.

In 1968, McCandless was asked to drive the Sox & Martin Plymouth Road Runner in Super Stock/F at the NHRA Winternationals. When the company he worked for wouldn't give him time off to make the event, he quit his job and became a full-time drag racer.

The 1969 season saw McCandless continue campaigning his Mr. 4-Speed LO23 Dart. He was increasingly drawing the attention of the Chrysler big hitters. His growing reputation as a fast and consistent stick shifter ensured offers began rolling in, and at times he drove for Dick Landy and Billy Stepp while still campaigning his Dart.

Partway through 1970, he was approached to drive the second Sox & Martin car, which was a newly constructed Pro Stock Plymouth Duster. The highlight being victory at the NHRA U.S. Nationals. For the 1971 season, McCandless stayed on at Sox & Martin, and drove Sox's 1970 'Cuda, while Sox switched to a new car.

McCandless was as handy on the tools as he was quick-firing a 4-speed, and he and Gale Mortimer built a new Sox & Martin Dodge Dart Demon. He dominated the AHRA Pro Stock series, but, like all the Mopar racers, he struggled in NHRA competition under the new weight breaks that handicapped the Hemi cars. In 1973 and part of 1974, he drove a Dart for the infamous Rufus "Brooklyn Heavy" Boyd and also had a brief stint in a Jack Roush Mustang II.

Eventually, "Mr. 4-Speed" established McCandless Performance and became a key component in Chrysler's Direct Connection Program, testing parts and combinations to help Mopar drag racers during the latter part of the 1970s and into the 1980s.

He continued to grow McCandless Performance, and these days still works on Chrysler cars, building motors, stocking and selling parts, and even performing Gen III Hemi engine swaps into classic Mopars. In addition, he helps one of his sons, Mike McCandless, run the McCandless Collection, which includes several "Forward Look" Chryslers of the 1955–1961 era, in addition to various vintage drag cars. Mike was instrumental in tracking down and purchasing some of Herb's old race cars, as well as building accurate tributes.

Now in his late 70s and still pulling long hours, Herb McCandless shows no sign of slowing down.

Herb McCandless entered his second year campaigning his 1968 Hemi Dart. The successful 4-speed driver also offered his talents as a work-for-hire driver in 1969 as well, piloting cars for Sox & Martin and Dick Landy. (Photo Courtesy McCandless Collection)

Ed Miller's BO29 Barracuda battles Sam Auxier's 1969 Mustang. (Photo Courtesy Alan Lewis)

which highlighted the wild new flopper Funny Cars. Although it was not an NHRA sanctioned event, it still drew teams and a strong crowd. A good entry of top Super Stock teams was on hand.

1969 NHRA Springnationals

Mid-June meant it was NHRA Springnationals time. The fifth running of this important event was hosted by the brand-new Dallas International Motor Speedway facility. The impressive new Lewisville, Texas, complex sported a growing trend for producing massive multi-purpose venues that boasted a paved, banked speedway and drag strip. In some cases, including this one, a road course employed sections of the speedway. Dallas hosted the final round of the 1969 SCCA Can-Am sports car series using the road course/speedway layout.

The Dallas complex was so new that parts of the pit area were still being built when the teams arrived to wage war upon each other at the Springnationals. More than 700 cars were entered to stake their claim for a share of the $190,000 prize purse.

The 32-car field that qualified for Super Stock Eliminator included Ronnie Sox, Dick Landy, Don Grotheer, Arlen Vanke, Ed Terry (Mustang), Randy Payne (Torino), Ron Mancini, Lance Hill (Camaro), Dick Arons (Camaro), Barrie Poole (Mustang), and Sandy Elliott (Mustang). Sox had won Super Stock Eliminator at the last two NHRA Springnationals, and sure enough, he went right through the final, where he met the 1969 Mustang of Poole, from Ontario, Canada. In the end, the Sox & Martin Barracuda blasted down the new track to become the first NHRA driver to win an Eliminator competition at the same event for three years running.

1969 NHRA U.S. Nationals

By the time the teams had reassembled for the next major NHRA national event at Indianapolis Raceway Park in late August, much had happened within the Super Stock ranks. Although it was not an official Chrysler event, a grid of Mopar Super Stocks got together at nearby Ohio on the Friday night prior to the Nationals and contested a Mini-Nationals event. Unlike the controversial NHRA Super Stock Eliminator competitions, the Mini-Nationals was heads-up racing only; both cars launch together, first to the finish line wins.

The Mini-Nationals were almost certainly targeting the NHRA to underline the unrest within the Super Stock group and the clumsy handicapping system the Eliminator contest was saddled with. Adding to the discontent was the qualifying format for Super Stock Eliminator. Some of the NHRA national events, including the big Indy race, had no class Eliminator competitions. The teams were all split into their respective classes and took part in qualifying runs from which the two cars that got closest to the existing class records would continue through to Super Stock Eliminator. The rest loaded up and went home.

Indeed, *Hot Rod* magazine approached leading Super Stock racer Dave Strickler for comment. He said, "We have a lot more Super Stockers racing these days, and they've added some classes, but as it stands right now, there are no class eliminations, which I think is definitely wrong. A lot of independents have spent a lot of money to come all the way out here and have no chance at all of elimination runs if they don't make qualifying."

Strickler had more to add on the much-despised break-out rule. He continued, ". . . there should be an answer to hitting the brakes at the end, thus barring the possibility of accidents. I think we should devise some way to come up with better records—records that would be more in the category of the cars' capabilities. Some of these cars have a shoo-in type record, where they can run four- or five-tenths under, which shouldn't be. It may take a driver's association or something to look it over, check these records, and change them as needed, or set up some group that could change a record we feel is too easy to run on. All this would make a better show for the spectators. They pay to see the show, and they should be pleased. And, of course, it's not good for the Super Stock driver to come out here and invest a lot of money and not be able to run."

As for the actual racing, Super Stock Eliminator featured 14 Fords, 3 Chevys, and a whole bunch of Mopars. Ten of the 14 Fords didn't make it beyond Round 1, and likewise 2 of the 3 Chevys, including Bill Jenkins's Camaro after the Grump triggered the red light. Dave Wren, driving an ancient 1964 Hemi Dodge, battled his way to the finals, having taken down Don Grotheer's Barracuda in the semifinals while Ronnie Sox did likewise to Ron Mancini. The final, however, was a fizzer; Wren broke an axle off the line, and Sox scorched to another victory.

Another beautiful paint scheme adorns John Hagen's BO29 Barracuda. Custom lace paint was all the rage during this era, and highly skilled artists were in high demand. Hagen is pictured at the NHRA World Finals in Dallas. (Photo Courtesy Geoff Stunkard Collection/Ray Mann Archive)

Chrysler engineer Dick Oldfield lines up his vintage 1964 Iron Butterfly *Dodge at the 1969 NHRA World Finals. (Photo Courtesy Geoff Stunkard Collection/Ray Mann Archive)*

Planning for the Future

At the conclusion of racing at the U.S. Nationals, several Super Stock drivers and teams met to discuss their concerns going forward. They nominated Buddy Martin, Dave Strickler, and Bill Jenkins to organize a meeting with NHRA president Wally Parks to discuss options for 1970 and beyond. The focus was to create a heads-up racing system and to use weight breaks to create an even playing field between the various makes and models and engine sizes. In doing so, they could finally ditch the much-despised handicapping system that had been blighting Super Stock Eliminator for the past few years.

1969 NHRA World Championship Finals

Following the drivers/teams meeting with Wally Parks in early September, the NHRA agreed to the terms of the new Super Stock heads-up system of flat-to-the-boards racing with applied weight breaks—almost to the letter. It was introduced in 1970.

To underline its confidence going forward, the NHRA applied a partial adoption of the new racing format at the 1969 World Finals—albeit with handicapping still in place based on the various Super Stock classes, as the weight breaks hadn't yet been applied.

So, race fans would get to see Super Stock drivers keep their foot in it without the fear of breaking out and being disqualified. There would be no braking right before the finish line. It was just all-out racing; class records be damned. The qualifying procedure still had the first two cars from each class going through, but this time it was based purely on elapsed times and not on who could get closest to the existing records.

The whole show proved to be a massive success. Furthermore, no less than eight Super Stock classes had their

Gary Ostrich was a longtime campaigner of Mopar products. His father, Chuck Ostrich, ran a Plymouth dealership out of Nevada, Iowa. (Photo Courtesy Geoff Stunkard Collection/Ray Mann Archive)

Bill Bagshaw gets set to take on a Cobra Jet Mustang in his Red Light Bandit *LO23 Dart at the 1969 NHRA World Finals in Dallas. (Photo Courtesy Geoff Stunkard Collection/Ray Mann Archive)*

existing records smashed, and several of them were by at least a quarter of a second. Finally, the Super Stockers were unleashed of their shackles and let loose to fully strut their stuff. The results were spectacular.

After qualifying on Saturday, the 16-car Super Stock Eliminator competition was set for Sunday prime time. It included 1 Chevy, 1 AMC, 4 Fords, and 12 Mopars. Better yet, by the time the field was sliced and diced, and only four cars remained: the lone Chevy (Ed Hedrick's Camaro), one Ford (Barrie Poole's Mustang), one Dodge (Dick Oldfield's 1964 Coronet), and one Plymouth (Ronnie Sox's Barracuda).

The Camaro and Mustang went by the wayside in the semifinals, leaving Sox to face Oldfield's classic Coronet in the final. Naturally, Sox soared to victory with a 10.23 at 135.13 mph.

These are the records that were set at the 1969 NHRA Super Stock World Finals:

- SS/B: Ronnie Sox, Plymouth (10.23)
- SS/E: Lou Downing, AMC (10.88)

- SS/H: Ken McLellan, Ford (11.14)
- SS/I: Barrie Poole, Ford (11.27)
- SS/BA: Don Grotheer, Plymouth (10.36)
- SS/CA: Dick Oldfield, Dodge (10.74)
- SS/DA: Ron Mancini, Dodge (10.92)
- SS/JA: Roger Caster, Ford (11.80)

1969 AHRA Competitions

Beyond the season-opening AHRA Winternationals where Chrysler took out the big Super Stock competitions and following Chevy victories at Detroit Dragway in May (Larry Kimball's Camaro) and Bill Jenkins's big win at the Spring Nationals, Sox beat Arlen Vanke in an all-Plymouth final at the AHRA U.S. Open at North Carolina Motor Speedway in late September.

By 1969, the Sox & Martin team had emerged as not only the leading Chrysler team but also the leading team in the Super Stock division as a whole. The 1970 season brought with it new rules, a new racing format, and a greatly expanded racing program. But would new heroes be born from it?

This is the famous Woodward Avenue 1968 Super Stock test mule, which carried out numerous passes while trialing parts and components for what would become the LO23/BO29 Super Stock production cars. It actually began life as a 1967 Barracuda Formula S updated with 1968 bodywork. (Photo Courtesy Geoff Stunkard Collection/Ray Mann Archive)

Larry Cooper launches his LO23 Dart during the 1969 AHRA Grand American Points Finale at Tulsa Raceway Park. (Photo Courtesy Geoff Stunkard Collection/Ray Mann Archive)

Larry Cooper competes against Don Grotheer in an all-Mopar battle at Tulsa. (Photo Courtesy Geoff Stunkard Collection/Ray Mann Archive)

Rich Thomas's BO29 Barracuda is pictured on the start line at Tulsa. The exquisite custom paint scheme typified late-1960s drag racing and the lengths to which many teams went in terms of aesthetic presentation. (Photo Courtesy Geoff Stunkard Collection/Ray Mann Archive)

THE DAWN OF PRO STOCK

In 1970, a new decade and a new era in Super Stock drag racing dawned. What emerged from the discussions between Wally Parks at the NHRA and the team owners and representatives immediately following the 1969 NHRA U.S. Nationals culminated not only in a new qualifying and racing format for 1970 but also a completely new set of regulations.

The NHRA had been trying (unsuccessfully) to juggle a handicapping system that amalgamated cars from its extensive repertoire of Super Stock categories and their wildly varying performances with the aim of producing close and unpredictable results. But it was all a bit of a fiasco.

For years, the biggest and best competition in Super Stock drag racing was the Eliminator contest, pitting cars from various categories against one another in a winner-takes-all epic. In the early and mid-1960s, Super Stock Eliminator was among the greatest highlights at any high-profile drag racing event. But by 1969, it had become a farce. That largely related to the bungling handicapping system introduced to try and even the odds and manipulate an equal finishing result between two unequal cars. It just didn't work.

Worse still was the introduction of stringent class records that dictated just how fast a car could get down the track. The set records determined the handicapping starting system and the length of time that the faster car was held before hunting down its slower opponent. In some classes, even the fastest cars couldn't get near the set time, so they could run flat out. In others, however, drivers had to brake aggressively before the finish line specifically so that they didn't break out. Scorching to a time lower than the class record resulted in instant disqualification. It was clumsy, largely unsuccessful, and everyone seemed to hate it.

Introducing Pro Stock

The new 1970 formula featured its own set of regulations designed to allow multiple makes and models of vehicles with different engine sizes to all compete on equal terms. It used a sliding scale weight system and loosened various strangleholds dictated by factory specifications. There would be no more handicapping—heads-up racing only. Both cars would leave the start at the same time, run side-by-side, and the first to the finish was the winner. It was racing in its purest form. The weight-break system ensured that the need for multiple classes was no longer required.

This new, heavily facelifted one-class Super Stock division was packaged under a new brand name: Pro Stock. Pro Stock removed the requirement for manufacturers to produce a dedicated drag racing–focused model each year and pushed the sport further toward that of silhouette racing.

The outgoing Super Stock formula, despite being superseded, still

Two great rivals in Ronnie Sox and Don Nicholson go at it during Eliminations at the 1970 NHRA Springnationals. Sox won this encounter and went on to take his first victory of the new Pro Stock season. (Photo Courtesy Geoff Stunkard Collection)

Once again, Dick Landy ran a full fleet of Dodge products in 1970, including the Charger that is driven here by his good friend Bob Lambeck. (Photo Courtesy Tom West/ Lou Hart)

This great color image captures the pair of Bill Tanner Mopars at rest. (Photo Courtesy Geoff Stunkard Collection)

boasted several positives. It required the manufacturer to commit by producing a turnkey car sporting a complete driveline, suspension, and braking system sourced from its own parts bin. This in itself was the definition of Stock. In addition, the requirement for a minimum number of cars produced (usually in the vicinity of 50 to 100) ensured a healthy influx of cars to bolster grid numbers at any given event. It was, seemingly, a win-win for all—but not quite.

The problem with the outgoing Super Stock regulations as they stood was the huge commitment required of the manufacturers if they wished to take part. If the manufacturer wasn't prepared to commit, there were no cars. If only a single manufacturer committed, the formula was heavily weighted toward that manufacturer. In 1962, Ford, General Motors, and Chrysler all unleashed performance models aimed at the thriving Super Stock division, and the category flourished as a result. By 1969, however, that was no longer the case.

What the Pro Stock rules did was sidestep the hefty manufacturer reliance. There was a general loosening of component parts, introducing a uniformity across all the brands, and as such, a more even playing field ensued.

1970 NHRA Pro Stock Regulations

The 1970 Pro Stock regulations called for 1968-or-newer American-made production vehicles with a minimum wheelbase of 97 inches and the original steel body. Sports cars, sedan deliveries, and trucks were not permitted. The stock wheelbase had to be retained, as did the stock length and width of the vehicle. No manipulation of the factory silhouette was allowed.

The hood, decklid, front fenders, and splash pan could all be replaced by exacting items made from fiber-

glass or other lightweight materials regardless of whether or not the vehicle already carried lightweight components as stock.

Furthermore, the hood and decklid could be lift-off pieces; no hinges were required. The firewall could be modified to make space for the engine, but otherwise, the underhood area had to remain stock. A hood scoop was permitted, but cars fitted with a scoop not supplied as factory equipment for that particular make and model could not extend more than 7 inches above the height of the hood surface.

The engine had to be a 1965-or-newer production item, and it had to be produced by the same manufacturer as the car. All internal modifications were unregulated, and carburetion was limited either to a pair of 4-barrels or four 2-barrels and had to be from an American manufacturer.

The driveline and rear end were unregulated, although the transmission had to be a stock-type unit and remain in the conventional location. Brakes were required in all four corners.

Exhaust systems were unregulated. Wheels and tires were also unregulated, although the tires couldn't extend more than 2 inches beyond the stock bodywork. The factory suspension had to be retained, but traction bars could be installed. Stock upholstery and windows were also required, although competition bucket seats could replace the factory front seat(s).

A roll hoop was mandatory as a safety measure, but full roll cages were also allowed.

Pro Stock employed a relatively simple one-size-fits-all weight system of 7 pounds per cubic inch with a minimum of 2,700 pounds, regardless of engine brand or design. The maximum allowable weight on the rear wheels was 55 percent of the car's total weight. In other words, there was 45-55 front-rear weight distribution.

The Jenkins & Rettig Brothers 1968 Hemi Dart faces off against "Fast" Eddie Schartman's 1970 Mercury Cougar. By 1970, most of the factory-connected Ford Pro Stock contingent had switched to the new pint-sized Ford Mavericks. (Photo Courtesy Wes Eisenschenk)

The concept behind Pro Stock was to produce close racing for a variety of makes and models where the engine and chassis setup were the difference makers. Some drivers took the freedoms quite literally. Wally Booth, for example, ran a Camaro fitted with a Chrysler transmission, driveshaft, and Dana rear end. The rules allowed this.

Each of the 1970 NHRA Pro Stock national events underwent a series of qualifying competitions for the field with only the fastest 16 cars making the cut. Those 16 cars would then compete in head-to-head elimination races until two cars remained to decide the winner.

Chrysler's All-New E-Body Cars

The arrival of Pro Stock coincided with Chrysler's introduction of its brand-new E-Body offerings: the Dodge Challenger and the Plymouth Barracuda. The new E-Body siblings were finally stand-alone models. This was a common theme in the pony car market, but it was a first for Chrysler. The Mustang, Camaro, and other alternatives shared nothing visually with any other model even if the underpinnings had originated in more mundane offerings.

Until 1969, Chrysler positioned its sporty two-door Dart and Barracuda as its gesture to the pony car market. But the 1969 Dart and outgoing Barracuda were based on a multipurpose platform with several bodystyles. The Dart could be ordered as a two-door sedan, a four-door sedan, and a convertible, as well as the two-door hardtop that Chrysler positioned in the pony car market. Likewise, the outgoing Barracuda was a sporty variant of the Plymouth Valiant, a model that included two-door and four-door sedan bodystyles (but no convertible).

The first rule of pony-car styling, as originally dictated by the Mustang, was aimed squarely at the unique buying behaviors of the new Baby Boomer generation: to ensure no visible relation to anything Mom might drive! The Dart and Barracuda broke these rules, and as such, were sometimes overlooked as a pony car buying alternative to a Mustang, Camaro, or Javelin.

The 1970 Dodge Challenger and Plymouth Barracuda finally embraced the pony car template as stand-alone models. Despite the arrival of the Challenger and Barracuda, the two-door hardtop Dart would carry on unaffected, while its Plymouth cousin would be the new Duster, which shared the Valiant platform and nose paired with a unique fastback body. Both the Dart and Duster were positioned in a cheaper market bracket than the Challenger and Barracuda.

The handsome new Challenger and Barracuda models embraced the popular Coke-bottle styling with great gusto. Although adhering to the almost-universal pony car 108-inch wheelbase (the Dodge was slightly longer at 110 inches), both new Mopar ponies were extremely broad at 76.1 inches wide. The 1970 Mustang by comparison was just 71.7 inches, and the new second-generation 1970½ Camaro was 74.4 inches. This gave the Chrysler pairing an assertive appearance, and it visually commanded significant real estate.

Styling for both models appeared similar at first glance, but there were in fact several subtle differences. While both feature prominent kicked-up rear quarters, the Dodge accentuated the effect with a sculpture line running just above the tops of the wheel openings, which mimics the curves of the waistline. The Plymouth's sculpture line runs straight as an arrow right down the flanks. The top rear corner of the Challenger's side windows follows a gentle curve, while the 'Cuda sports a sharper edge. A more rounded rump completed the overall curviness of the shapely Dodge, which of course carried four headlights in its broad, full-length grille, while the cheaper Plymouth had two.

E-Body buyers could choose from two bodystyles: two-door hardtop or convertible. There was no fastback, but the styling really didn't warrant it. The Dodge range included the base model Deputy, the upmarket Special Edition (SE), and the sporty Road and Track (R/T).

Meanwhile, the Plymouth opened with the base-model Barracuda (it was just called Barracuda) followed by the upmarket Gran Coupe and the sporty 'Cuda.

The list of options, however, was almost endless. Engine choices started with the anemic 198-ci inline-6, the tough little 225-ci inline-6, a 318- and 340-ci LA-based V-8, a trio of 383-ci V-8s, two 440-ci RB-based V-8s (Magnum and Six Pack), and the 426-ci Hemi.

Transmission options included the base 3-speed manual, the 3-speed automatic, the 727 TorqueFlite automatic, or the 4-speed manual. The 4-speed featured the creative Pistol Grip shifter, which was a wooden shift handle shaped like a hand-gun grip.

Chrysler's list of optional axle packages was extensive. It included the Performance Axle Package (A36) for cars with 4-barrel or multiple carburetors, which featured 3.55:1 gears with Sure Grip, an 8.75-inch axle, and heavy-duty suspension. The A31 option (High Performance Axle Package) was available on 340- or 383-ci 4-barrel cars and included 3.91:1 gears, Sure Grip, and heavy-duty suspension. The A32 (Super Performance Axle Package) was available on the 440- and 426-ci cars with an automatic transmission, and it had the Dana with 9.75-inch axle, 4.10:1 gears, and Sure Grip. The A33 (Track Pack) was available on 440-ci cars but mandatory on Hemi cars with the 4-speed manual transmission, and it included 3.54:1 gears, Dana 9.75-inch axle, and Sure Grip. Finally, the A34 (Super Track Pack) was similar to the A33 but with 4.10:1 gears and power front disc brakes.

The suspension featured torsion bars and independent lateral non-parallel control arms in the front, while rear suspension was asymmetric semi-elliptical leaf springs. A front anti-roll bar was standard equipment on R/T models, while a rear anti-roll bar was an option.

By late 1969, when the Challenger and the Barracuda went to market, Chrysler's marketing team had reached full bloom. The array of exterior high-impact hues was immense, and some of the colors themselves were unashamedly brash. Furthermore, marketing had concocted names for the colors that were as colorful as the colors themselves. There was also an array of stripe packages to further invigorate an already highly invigorated vehicle. The arrival of the 1970 Dodge Challenger and Plymouth Barracuda was one of fun, adventure, exploration, and the open road.

Prices for the new E-Body siblings was competitive with that of the pony car competition. Dodge Challenger prices started at $2,851. Sadly, the Challenger and new Barracuda arrived on the scene just as the pony car/muscle car party was beginning its decline. Regardless, Chrysler Corporation went at the 1970 racing programs with all-guns blazing.

NASCAR

As well as the drag racing operations, Chrysler expanded its NASCAR Grand National operation by producing a second "winged warrior" in the Plymouth Superbird, which was based on the Road Runner. This provided the company with a two-pronged attack on stock car racing that would see it completely dominate, winning the 1970 Daytona 500, Southern 500 (at Darlington), and Talladega 500. It missed out on the Charlotte 600 when its top cars struck trouble, gifting Ford a rare win.

Bill France invited Chrysler to attempt a top speed record run at his new Talladega Superspeedway. Buddy Baker made history by becoming the first driver to break the 200-mph closed-course speed barrier when he ran an average speed of 200.447 mph aboard a Dodge Daytona in March 1970. The marketing mileage from this achievement alone was virtually endless.

Chrysler directly supported six teams in the 1970 NASCAR Grand National while countless independents also campaigned Chrysler machinery.

Trans-Am

In addition, Chrysler funded a genuine factory effort in the SCCA Trans-Am road racing series for the first time. It employed Dan Gurney's All-American Racers to run a pair of Plymouth 'Cudas for Gurney and his young protégé Swede Savage to drive. A second team, owned by Ray Caldwell of Autodyamics with the young racing driver Sam Posey, fielded a single Dodge Challenger for Posey.

Chrysler's commitment to the Trans-Am extended to the design and production of a pair of factory street cars. The Plymouth 'Cuda AAR and Dodge Challenger T/A were built specifically to homologate parts for the Trans-Am race cars. Incidentally, while Caldwell/Posey were instructed to paint their Challenger factory Sublime (a color Posey hated), the high-profile Gurney was allowed to paint his 'Cudas in his traditional dark metallic blue, itself a non-Chrysler exterior color.

So, despite the downward turn in performance car sales, Chrysler was set to embark on its biggest and most widespread motor racing program yet. Its drag racing ambitions were just as lofty. Naturally, the new Dodge Challenger and Plymouth 'Cuda E-Body cars were well represented. But so too were the Dodge Dart and Plymouth Duster. Some Pro Stock teams campaigned multiple cars and might even have one of each from the same manufacturer. In addition to the new-1970 models were numerous older 1968/1969 Dart and Barracuda models.

Leading Chrysler Factory Drag Teams

The expected lead protagonists in the Chrysler camp were Sox & Martin and Dick Landy. Sox & Martin ran a new 1970 Plymouth 'Cuda, while Landy campaigned a new Dodge Challenger.

Pro Stock differed from Super Stock in that it introduced a variety of technical freedoms, which meant each team built its own car from the ground up rather than campaign and tweak a turnkey factory-built race car, as was common in the Super Stock era. To that end, each car was different from the next, even if it was the same make and model because every team incorporated its own tricks and mastery into its car(s). Despite no longer being required to build turnkey race cars as it had done in previous years, Chrysler was still on hand to provide support.

Chrysler supplied acid-dipped bodies to its teams in addition to a complete road car so that important componentry, including trim pieces, interior, various brackets, hinges, lights, and other parts that ensured the race cars were correctly presented, were also harvested.

Both the Sox & Martin 'Cuda and the Landy Challenger were equipped with a fiberglass lift-off hood and decklid, and both had a front-opening scoop molded into the hood. Landy arrived at the opening NHRA event at Pomona sporting a set of Hemi heads that featured twin sparkplugs and dual ignition. Both cars ran twin Holley carburetors and experimented throughout the season with carburetor sizes, intake manifolds, and spent gases exiting through Hooker Headers that dumped down just behind the front wheels. Both Sox and Landy preferred manual shifting, so both ran the Chrysler A833 4-speed, which transmitted power to the rear wheels via a Dana 60 rear end.

The Sox & Martin 'Cuda was finished in the team's traditional red, white, and blue livery, while Landy built on his traditional silver and red hue by adding blue stripes down the center. Both the Sox & Martin 'Cuda and Landy teams were sponsored by

The Sox & Martin Plymouth Duster of Herb McCandless is serviced in the Gainesville pits during an NHRA Division II Points event. (Photo Courtesy Charlie Suggs)

Bill Tanner's beautiful new Dodge Challenger Pro Stock is pictured alongside his 1968 LO23 Dart in the Gainesville pits. (Photo Courtesy Charlie Suggs)

Herb McCandless and a fleet of 1968 LO23/BO29 Hemi Mopars roll up for battle during an NHRA Division II points event at Gainesville. Even these regional events drew fierce grids and strong crowds. (Photo Courtesy Charlie Suggs)

Cragar wheels, and while the 'Cuda rolled on Keystones, Landy switched between running Cragar SSs and STs (Super Trick), and sometimes a combination of the two.

Landy appeared to experiment more with aerodynamic aids throughout the year, which suggests he was looking for better balance or more downforce. His Dodge ran a factory chin spoiler at most events, and while it ran without a deck spoiler (as the Sox & Martin 'Cuda did) in the early races, eventually it was equipped with a Challenger T/A Trans-Am spoiler and even an adjustable spoiler from a Ford Mustang.

What was notable also was the aggressive rake that all the new Chrysler Pro Stock cars ran. While just a few years earlier teams lifted the noses up to transfer weight to the rear tires, now they had them stuffed into the pavement, to better help them slice through the air and reduce drag.

1970 NHRA Drag Racing Highlights

For 1970, the NHRA announced an expansion of its Super Season, which would swell from four to seven National racing events, as well as recognition of the Funny Car division, which co-headlined along with Top Fuel and the new Pro Stock category. The 1970 NHRA Super Season schedule was as follows with the dates listed as those when Eliminations for Top Fuel, Funny Car, and Pro Stock were all contested:

1970 NHRA Events			
Date	**Event**	**Track**	**Location**
February 1	Winternationals	Auto Club Raceway	Pomona, California
February 15	Gatornationals	Gainesville Raceway	Gainesville, Florida
June 14	Springnationals	Dallas International Motor Speedway	Lewisville, Texas
July 19	Summernationals	York U.S. 30 Dragway	Thomasville, Pennsylvania
September 7	U.S. Nationals	Indianapolis Raceway Park	Clermont, Indiana
October 25	World Finals	Dallas International Motor Speedway	Lewisville, Texas
November 22	Supernationals	Ontario Motor Speedway	Ontario, California

For the first time, an outright NHRA National Champion would be declared rather than a Champion being awarded at each high-profile event. The driver who emerged at the top of the Pro Stock pile would be crowned 1970 NHRA Pro Stock Champion. Weirdly, however, the Championship was not decided by way of a points-paying system spread across all seven events. Instead, the driver who won the World Championship Finals at Dallas Motor Speedway would be Champion. The obvious pitfall of this system was that a driver could dominate the entire season but suffer mechanical failure in Round 1 at the World Finals. But such was life. A points-paying Championship wouldn't see the light of day until 1974.

1970 NHRA Winternationals

The NHRA Super Season was launched at Pomona for the annual Winternationals. A field of 750 competitors were entered throughout the spread of classes to claim their stake of the substantial $266,000 prize purse. The new Pro Stock division was one of the most highly anticipated competitions on the roster.

The big field of Pro Stock had more than 40 cars and consisted of newly built 1970 machinery and existing/updated Super Stocks. Included among the Chrysler contingent were Sox & Martin's Plymouth 'Cuda, Dick Landy's Dodge Challenger, Bill Bagshaw's Dart, Don Grotheer's 1970 'Cuda, Reid Whisnant's Duster, Ed Miller's Duster, Arlen Vanke's 1968 Barracuda, Don Carlton's 1968 Barracuda (the second Sox & Martin car), Herb McCandless's 1968 Dart, and a host of others.

Beyond the eye-candy, there was plenty of cutting-edge technology introduced. As well as Landy's trick twin-plug heads, Vanke ran a flat-plane crankshaft, offering a completely unique soundtrack in the quest for more horsepower.

Meanwhile, the Chrysler competition included "Dyno" Don Nicholson's new SOHC Ford Maverick, Sam Auxier Jr.'s SOHC Maverick, Bill "Grumpy" Jenkins's 1968 Camaro, Wally Booth's 1968 Camaro, Bill Heilscher's 1968 Camaro, Butch Leal's 1970 Camaro, Mike Fons's 1968 Camaro, Bob Glidden's SOHC Mustang, and Hubert Platt's SOHC Mustang. The list went on and on. Quality machinery abounded throughout.

In addition to the manufacturer wars, there was also a full-blown tire war, as Goodyear, M&H, and Firestone were all busy developing the stickiest rear boots they could devise to give their contracted teams an edge. Most Pro Stock cars were running 15 x 12-inch rear slicks in 1970.

The big field spent Friday and Saturday running as hard as they could and vying to make the top 16 to qualify for racing on Sunday. Ronnie Sox was the fastest qualifier both days, leading the time sheets on Friday with a 10.00 at 139.10 mph. He was chased by Jenkins on a 10.08 and Landy with a 10.11. On Saturday, Wally Booth pushed Landy down to fourth, punching out a 10.09, while Carlton ran fifth on 10.17. Next was Vanke (10.20), Fons (10.21), Grotheer (10.22), Bagshaw (10.26), and Auxier Jr. (10.49). Nicholson was struggling, lunching two motors, but popped in a 10.47 best to barely make the show. In the end, six Plymouths, five Chevys, three Fords and two Dodges made up the 16-car field.

Sox & Martin looked like the favorites heading into Eliminations, and Sox took out Vanke in Round 1. But the world was turned on its head a few minutes later, when Jenkins faced Heilscher. The Grump scorched a 9.98 on his way to victory, recording the first sub-10-second time ever for a Stock car. The massive audience went crazy. This was heady stuff.

None of the Fords made it past Round 1, while Sox faced off against Ed Miller and went to the next round. Meanwhile, Jenkins beat Fons in an all-Camaro match. Landy was also going rounds, taking out Bagshaw, while Booth scored an easy victory when Grotheer redlit.

That left four cars: two Chevys and two Mopars. Sox faced Booth first, and it was the Camaro driver who held a narrow margin early, until his clutch began slipping when he grabbed second gear. The Sox 'Cuda romped home with a 10.09 at 137.61 mph. Meanwhile, Jenkins's 9-second thumper in Round 1 must have rattled Landy because the big Dodge left early. Grumpy underlined his pace by scorching to another 9.98 to face Sox in the final.

In the big one, Jenkins popped another sub-10 time, blasting home a 9.99 at 139.53 mph to Sox's fading 10.12 at 138.67. With the first event done, it was Jenkins who put the competition on notice. He would be hard to beat in 1970.

1970 NHRA Gatornationals

Just two weeks after the epic Winternationals, the teams reassembled on the other side of the country for the Gatornationals. The new Pro Stock division and its heads-up racing was already proving to be a highlight of the 1970 NHRA Super Season.

As at Pomona a fortnight earlier, it was Sox and Jenkins who looked strongest in qualifying. Other than this pairing, others to make the show included Landy, McCandless, Miller, Fons, Carlton, Platt, Grotheer, Vanke, and former Funny Car ace Dick Loehr (1969 SOHC Mustang).

As at Pomona, Sox and Jenkins marched their way through Eliminations without actually encountering one another. In Round 1, Sox beat Loehr, while Jenkins beat Platt, both knocking out sub-10-second runs as they did so. Also to progress was McCandless (beating Miller), Carlton (beating Fons), Landy, Grotheer, and Vanke.

Round 2 of the 1970 NHRA Super Season was held at Gainesville Raceway in Florida just two weeks after the Winternationals. The wording on the license plate cover on the Sox & Martin Plymouth 'Cuda reads: "Plymouth Makes It." (Photo Courtesy Charlie Suggs)

Don Grotheer's beautiful Plymouth 'Cuda sits alongside his transporter while his BO29 1968 Barracuda lurks behind. (Photo Courtesy Charlie Suggs)

A rear view of the Sox & Martin 'Cuda in the Gainesville pit is shown here. One of the areas that would see the biggest technical gains throughout 1970 was tires. They became bigger and stickier in 1970. (Photo Courtesy Charlie Suggs)

There was a new breed of tiny Stockers. For 1970 Pro Stock competition, Ford factory teams ran a fleet of SOHC Ford Mavericks. This is Dick Loehr's example resting in the pits during the 1970 Gatornationals. (Photo Courtesy Charlie Suggs)

Dick Landy had a gorgeous new Dodge Challenger Pro Stock. A lot of the Mopar contingent opted not to fit the front and rear spoilers, including the Sox & Martin team, but Landy did. (Photo Courtesy Geoff Stunkard Collection)

When the field was whittled down to four cars, it was Sox to face his teammate Carlton and Jenkins against Landy. The Sox & Martin pairing put on an epic display with both cars dipping into the 9s. But Sox came out just in front, punching a 9.88 to Carlton's losing 9.94. Jenkins enjoyed a slightly easier road to the final, winning with a 9.84 to Landy's 10.13.

So, it was a repeat of Pomona—only now the 'Cuda was much stronger. In the end, it didn't matter. Sox was slow out of the gate, and Jenkins got the holeshot and was gone. Sox made a slightly quicker pass at 9.86 to Jenkins's 9.90, but the white Chevy was still ahead at the finish.

Notch up 2 for Sox and 0 for the Grump.

As if to underline the mass popularity of the new Pro Stock division, after Jenkins and Sox faced off in the final, hundreds of fans got up and left for home, despite Top Fuel, Funny Car, and Top Gas finals still to run. The Stockers were back, and the fans were loving it!

1970 NHRA Springnationals

In mid-June, the teams gathered once more for the Springnationals. The third round of the Super Season took place at Dallas International Motor Speedway. Of course, everything is bigger in Texas, and the Springnationals was touted as the richest drag race ever, with over $300,000 in prizes. In addition, it was hot and humid. To counter the heat and humidity, some of the action took place in the evening under lights. This was the first NHRA night race in history.

The four months that separated the Gatornationals and Springnationals appeared to tip the scales in favor of the Sox & Martin squad. Jenkins was never really in the running. He made the 16-car show but qualified a relatively poor (for him) seventh. Sox, by contrast, was blazing. He was top qualifier and took down Loehr's Mustang in Round 1.

For the second race in succession, Ronnie Sox met Bill Jenkins in the final. Much like the previous encounter at the NHRA Winternationals, the Camaro was first to the finish. But this was as good as it got for Jenkins in 1970, and for that matter, this was as good as it got for anyone not running a Mopar. (Photo Courtesy Charlie Suggs)

Gene Graham, in Joe Ralph Thompson's LO23 Dodge Dart, launches hard against Bill Jenkins at the NHRA Springnationals. Jenkins had now switched to a 1969 Camaro. (Photo Courtesy Geoff Stunkard Collection)

Others to progress to the second round were Nicholson, who beat Bill Tanner, while Ed Terry's brand-new SOHC Maverick was put on the trailer when he redlit against Bagshaw.

Jenkins made it as far as Round 2 before he was beaten by Lee Smith's Barracuda, while Sox took down Smith in the next round to face Wally Booth's rapid Camaro in the final. But Booth's big shot at the $14,000 winner's check went up in smoke when he was a little too trigger-happy off the line, gifting Sox the win with a 10.02 and the first Pro Stock Super Season victory for Chrysler.

1970 NHRA Summmernationals

A little over a month after the Springnationals, everyone assembled at York U.S. 30 Dragway in Pennsylvania for the first annual Summernationals.

The 350-car entry for the event was a little disappointing following previous NHRA competitions, and car numbers in both Top Fuel and Funny Car were poor. Fortunately, Pro Stock came to the party and was bursting at the seams. Nearly 60 cars went into battle to try and qualify for the impossibly small 16 Elimination spots. A lot of teams went away unhappy.

John Hagen switched to a new Plymouth 'Cuda for 1970. The Minnesota racer is pictured here at the NHRA Springnationals, where he was put on the trailer by Ronnie Sox. (Photo Courtesy Geoff Stunkard Collection)

"Mr. 4-Speed" Herb McCandless jumped aboard the second Sox & Martin Pro Stock, which was a new Plymouth Duster. McCandless very quickly repaid the team's faith in him. (Photo Courtesy Geoff Stunkard Collection)

With Chrysler no longer building turnkey drag cars, Don Grotheer built this beautiful 1970 Plymouth 'Cuda Pro Stock in his own shop. (Photo Courtesy Geoff Stunkard Collection)

The engine compartment of Don Grotheer's immaculate Plymouth 'Cuda is shown here. (Photo Courtesy Geoff Stunkard Collection)

Dick Landy's Pro Stock Challenger sits alongside his hauler. Landy's truck clocked up a lot of miles taking in racing events all over the country. (Photo Courtesy Geoff Stunkard Collection)

Ed Miller's beautiful new Plymouth Duster arrives on the back of the team's transporter. The Duster was slightly narrower than the 'Cuda and Challenger, but the E-Body Mopars did most of the winning in 1970. (Photo Courtesy Geoff Stunkard Collection)

Another of the new Plymouth Duster fleet was Bobby Yowell's 1970 Plymouth Duster, rolling on Keystone wheels. (Photo Courtesy Geoff Stunkard Collection)

Surely one of the most charismatic drag cars of all was the Sox & Martin Plymouth Superbird. It ran in the Super Stock/E class. The Superbird was designed specifically for competing at 200 mph on NASCAR superspeedways. In reality, the aero bodywork probably offered little advantage on a drag racer that wouldn't get near those speeds, but it sure looked good! (Photo Courtesy Geoff Stunkard Collection)

Dick Landy's Dodge Challenger switched to running Cragar ST (Super Trick) wheels with their smooth surface by mid-season. He was something of a pioneer with trialing new tricks to gain an advantage. (Photo Courtesy Geoff Stunkard Collection)

Adding to the woes were a variety of problems with the track surface, including a severe bump just beyond the start line in one of the lanes, forcing NHRA officials to move the start line forward by 20 feet.

When the Pro Stock cars came out to strut their stuff, it was Dick "Barney" Oldfield in the beautiful black *Motown Missile* Dodge Challenger that captured everyone's attention. He laid down a 9.936 to head the 16-car field as top qualifier. The only other driver to dip into the 9s was Ronnie Sox.

Bill Jenkins debuted a new 1970-model Camaro at the Summernationals, which was being piloted by his former teammate Dave Strickler. Herb McCandless had now switched to driving the new Sox & Martin Plymouth Duster, which first debuted in early May. Jenkins, meanwhile, was at the helm of a 1969 Camaro.

Sox, to everyone's surprise, went out in Round 1. The 'Cuda nosed-over mid-pass when it ran a bearing and lost to Billy "the Kid" Stepp's Dodge Challenger. McCandless went rounds in the second Sox & Martin machine, and he met "Dandy" Dick Landy in the final. Landy had been flying all day and taking names, but in the end, his path to victory was ensured when McCandless redlit, and Landy bagged

The Good Guys LO23 Dodge Dart was now into its third season of Super Stock competition. (Photo Courtesy Geoff Stunkard Collection)

Pictured at York U.S. 30 Drag-O-Way are the Super Stock *magazine giveaway Plymouth 'Cuda and Ed Miller's 1968 BO29 Barracuda. (Photo Courtesy Geoff Stunkard Collection)*

$8,000 as the third Pro Stock winner in four events.

So, after four rounds, Chrysler and Chevrolet were all even.

1970 U.S. Nationals

Despite the increased schedule, the U.S. Nationals at Indy was still the biggest and most coveted event on the drag racing calendar. The five-day epic began with cars cutting timed runs on Thursday. The show-stopper classes, including Top Fuel, Funny Car, and Pro Stock, all held their Eliminations on Monday, the final day of the event.

Once again, a sizable field of Pro Stock machines all converged on Indy to fight over the 16 grid slots for the finals. This time around, Don Nicholson had the hammer down in his SOHC Maverick to blast out a best run of 9.90 and narrowly beat Jenkins on a 9.91. Others to

make the show included Sox, Landy, McCandless, Loehr, Platt, Vanke, Bagshaw, Schartman (Maverick), Oldfield in the *Motown Missile* Challenger (which also won Best Engineered Car), Paul Longenecker, Sam Carroll, Jim Hayter, Ed Hedrick, and Ed Terry.

Jenkins was eliminated in Round 1 when the left rear wheel broke during the burnout. He ran spacers but hadn't installed longer studs. Those to advance included Longenecker, who narrowly edged out the *Motown Missile*, Sox, Vanke, McCandless, Carroll, Bagshaw, and Hedrick.

Hedrick then took a surprise victory in Round 2 against Sox, when the 'Cuda's transmission broke, and Hedrick then defeated Bagshaw. He was ultimately beaten by Vanke in the semifinals. Vanke faced McCandless for an all-Duster final, which ultimately played out as one of the all-time epic races.

Both drivers ran the exact same time and mph (9.98 and 138.03), but the Sox & Martin–equipped pilot cut a marginally better light at the start and held his minimal advantage all the way down the shoot. The massive crowd went berserk, and the Pro Stocks further cemented their place as one of NHRA's most prominent categories.

1970 NHRA World Championship Finals

While the U.S. Nationals was the most coveted event in drag racing, in many ways, the World Finals at Dallas International Motor Speedway carried more significance. For it was here that an NHRA National Champion was crowned. For the Pro Stock division, the 1970 NHRA

BO29 Barracudas were still hugely popular Super Stock racers in 1970. Bill Stiles, parked alongside the Car Center example, had owned his Stiles Performance Barracuda since 1968. (Photo Courtesy Geoff Stunkard Collection)

Another great 1968 Chrysler Super Stock was still racing hard and still looking a million bucks. Charlie Castaldo's LO23 Dart rests in the pits at York U.S. 30 Drag-O-Way. (Photo Courtesy Geoff Stunkard Collection)

BILLY "THE KID" STEPP

The introduction of NHRA Pro Stock in 1970 brought with it something of a change, as a few of the traditional Super Stock drivers drifted away while new characters stepped forward. One of the most colorful of the new arrivals was Billy "the Kid" Stepp.

William Stepp hailed from Dayton, Ohio, and was the son of an Appalachian lay minister. He was as smart, polite, and ingratiating as he was tough. As a young boy, his father took him to the docks in Cincinnati and bet on him in fights against adults.

Stepp's business practices were not necessarily aboveboard. Interestingly, he was an underworld figure who also enjoyed and sought a high-profile life. He drove an imposing black Mercedes-Benz and was an ominous yet charismatic figure on the streets of Dayton. He was also a keen drag racer, and although he was racing long before the advent of Pro Stock in 1970, somehow, it was in Pro Stock that he shot to stardom.

Stepp arrived in 1970 with a beautiful Dodge Challenger painted in an intricately detailed custom candy mix paint scheme. Rather than shy away from publicity, he instead played off his reputation with joyous abandon. In recognition of the notorious Wild West fugitive and gunslinger William H. Bonney, and almost certainly his own dubious background, Stepp had "Billy the Kid" lettering emblazoned along the flanks of the Challenger. At the track, he handed out hero cards titled "The Saga of Billy the Kid."

Stepp loved the attention, and he happily agreed to a photoshoot suggested by Don Green for *Car Craft* magazine in 1972, playing out a 1930s gangster scene. Stepp, his two crewmembers, and a blonde girl were all adorned in period attire with Stepp's new *Billy the Kid* Plymouth Duster as the centerpiece. Stepp, naturally, was toting a Tommy gun. It was pure Hollywood.

Stepp drove the Challenger himself initially and performed well against the seasoned campaigners. Ultimately, he opted to plug a hired gun into the hot seat. Among the celebrated names that drove for and partnered with him were Bobby Yowell, Stu McDade, Don Carlton,

Billy Stepp's Billy the Kid BO29 Barracuda is pictured. He ran this car in Pro Stock alongside a new Dodge Challenger. (Photo Courtesy Geoff Stunkard Collection)

Melvin Yow, and even "The Boss" himself, Ronnie Sox.

Stepp's cars weren't just chrome and candy paint. They were the very best equipment that money could buy, and he employed top crewmembers. As such, his cars won silverware.

Despite there being arrests and indictments, Stepp was never imprisoned.

Bill "the Kid" Stepp died in 2008 at age 73.

Billy Stepp's hauler was just as beautiful as his Challenger. (Photo Courtesy Jim Simmons/Allen Tracy)

MOTOWN MISSILE

The *Motown Missiles* will forever be linked with Don Carlton, but in fact, the first *Missile* was campaigned a full season before Carlton was brought in to take the reins. The first *Motown Missile* appeared in 1970. It was a direct Chrysler Corporation effort, and throughout the team's existence, boasted some of the smartest drag racing boffins in the industry, including Joe Pappas, Tom Coddington, Ted Spehar, Tom Hoover, Al Adams, Dick Oldfield, Len Bartush, and Ron Killen, who worked for Chrysler, as did Dick "Barney" Oldfield, who drove the first season.

The Motown Missile *poses in staging with Barney Oldfield behind the wheel. (Photo Courtesy Geoff Stunkard Collection)*

The cars were highly advanced technically and were among the very first race cars designed with the use of computers. The first *Motown Missile* was a 1970 Dodge Challenger driven by Oldfield. It debuted partway through the season but was quickly on the pace. As the season progressed, the car got closer to the sharp end of the field, and Oldfield progressed to the semifinals at the season-ending NHRA Supernationals.

For the 1971 season, the Challenger was updated as a 1971 model and upgraded with more technical wonderment. In addition, young hot shoe Don Carlton was ushered in as the driver. He brought with him longtime friend Clyde Hodges, who added further value to the program.

Carlton was quickly gunning for the top spot. He was top qualifier at two NHRA national events during the year, made the semifinals twice, and also went to the finals twice, where on both occasions he faced Sox and lost. But he won two IHRA national events in the U.S. Open and World Finals.

For 1972, a new *Motown Missile* was built: a Plymouth 'Cuda. Unfortunately, the team was hit with the NHRA's new weight-break system that handicapped the Chrysler teams. Regardless, Carlton won the Gatornationals and was the leading Mopar runner at several events. He won the IHRA Longhorn Nationals and Dallas Nationals to round out what had been another successful season, despite the challenges.

For 1973, another all-new car was built: a Plymouth Duster. However, this one was named the *Mopar Missile* because of confusion over the Detroit record company Motown Records.

Again, Carlton enjoyed success with the new *Missile*, including winning the NHRA Springnationals and losing to Don Nicholson in the final at the Winternationals. In IHRA competition, he won the Winternationals, Longhorn Nationals, Pro Am Nationals, Northern Nationals, and Springnationals. It had been a truly impressive year.

When Chrysler stepped back from Pro Stock racing, the Duster was handed over to Carlton, along with the infamous "wire car" and scores of parts. The wire car was a state-of-the-art Plymouth Duster designed around Chrysler's small-block motor.

It was introduced for NHRA competition because of the hefty weight disadvantages beset upon the big Hemi. It made extensive use of titanium and magnesium. The rear suspension was titanium, with the exception of the magnesium pig. It also included an early floating rear axle setup. Because the chassis effectively ended at the back axle, a steel cable tensioning system held the rear bodywork in place, hence the name wire car. It was light and innovative, but it never raced under Chrysler ownership as a *Mopar Missile* because the company got out of direct involvement with the sport.

The Motown/Mopar Missile program was relatively brief, lasting just four seasons. But it was hugely successful and introduced many firsts to the sport.

As an aside, 1971 NHRA World Championship winner Mike Fons purchased the 1972 *Motown Missile* 'Cuda along with the copyrighted name and continued racing it as the *Motown Missile*. He then purchased from Irv Beringhaus a former Dick Landy Dodge Demon built by Ken Fuller and raced that also as a *Motown Missile*.

National Champion was the first ever.

From the first five Pro Stock Super Season races contested in 1970, four different winners had emerged: Bill Jenkins, Ronnie Sox, Dick Landy, and Herb McCandless. Jenkins was the only multi-race winner.

The NHRA World Finals boasted 350 entries and a prize pool of $225,000. The Pro Stock division offered a large field of fiercely competitive cars with little to separate the top runners in performance.

The cars were due to hit the track on Friday morning, but persistent rain throughout the day meant everyone was forced to wait patiently in the pits until it relented. The action got underway at 3 p.m.

For Pro Stock, the big entry was whittled down and the 16-car field was established. When the engines fell silent, Dick Oldfield sat on top of the pile. He bombed home a strong 9.954 at 137.82 mph to emerge just ahead of Sox, who ran a best of 9.959 (just 0.005 shy of the *Motown Missile*). Next were the Camaros of Wally Booth and Jim Hayter, as the only other drivers to dip below 10 seconds. Booth ran a 9.97, and Hayter ran a 9.99.

It's an impressive sight! Dick Landy's full-race hauler, complete with Dodge Charger Super Stock and Dodge Challenger Pro Stock, arrives at Dallas International Motor Speedway for the 1970 NHRA World Finals. The twin-axle trailer carrying the Challenger rolls on Cragar wheels, which was one of Landy's sponsors. (Photo Courtesy C. Mike Cook)

The incredible Motown Missile *Dodge Challenger arrives to battle at the World Finals. Dick "Barney" Oldfield was at the controls here. By 1970, it was rare to see a Pro Stock car arriving on an open trailer pulled by a station wagon. Dick Landy's 1969 Charger can be seen in the background. (Photo Courtesy C. Mike Cook)*

Jake King, seen here tending to Sox's steed, played a significant role in the Sox & Martin team's success. (Photo Courtesy C. Mike Cook)

Partway through 1970, Herb McCandless stepped aboard the Sox & Martin Plymouth Duster and never looked back. He won the U.S. Nationals at Indy, beating Arlen Vanke in the process. Here, at the World Finals in Dallas, McCandless again met Vanke, this time in the semifinal, and "Akron" Arlen turned the tables on him. (Photo Courtesy C. Mike Cook)

Dick Landy tends to his Dodge Challenger at the 1970 NHRA World Finals. This shot with the hood off shows Landy's trick twin-plug cylinder heads. (Photo Courtesy C. Mike Cook)

Dick Landy works with the finesse and precision of a surgeon as he tweaks one of the massive carburetors sitting atop his Hemi. (Photo Courtesy C. Mike Cook)

Bill Tanner's beautiful Dodge Challenger and matching hauler looked a treat. Hailing from Atlanta, Tanner is seen here at the World Finals. He ran strong, too, making the field and working through to the quarterfinals, where he faced Herb McCandless. On this occasion, McCandless came out on top. (Photo Courtesy C. Mike Cook)

Jim Thompson's beautiful new Rod Shop Plymouth 'Cuda ran C/Gas at the NHRA World Finals. For 1971, this team gained backing from Dodge and massively expanded to include a fleet of cars and drivers. (Photo Courtesy C. Mike Cook)

By late 1970, Ronnie Sox had become drag racing royalty, but he could still be found polishing the wheels on his race car between rounds. (Photo Courtesy C. Mike Cook)

Jenkins lost some of the early season form he'd shown in his 1968 Camaro after he switched to a 1969 model. His best time was 10.07. The Grump did, however, tie Oldfield for top speed. Strickler also qualified for the top 16 in Jenkins's 1968 Camaro. Both McCandless and Vanke also made the show, while Landy and Nicholson missed the cut. Pro Stock racing in 1970 was tough!

As the 16-car field went through Eliminations, it was Sox, Hayter, Vanke, and McCandless who continued through to the semifinals. In the first heat, Vanke took down McCandless, while Sox knocked the last Chevy out of the competition in the second. Two Mopars faced off in the final, which was something that was becoming increasingly common in 1970.

The 31-year-old Sox was unbeaten at Dallas International Motor Speedway, having won the 1967, 1968, 1969, and 1970 NHRA Springnationals as well as the 1969 NHRA World Finals. Against Vanke in the opposite lane, he added the 1970 NHRA World Finals to the list. With that win, Sox was crowned 1970 NHRA Pro Stock Champion.

Incidentally, Ronnie Martin was crowned 1970 NHRA Top Fuel Champion, and Gene Snow was the Funny Car Champion. All three were Mopar propelled.

After Bill Jenkins blitzed everyone in the first two Pro Stock races of 1970, the Sox & Martin squad established itself as the high watermark of the class, going on a winning spree. While Ronnie Sox took the lion's share of victories aboard the team's 'Cuda, Herb McCandless, aboard the team's Duster, often gave the Boss a whooping. He won the World Championship Finals at Dallas. Here, during the NHRA season-ending contest Supernationals at Ontario Motor Speedway, the pair met again during eliminations. This time, Sox came out ahead, and indeed, went to the final, where he defeated Dick Oldfield in the Melrose Missile. (Photo Courtesy Geoff Stunkard Collection/Ray Mann Archive)

Arlen Vanke guns his beautiful Duster off the start line at Dallas International Motor Speedway, where he went deep into the Pro Stock Eliminator competition. (Photo Courtesy Geoff Stunkard Collection/Ray Mann Archive)

The beautiful Sox & Martin 'Cuda is on the start line at Dallas. As 1970 rolled forward, the Pro Stock teams lowered the nose of their cars more and more. (Photo Courtesy Geoff Stunkard Collection Courtesy Ray Mann Archive)

Bill Stepp's beautiful custom candy painted Billy the Kid Dodge Challenger runs against the Campbell & Ashley 1968 Camaro driven by Rick Campbell. (Photo Courtesy Geoff Stunkard Collection/Ray Mann Archive)

Another beautiful new Dodge Challenger built for the 1970 Pro Stock season was Bill Bagshaw's Red Light Bandit. (Photo Courtesy Geoff Stunkard Collection/Ray Mann Archive)

Among these chatting in the pits during the NHRA World Finals are Jake King, Ronnie Sox, and Buster Couch. (Photo Courtesy C. Mike Cook)

1970 NHRA Supernationals

The stellar 1970 NHRA Super Season concluded at the impressive new $25.5-million multipurpose Ontario Motor Speedway in California called the "Dragstrip in the Sky."

In Pro Stock, it was Ronnie Sox who set the pace in qualifying, busting out a series of runs in the 9.8-second bracket, which must have been demoralizing for the opposition. Except, that is, for Oldfield, who really had the *Motown Missile* humming.

Arlen Vanke was also cooking in his yellow and black Duster. He blazed a trail to the finals, where he met Sox for the second event on the trot as well as the third in which he faced a Sox & Martin Plymouth. Other notables were Bill Bagshaw's beautiful *Red Light Bandit* Dodge Challenger, which knocked Jenkins out in Round 2. Certainly, the best matchup was Sox versus Oldfield in the semifinals.

Sox edged his rival with a jaw-dropping 9.83 to set the Pro Stock low ET, while the *Motown Missile* was almost as impressive with a 9.86. Had Oldfield met anyone other than Sox during Eliminations, he would have found himself in the finals. But as it was, Sox faced Vanke, just as they did at the World Finals, and just as he did at the World Finals, Sox came out on top.

Really, it couldn't have been anyone else.

1970 AHRA Highlights

The Sox & Martin team had been immense in the second half of the 1970 NHRA Pro Stock campaign, but equally, its AHRA performances were just as impressive. Ronnie Sox ran amuck in AHRA competition, winning the Winternationals at Beeline Dragway in Scottsdale, Arizona, and then continued his winning form in the Pro-Am Nationals at North Carolina Motor Speedway in April. He won again at Frontier Lake Raceway in May and again one week later at Detroit Dragway.

Sox won the AHRA Spring Nationals at Bristol International Dragway in June as well as at New York National Speedway in late August. A month later, he won the U.S. Open at North Carolina Motor Speedway and topped off an immensely successful campaign with another victory at Beeline Dragway in mid-November.

By the time 1970 had concluded, the Sox & Martin team had racked up thousands of miles traveling the length and breadth of the country, and the trophy cabinet was heaving under the weight of all the silverware. It had been a year of epic proportions, immense speed, and enormous success. Chrysler Corporation was the undisputed king of speed.

Dave Koffel of Chrysler, Ronnie Sox, and Bill Jenkins discuss the highlights of the NHRA World Finals. Sox and Jenkins are drinking Schafer beer, so the day's action has clearly ended. While Sox won the event, Jenkins, the season's early pacesetter, went out in the quarterfinals. (Photo Courtesy C. Mike Cook)

CHAPTER 11

1971

CHRYSLER GOES ON A RAMPAGE

In automotive sales terms, performance cars were on their way out by 1971. When Ford Motor Company launched the Mustang in April 1964, it commanded massive interest and excitement, which generated record-breaking sales. During its first two years of production, the Mustang accounted for more than 25 percent of total Ford sales. It was phenomenal.

The Mustang's sales success sparked immediate reaction from rival manufacturers. GM engineers and bigwigs were initially unimpressed by the new Mustang when an early example was sourced and assessed. Many within the company confidently predicted the new 1965 Chevrolet Corvair would comfortably deal with the Mustang when it came to market, but when the Ford pony car sold 100,000 units within four months of its launch, General Motors couldn't ignore it any longer. In August 1964, a program was launched to design and build a Chevrolet variant of the Mustang and have it on sale by September 1966.

General Motors met its goal, and the Chevrolet Camaro was launched in September 1966. Four days later, Lincoln-Mercury unveiled the Mercury Cougar, an upmarket and slightly longer variant of the Mustang. By February 1967, Pontiac introduced another pony car offering to tempt buyers, and later that year, AMC came to market with its own pony car: the Javelin.

By 1967, pony car sales accounted for 13 percent of total vehicle sales in the United States. By any standard, that was significant. In addition, the muscle car market was also booming, and the manufacturers were all-in. When Chrysler greenlighted its dedicated E-Body models, it confidently predicted combined sales of 225,000 units per year. But when the new Dodge Challenger and

The resplendent Motown Missile *with Don Carlton at the controls faces Dick Brannan's SOHC Maverick. (Photo Courtesy Geoff Stunkard Collection)*

Having raced Chevy products since he began racing, Mike Fons switched to this newly constructed Dodge Challenger in 1971 as part of the rapidly expanded Rod Shop team, which was supported by Dodge. Fons quickly established himself as a genuine contender in the tough Pro Stock division. (Photo Courtesy Geoff Stunkard Collection)

Plymouth Barracuda hit the market in the fall of 1969, pony-car sales had already slipped to 9.2 percent. Sadly, that downward trend continued into the early 1970s.

1971 Dodge Challenger and Plymouth Barracuda

For the 1970 model year, Chrysler sold just shy of 77,000 Challengers and just under 49,000 Barracudas. Combined, the Dodge and Plymouth pony car siblings accounted for nearly 126,000 units sold, which was an encouraging figure given the market-leader Mustang sold 190,000 units. With that being said, Ford sold 607,000 Mustangs in 1966, and although the pony car market was a busy place by 1970, there were already worrying signals that customers were losing interest.

Certainly, the Chrysler division offered several models that might tempt buyers away from a Challenger or a Barracuda, such as the cheaper Dart and Duster. But even in early 1970, many pundits within the motoring industry, including the press, were predicting dark times ahead for performance and sporty car sales. The manufacturers responded by tightening their belts.

For 1971, Chrysler changed little on its Dodge Challenger and Plymouth Barracuda street cars. Minor trim and interior changes took place, while the entry-level Challenger Deputy name was dropped and replaced with the Challenger Coupe. The 340 ci with three 2-barrel carburetors engine option was no longer available nor was the 4-barrel 440.

The most notable exterior changes centered around the nose. The Challenger received a new grille, and the Barracuda was gifted an extra pair of headlights. Typically, when a manufacturer brings a new model to market, it makes very few aesthetic changes in the second year. Besides,

Part of the expanded Rod Shop team in 1971 was this wild little Dodge Colt station wagon, which competed in D/Altered. The stubby little monster was powered by a 340 motor that was destroked to 319 ci. (Photo Courtesy Geoff Stunkard Collection)

Another addition to the Rod Shop 1971 fleet was Bob Riffle's B/Modified Production Dodge Dart. (Photo Courtesy Geoff Stunkard Collection)

Jim Wick in the Matchmaker *Duster launches against "Dyno" Don Nicholson's SOHC Maverick at U.S. 131 Dragway. (Photo Courtesy Geoff Stunkard Collection)*

Mike Fons gets the nose right up off the deck in his duel with the Johnson & Hauri Camaro. (Photo Courtesy Geoff Stunkard Collection)

Don Grotheer's 1970 Plymouth Cuda was purchased by Irv Beringhaus, repainted in a beautiful new custom hue, and updated with 1971 beak. (Photo Courtesy Grant Bittner)

Billy Stepp's beautiful Dodge Challenger, Billy the Kid, had Stu McDade as designated pilot in 1971. McDade's performance was impressive. (Photo Courtesy Geoff Stunkard Collection)

Reid Whisnant, the "Flying Plumber," ran this beautiful two-tone gold Plymouth Duster throughout the 1971 season, and he was a regular top gun. Some wheelie bar adjustments are being made to Whisnant's Duster at the Gatornationals. (Photo Courtesy Charlie Suggs)

the new E-Body Chrysler siblings were both strong designs that were well received.

Changing Times in Auto Racing

In 1970, the SCCA Trans-Am road racing series reached its peak. It boasted fully fledged factory-supported race teams representing the Ford Mustang, the Chevrolet Camaro, the Plymouth 'Cuda, the Dodge Challenger, the AMC Javelin, and the Pontiac Firebird. Detroit was putting literally millions of dollars into the Trans-Am. But by 1971, they'd all left. All, that is, except for American Motors, who'd signed a three-year deal with Penske Racing beginning with the 1970 campaign.

Indeed, Chrysler reduced its funding of Dan Gurney's AAR equipment partway through the 1970 campaign, forcing Gurney himself to step aside from driving duties. The team ran a single car for Swede Savage throughout the remainder of the 1970 season—other than the final at Riverside. It was here that Gurney returned, as the team expanded once again to a two-car team in an effort to win a race (which it hadn't managed to achieve yet) and hopefully win an extended Chrysler contract for the 1971 season. It was all to no avail.

The same was true in the NASCAR Grand National. Chrysler greatly reduced its funding, cutting back from six teams to two, both of which operated out of Petty Enterprises.

Ford, the only other manufacturer invested in the Grand National, was even more forceful in its exit and announced a total withdrawal in November 1970, going as far as to change the locks on the doors at Kar-Kraft, its skunkworks facility. Having pumped many millions of dollars into an extensive range of racing programs spanning much of the 1960s, Ford was conscious of a change in buyer patterns and an increasing shift away from high-performance vehicles. As such, it terminated its remaining projects and severed ties with its teams.

Further adding to the aggravation was the intro-duction of carburetor restrictor plates in August 1970, which severely limited the breathing abilities of the big purpose-built engines. NASCAR was targeting the Chrysler Hemi and Ford Boss 429. Several of the Ford teams switched to the older 427, which worked better under the restrictor plate regime. But the Chrysler teams stuck determinedly with the Hemi.

For 1971, NASCAR announced the arrival of a new title sponsor: R.J. Reynolds. It also rebranded the NASCAR Winston Cup, which would be its official title. The introduction of cigarette funding filled the void left by the departing automotive manufacturers.

The same was true of Pro Stock drag racing. The manufacturers were jumping ship, but fortunately, the rules were designed in such a way that emphasis was placed on individual team performance rather than the commitment made by the automakers to design the best possible performance street car that translated across into a competitive race car.

1971 NHRA Drag Racing Highlights

The new-for-1970 NHRA Pro Stock regulations may have shifted the cars ever further from their stock roots. In fact, the rules themselves, and the mechanical freedoms they allowed, were the likely savior of the category. They sidestepped the requirement for manufacturers to produce homologation specials, which was important in a time when manufacturers were moving away from automobile racing as a whole. With that being said, it seemed that Chrysler's mighty Hemi engine, despite its age, was still the pinnacle of Stock drag racing.

It was fortunate also that, despite waning sales of performance and sporty cars, enthusiasm for racing continued to soar. As such, the NHRA expanded its Super Season beyond that of 1970 to eight events and for the first time ventured into Canada.

Notable was the switch from U.S. 30 Drag Strip to Madison Township Raceway Park (later known as Old

1971 NHRA Events			
Date	**Event**	**Track**	**Location**
February 7	Winternationals	Auto Club Raceway	Pomona, California
March 21	Gatornationals	Gainesville Raceway	Gainesville, Florida
June 13	Springnationals	Dallas International Motor Speedway	Lewisville, Texas
July 18	Summernationals	Madison Township Raceway Park	Englishtown, New Jersey
August 15	Le Grandnationals	Sanair Super Speedway	St. Pie, Québec, Canada
September 6	U.S. Nationals	Indianapolis Raceway Park	Clermont, Indiana
October 24	World Finals	Amarillo Dragway	Amarillo, Texas
November 21	Supernationals	Ontario Motor Speedway	Ontario, California

Butch "the California Flash" Leal returned to the Chrysler fold in 1971, having tried unsuccessfully to campaign a second-generation Camaro in the 1970 Pro Stock national races. He had Ron Butler build the new Plymouth Duster chassis, while Joe Allread built the motor with Leal's assistance. It was fast! As the 1971 season trucked along, Leal emerged as one of the true heavy hitters in the Pro Stock ranks. (Photo Courtesy Tom West/Lou Hart)

Bridge Township Raceway Park) for the Summernationals.

Just as it had done in 1970, the NHRA awarded the winning driver of the World Finals as the Pro Stock National Champion.

Although Camaro racer Bill Jenkins shot out of the gates to dominate the first two events in 1970, he was soon overhauled by the fleet of top-performing Mopar teams. From Round 3 onward, Pro Stock was dominated by Hemi-powered Chryslers. In almost every case, the two cars scrapping out the final at each event were either Dodge or Plymouth. For 1971, the Mopar contingent got even bigger and even more potent.

The reigning Champions, Sox & Martin, were back of course. Ronnie Sox drove a brand-new 'Cuda, while his 1970 multi-race winner was updated to 1971 trim and campaigned by Herb McCandless. Don Carlton was now at the helm of the *Motown Missile*, while Don Grotheer switched to a new 1971 Plymouth Road Runner equipped with a Hemi, of course.

Dick Landy returned, again driving a Dodge Challenger, while Plymouth Duster driver Arlen Vanke, who reached the finals in three 1970 Super Series events, was also back. Bobby Yowell ran a Plymouth Duster, as did Butch Leal, who returned to the Chrysler fold after running a Camaro in 1970. Mike Fons was another to switch brands, having run a Camaro in 1970. For 1971, he joined the expanding Rod

The incredible Motown Missile *Dodge Challenger was back for the 1971 season. Don Carlton replaced Dick Oldfield in the hot seat, and he went on a run. He regularly top-qualified and likewise made the final. He won two IHRA competitions late in the year, but like a lot of the Pro Stock contingent in 1971, he came up just marginally short of the Sox & Martin squad. (Photo Courtesy Tom West/Lou Hart)*

Dick Landy launches the nose as he sets off on a fast run in his Dodge Challenger. Again, Landy had a busy year, campaigning multiple cars as well as running his supercar clinics and overseeing his business. (Photo Courtesy Tom West/Lou Hart)

Shop team to race a Dodge Challenger. John Petrie ran a new Dodge Demon, while Bob Lambeck had a 1968 Dart.

Once again, the opposition was tough and included Ed Schartman (SOHC Mercury Comet), Don Nicholson and Dick Brannan in SOHC Mavericks, as well as Bill Jenkins, Wally Booth, Jim Hayter, Ron Hutter, and Carroll Caudle in Camaros.

Ronnie Sox is in the latest Sox & Martin Plymouth 'Cuda built for the 1971 season. The 1971 models switched to a four-headlight front, while the hood scoop on the Sox & Martin car also grew several inches over the 1970 variant. (Photo Courtesy Tom West/Lou Hart)

NHRA Division 7

One week before the Winternationals, the NHRA hosted its Division 7 event at Orange County Raceway. It attracted several of the big-name teams that were eager to get in some track time before the championship began.

Having campaigned a wild silver with metallic rainbow candy-striped Hemi-propelled 1964 Plymouth Belvedere station wagon called the Whackee Wagon, Lee Smith switched to a new Plymouth 'Cuda to tackle Pro Stock. The 'Cuda sported a similar custom paint scheme to the Belvedere wagon and was aptly named the Crazee 'Cuda. (Photo Courtesy Tom West/Lou Hart)

For the 1971 season, Don Grotheer sold his 1970 Plymouth 'Cuda and commissioned Don Hardy Race Cars to build him a brand-new car. (Photo Courtesy Tom West/Lou Hart)

In addition to his new Pro Stock 'Cuda, Don Grotheer also campaigned this stout 1971 Plymouth Road Runner in B/Modified production. Butch Leal had a couple of races in the Road Runner while his new Plymouth Duster was being finished. (Photo Courtesy Tom West/Lou Hart)

Irv Beringhaus wrinkles the rear tires as he launches at Orange County Raceway during the hotly contested NHRA Division 7 event. (Tom West Photo Courtesy Lou Hart)

Herb McCandless launches in the Sox & Martin Plymouth Superbird at the 1971 NHRA Winternationals at Pomona. McCandless won C/Modified Production. Sox & Martin campaigned at least two Superbirds. The cars looked incredible, but the long beak and tall rear wing were of little use in a drag racing environment where top speeds fell well short of those for which the car was designed. (Photo Courtesy Tom West/Lou Hart)

1971 NHRA Winternationals

The new Sox & Martin 1971 Plymouth 'Cuda was, by all accounts, a weapon, and faster than the car that dominated much of the 1970 campaign. When the Pro Stock field gathered for qualifying, Ronnie Sox again headed the charge, clocking a 9.81. Vanke, Petrie, Jenkins, Booth, Hayter, Schartman, Nicholson, Brannan, and Lambeck also made the show. The Chevy contingency was headed not by Jenkins but by Ron Hutter.

Interestingly, many of the cars punched out faster times in Eliminations than they did in qualifying. The four cars that remained included Sox, Petrie, Booth, and Vanke. The first semifinal had Booth facing Vanke. As the pair blasted through the traps, it was the Chevy in front and heading to the final. Booth ran a 9.87 to Vanke's los-

ing 9.93. Meanwhile, Sox had an easier road to the final, when Petrie suffered a failed spark plug.

So, it was a repeat of the 1970 NHRA Winternationals Pro Stock final with a Mopar facing a Chevy. Only this time, it wasn't one of *Grumpy's Toys* lining up against Sox. It was the Plymouth that reached the finish first; Sox scorched to a 9.86 (141.20 mph) to Booth's 10.02. It was later discovered the Camaro had a cracked block, but regardless, Sox again stood in victory circle and got his 1971 campaign off to the best possible start.

1971 NHRA Gatornationals

When the Pro Stock contingent gathered for the NHRA Gatornationals six weeks later, Sox & Martin looked to have extended its advantage over the opposition. In March 1971, the NHRA lowered the minimum weight by 300 pounds (from 2,700 to 2,400 pounds), and the mega new elapsed times recorded at Gainesville Raceway reflected this.

During qualifying, Sox scorched to an epic 9.57 at 142.76 mph to lead the field once again. Certainly, the 'Cuda was running hard, but in addition to the dumped weight, Firestone introduced a new set of super trick tires that also upped the speed of the Pro Stock cars. But even still, Bill Jenkins punched out the first sub-10-second run at the NHRA Winternationals in February 1970, and everyone went crazy. Just 12 months later, running in the 9s didn't even guarantee a birth in the top 16. The evolution was intense.

Chasing Sox was Don Carlton in the *Motown Missile* at 9.60 followed by Stu McDade, who was now at the helm of the *Billy the Kid* Challenger. McDade ran 9.68. Don Grotheer was next at 9.70, then Vanke (also on 9.70), Petrie (9.71), and Landy (9.71), while Jenkins was the first non-Mopar driver at 9.77, just ahead of Booth (9.80). Nicholson was the fastest of the Fords with 9.82. Reid Whisnant also went through in his beautiful gold Duster. Brannan didn't actually make the cut. He qualified 17th but was promoted when McDade's Challenger was withdrawn due to engine failure.

When Eliminations came, Vanke took down Nicholson before Sox put Vanke on the trailer in Round 2. Sox then beat Booth's Camaro, and Carlton did likewise to the Grump. Indeed, Carlton was blazing. He also eliminated Petrie and Whisnant to meet Sox in the final.

Heading through Eliminations, the numbers were unbelievably close. Carlton ran a best of 9.60; Sox ran a 9.61. The final was sure to be an epic. But sadly, it wasn't. As the Mopar pairing razed the tires during the burnout and then backed into their boxes, Carlton somehow clunked his shifter into second gear without realizing it. Sox was up for the fight and blazed to a winning 9.60 at 141.95 mph, while the *Missile* crossed the line nearly a second in the arrears.

1971 NHRA Springnationals

First, neither Jenkins nor Booth attended this event with their Camaros. Grumpy was having a tough year. At the 1971 Springnationals, it was "Dyno" Don Nicholson who upped the ante and best challenged the Chrysler contingent. Meanwhile, Don Carlton switched from running a 4-speed manual to a new Clutchflite in the *Motown Missile.*

Sox again qualified fastest for Eliminations and took down the likes of Butch Leal on his way to the finals. Landy and McCandless struggled with sick motors, while Mike Fons made his debut with his newly built Rod Shop Dodge Challenger and progressed through to the second round. Carlton made the semifinals, as did Grotheer, but it was the SOHC Maverick of Nicholson that faced Sox for the big one. It was a barnstormer.

Nicholson busted out of the gates and ran faster than he'd ever gone, scorching to a 9.78 ET. But it still wasn't enough. Sox wore him out with a 9.70, and said after the match, "That was the hottest race I've ever had. We both dropped the clutch at the same time. I pulled him mostly in third and high gear."

The big high-revving Chrysler Hemi made all the difference.

Having raced a Plymouth Duster in 1970, Arlen Vanke switched to a Cuda for 1971. It was a fast car too. Unfortunately for Vanke, however, he couldn't topple the dominant Sox & Martin outfit. (Bryan Wall Photo, Courtesy Gilbert Ramsey)

1971 NHRA Summernationals

The big news in Pro Stock at the Summernationals was that Ronnie Sox didn't enter Eliminations as top qualifier. Don Carlton did, and he mowed through his new stick shifter with immense speed and accuracy to post a staggering 9.502 at 145.39 mph, which was a new low ET for the category. Sox, by contrast, produced a relatively tardy (for him) 9.640 at 143.31 mph.

But all would be put to right come Eliminations, right? Nope. Sox went out in Round 2, not due to driver error or mechanical failure but because of a tire getting punctured during the burnout.

Nicholson was flying in the Maverick, as was Mike Fons, making his second appearance in the Rod Shop Challenger. Fons comfortably made the top 16, and in Round 1 was the only driver other than Nicholson to run in the 9.6-second bracket (Fons 9.66, Nicholson 9.68).

Jenkins and Booth went out in Round 2. Then, top-qualifier Carlton produced a 9.67 to send Bobby Yowell home, while Fons and Dyno went faster still at 9.63 and 9.64. But three into two doesn't work, and Carlton met Nicholson in the semifinal. There was almost nothing between them—almost nothing being 0.005 seconds to be exact. Nicholson got the holeshot, and that decided the race. He ran a 9.665.

The impressive Fons blasted his way through to the final to face Nicholson. Again, it was an impossibly close contest, which went the way of the little Ford. "Dyno" Don produced a 9.638 to Fons's 9.689 to score the first NHRA National Pro Stock win for the Blue Oval. Fons, however, had put the Pro Stock contingent on notice and thrown his hat into the ring as yet another contender for race wins.

1971 NHRA Le Grandnationals

The NHRA circus traveled up to Québec for the first Le Grandnationals in August. It was the first Canadian National event since the inception of NHRA's Super Season.

Naturally, fewer teams made the pilgrimage from the United States, but those who did found the track surface and grip to be mind-blowingly sticky.

Jere Stahl made a much-heralded return to Stock drag racing—only to be put on the trailer by the scorching Ronnie Sox, who was punching out times in the 9.5-second range all weekend.

The 16-car field was eventually whittled down to four Mopars in the semifinals, including Sox, Vanke, Carlton, and Petrie. Sox put Petrie away in their matchup, and Carlton did likewise to Vanke, but the *Motown Missile* Challenger had nothing for the Sox & Martin 'Cuda. Sox scorched through the traps to record another major win.

The Hemi motor is nestled in the nose of Ronnie Sox's Cuda. Note the twin-plug heads and second distributor. (Bryan Wall Photo, Courtesy Gilbert Ramsey)

It's all in the details. Note the personalized front tires on the Ronnie Sox Cuda. (Bryan Wall Photo, Courtesy Gilbert Ramsey)

At Le Grandnationals, Don Carlton and the stout Motown Missile Challenger went all the way to the final, where they met and were beaten by Ronnie Sox. (Bryan Wall Photo, Courtesy Gilbert Ramsey)

1971 NHRA U.S. Nationals

Onward to the big one: the U.S. Nationals at Indianapolis. This event began in 1955, and Calvin Rice, driving a 10-second Ford flathead-powered slingshot dragster won Top Eliminator (now Top Fuel). By 1971, any Pro Stock car running the same times as Rice's dragster 16 years earlier wouldn't have made the show. That's how quick the big banger Stockers were running now, and the competition was only getting tougher.

How popular had the Pro Stocks become? Many considered them to be the highlight of the NHRA national schedule, and the prize purse that was posted backed this up. While the

Bobby Yowell's beautiful Plymouth Duster rolls into the Indianapolis pits aboard the team transporter. (Photo Courtesy C. Mike Cook)

Irv Beringhaus's beautiful Plymouth 'Cuda, sporting its glorious custom candy paint, is pictured at the 1971 NHRA U.S. Nationals. (Photo Courtesy C. Mike Cook)

Butch Leal's stunning new Plymouth Duster was a force to be reckoned with during the latter part of 1971. Here, it's pictured in the Indianapolis pit area during the NHRA U.S. Nationals. (Photo Courtesy C. Mike Cook)

Judy Lilly's SS/AA 1968 Plymouth Barracuda arrives for the 1971 U.S. Nationals. (Photo Courtesy C. Mike Cook)

The extraordinary artwork on Bobby Yowell's Plymouth Duster, as produced by Greg of Akron, differed on each side. Early Pro Stocks were true rolling art. (Photo Courtesy C. Mike Cook)

"Wild" Bill Shrewsberry's crazy blown Hemi-powered rear-engined L.A. Dart, resting in the pits at the U.S. Nationals. One stab on the throttle and the front wheels on this thing are going straight up! (Photo Courtesy C. Mike Cook)

The stunning Dodge Challenger of Charlie Castaldo is pictured in the Indianapolis Raceway Park pit area during the 1971 NHRA U.S. Nationals. Castaldo ran in the highly competitive Super Stock/D Automatic class. (Photo Courtesy C. Mike Cook)

Dave Boertman's infamous Rod Shop Dodge Coronet wagon was built in two weeks as part of Gil Kirk's ambitious 1971 Chrysler drag racing program. Dodge hit the green light on the project so late that this was the only Rod Shop car ready for the opening NHRA event at Pomona, and it was only there because Boertman built it in just two weeks. The giant wagon went on a winning streak throughout 1971 in Stock Eliminator, and it racked up the trophies and a stack of prize money. So successful was this car that the NHRA changed its Stock Eliminator format for 1972, withdrawing all prize and contingency money and offering only trophies to the winners. Boertman, therefore, made the switch to Super Stock so he could continue to fund his racing. (Photo Courtesy C. Mike Cook)

Reid Whisnant's beautiful gold Duster is at rest in the Indy pits for the 1971 NHRA U.S. Nationals. (Photo Courtesy C. Mike Cook)

"The Boss" Ronnie Sox's Plymouth 'Cuda is pictured in the Indy staging lanes. (Photo Courtesy Don Webber)

The second Sox & Martin Plymouth 'Cuda was driven by Herb McCandless. This was the team's 1970 car updated as a 1971 model. (Photo Courtesy Don Webber)

Having raced a Plymouth Duster in 1970, Arlen Vanke switched to a 'Cuda for 1971. It was a fast car too. Pictured at the U.S. Nationals, Vanke can be seen in the white shirt standing in front of his 'Cuda. (Photo Courtesy C. Mike Cook)

Don Grotheer is pictured heading toward the staging lanes in his 1971 Plymouth 'Cuda. Grotheer was a force to be reckoned with in 1971 and was among the top cars on the Pro Stock circuit all year. (Photo Courtesy C. Mike Cook)

Butch "the California Flash" Leal, like so many great racers of the era, was as handy with the tools as he was at the controls. He was one of the top-performing Pro Stock racers throughout 1971. (Photo Courtesy Mike Cook)

Bill Bagshaw's magnificent Red Light Bandit Dodge Challenger Pro Stock is sparkling in the Indianapolis sunlight. (Photo Courtesy Don Webber)

Billy "the Kid" Stepp's beautiful Dodge Challenger is in the pits at the 1971 NHRA U.S. Nationals. Driver Stu McDade impressed here by qualifying in the number-2 position. Stepp was one of the few Mopar teams to run the rear spoiler that was homologated for Chrysler's 1970 SCCA Trans-Am program. Stepp's Barracuda Super Stock can be seen in the background on a trailer. (Photo Courtesy C. Mike Cook)

Bob Riggle's incredible Hemi Under Glass *Plymouth Barracuda wheelstander gets unloaded in the Indianapolis pits. (Photo Courtesy Don Webber)*

Billy the Kid was a showman, certainly. His transporter was as flamboyant as his race car. But beyond the showiness was a dedicated racer who spent his money well and had the best equipment. His cars were genuine contenders. (Photo Courtesy Don Webber)

winner for Top Fuel at the U.S. Nationals would bag $9,750, and Funny Car $9,700, the Pro Stock driver who could beat all before them would take home $14,600. That was quite a statement!

The U.S. Nationals followed a different system from the regular NHRA events in that 32 cars qualified for Eliminations rather than 16. But that didn't make it any easier to progress. There were 86 cars entered!

When qualifying was run and won, Carlton topped the times with an epic 9.559 in the *Motown Missile*. He was followed by Stu McDade, who surprised many in Billy Stepp's *Billy the Kid* Challenger. In fact, some had genuine concerns that something may be amiss with the fast Dodge, and a protest was lodged. The NHRA tore the motor down but found it to be under the legal 429-ci maximum limit.

McDade produced a 9.562, which bettered Ronnie Sox's best run of a 9.688, back in third. Butch Leal was

next, posting the exact same time as Sox. Then came Don Nicholson in fifth with a 9.691 in the first non-Mopar.

Bill Jenkins was back in tenth, running a 9.777, while of interest was Wally Booth's brand-new 1971 Camaro (9.910) and the equally new factory-backed AMC Hornets of former Chrysler racers H. L. and Shirley Shahan.

But whether it was a 16-car field, a 32-car field, or even a 64-car field, the top four qualifiers were also the final four to progress through to the semifinals: Carlton, McDade, Sox, and Leal. All the Fords and Chevys had been sent packing.

First up, Sox faced Carlton, and the atmosphere was electric. But then everything went haywire with Sox busting out of the gates first, even though Carlton was showing as having redlit. NHRA starter Buster Couch reviewed the system and found an inadvertent handicap had been dialed into the tree. So, he called for a re-run. The cars headed back to the pits, where the crews got

Racers lined up on Eliminations days at the NHRA U.S. Nationals, hoping to see some action. But the weather had other ideas. The event was delayed a day as a result. (Photos Courtesy Don Webber)

In 1971, Ronnie Sox could seemingly walk on water, but even he couldn't race in the rain. (Photo Courtesy Don Webber)

Mopar wheel-stand legends Bob Riggle in Hemi Under Glass *and Bill Shrewsberry in* L.A. Dart *turn it on for the crowds. (Photo Courtesy Don Webber)*

Dave Wren's ragtop 'Cuda takes on Ray Allen's ragtop Chevelle in Super Stock/EA. On this occasion, the Chevy pilot took the spoils. (Photo Courtesy Don Webber)

Another photo of the impressive Rod Shop team shows Bill McGraw's striking 1971 Dodge Charger as it hurtles to a Super Stock/E class win at Indy. (Photo Courtesy Don Webber)

The hood on Lee Cameron's Dodge Challenger is starting to lift as he takes on Gene Boitnott in the Boitnott Brothers 'Cuda in SS/DA at the U.S. Nationals. The handsome blue and white 'Cuda was the former Sox & Martin 1970 AHRA GT1 World Championship winner. (Photo Courtesy Don Webber)

Ronnie Sox (#4) and Herb McCandless (#44) are in the two Sox & Martin 'Cudas at the U.S. Nationals. It's interesting to note the quite different hood-scoop designs. (Photos Courtesy Don Webber)

Butch Leal's Plymouth Duster is shown here at Indy. Throughout the 1971 racing season, the angle of rake on this car became ever more dramatic with the nose getting very low to the ground to help it slip through the air cleaner. This car also sported unconventional diagonal roll-cage bars spanning the A-pillar and B-pillar area. This was certainly one of the earliest cars to feature a robust roll cage to improve body rigidity and better exploit chassis adjustments. (Photo Courtesy Don Webber)

Dick Landy's Challenger lines up in the staging lanes at Indy. Landy was constantly experimenting, and his cars sported changes from race to race. He was a pioneer in the use of smooth wheels, and he started running Cragar Super Tricks (STs) on the front of his Challenger in 1970. This he continued into 1971. Within a couple of years, virtually every drag car featured similar flat-face wheels in favor of the attractive Cragar SSs, Keystones, slot mags, and other custom wheels that adorned the early Pro Stocks. The year 1971 was also the first year that tire manufacturers started going to larger lettering (as was demonstrated here by Goodyear) so that their products were easier to identify on TV and in magazines. (Photo Courtesy Don Webber)

Stu McDade in Billy Stepp's Dodge Challenger gets a run against Hubert Platt's SOHC Ford Maverick during U.S. Nationals Eliminations. (Photo Courtesy Don Webber)

to work preparing them again. During his run, Carlton's clutch failed, and his team asked permission to be given extra time to repair it, which was duly granted. But when they went to stage, were told they were too late. It was a disappointing conclusion.

In a much less controversial second semifinal bout, McDade took down Leal and faced Sox in the final.

So, it was Sox versus McDade. Sox was in the right lane, and McDade was in the left. The pair erupted off the line at the first light and thundered down the chute side by side with almost nothing separating them. In the end, it was almost too close to call, but Sox narrowly edged ahead, with a winning 9.586 to McDade's losing 9.588. What a race—and what a showcase of Pro Stock!

Ronnie Sox gets the jump on Gene Graham in Joe Ralph Thompson's vibrant red Dodge Dart Demon. Thompson, of Rison, Arkansas, was a longtime Mopar racer, having entered the sport 10 years earlier with a Dodge Polaris. His cars won multiple Arkansas State championships, and although he received support from Chrysler, he was really an independent. As such, he didn't follow the full NHRA Pro Stock circuit. (Photo Courtesy Don Webber)

Dave Wren battles Dick Landy in a closely fought Mopar contest at the 1971 NHRA U.S. Nationals. The different nose heights on these two cars shows how Pro Stock evolved throughout 1971. The cars running the full NHRA Super Season all began slamming the fronts into the ground to help slice through the air a little cleaner and achieve a greater top-end speed. No doubt, the heavy rake aided in downforce. Wren was another longtime Mopar campaigner who had a busy weekend at the U.S. Nationals, competing in both Super Stock and Pro Stock. (Photo Courtesy Don Webber)

Larry Griffith in the blue Plymouth Duster takes on Herb McCandless in the Sox & Martin 'Cuda in a Round 1 scrap at the NHRA U.S. Nationals. Both drivers had been loyal Mopar competitors for many years. In this contest, McCandless came out on top. (Photo Courtesy Don Webber)

Dick Landy heads up the return road at the 1971 NHRA U.S. Nationals. From here, the twin front chin spoilers fitted to his Dodge can be seen. Landy was one of the few Mopar racers to experiment with aerodynamics in 1971. Pro Stock regulations only allowed factory front and rear spoilers, but few took the opportunity to help stabilize the front end by fitting these components. (Photo Courtesy Don Webber)

McCandless makes his way up the return road. He'd been dynamite throughout the 1971 campaign, but at the U.S. Nationals, his day ended early when Don Carlton in the Motown Missile put him on the trailer in Round 2. (Photo Courtesy Don Webber)

The dramatic Hemi Mopar battle was between Don Grotheer and Butch Leal. The California Flash has a nose in front and was still ahead at the finish. He made it as far as the semifinals, where he was taken out by the Motown Missile. (Photo Courtesy Don Webber)

Bobby Yowell and Butch Leal face off at Indy in their Dusters. Leal won on this occasion. (Photo Courtesy Geoff Stunkard Collection/Ray Mann Archive)

Don Carlton and the Motown Missile were a force in 1971. (Photo Courtesy Geoff Stunkard Collection/Ray Mann Archive)

Bob Riffle, his crew, and his Dodge Dart Demon in the winner's circle at the U.S. Nationals. Rod Shop team member Riffle had just won B/MP. (Photo Courtesy C. Mike Cook)

Ronnie Sox (left), Buddy Martin, and a friend celebrate yet another victory, this time at the U.S. Nationals at Indy. This was a regular scene throughout the first two years of Pro Stock. (Photo Courtesy C. Mike Cook)

1971 NHRA World Championship Finals

Of the six races to date, Ronnie Sox won five of them. The scintillating form he'd displayed throughout the latter half of 1970 carried across to the new season and the new car, and it seemed that no one could catch him. Heading into the NHRA World Finals at Amarillo Dragway in late October, he was sure to add another NHRA Pro Stock Championship to his list of accomplishments, wasn't he?

The World Finals was an invitation-only event. Only the drivers who scored points during the NHRA qualifying races were eligible to compete. This was an elite event, and the final outcome mattered.

The problem with the Amarillo track was that it was 3,700 feet above sea level. The lean air created yet another challenge for the teams.

There were 29 cars entered to run in Pro Stock, and it was Butch Leal who emerged at the top of the pile once qualifying was done. His 10.04 ET showed how much the elevation affected horsepower and, consequently, speed. McDade was fast again, and again the NHRA tore his motor down and found it to be legal.

When Eliminations got underway, Mike Fons drew the lucky straw. He got the bye run in Round 1. He then beat John Hagen's 'Cuda to advance through to the next round, where he met top-qualifier Leal. Fons ran a 10.15 against Leal, which, given Leal's qualifying times, should have sent the Rod Shop Challenger home, but it didn't. The California Kid redlit, and Fons continued his march. In the semifinals, Fons faced Ronnie Sox. Surely his good fortune was about to come to end? Nope. Fons was up for the fight. He laid down an epic 10.06 to Sox's 10.14 and advanced to the final.

Meanwhile, McDade had stormed through Eliminations, running some of the fastest times of the day, including a 9.96, 9.98, and 10.04. But his luck ran out in the semifinals when he faced McCandless in the second Sox & Martin 'Cuda. McCandless didn't outrun him, however. A broken eyebolt on the pressure plate kept the clutch engaged, and he struggled down the lane to a losing 12.73.

So, a Sox & Martin 'Cuda lined up in the finals against the come-from-nowhere-guy Fons. But it wasn't Ronnie Sox in the right lane, it was McCandless. Fons was in the final because he'd taken down the top driver of the past 18 months. When the lights triggered, it was the Rod Shop Challenger first out of the hole, and Fons ran it hard all the way down the track, scratching out a small margin to take the win and the championship. His 10.05 comfortably beat McCandless's 10.40, and Fons was crowned 1971 NHRA Pro Stock Champion.

1971 NHRA Supernationals

The heat and the smog of early 1970s California greeted the teams for the final round of the 1971 Super Season in late November. Ontario Motor Speedway hosted its second NHRA Supernationals.

Butch Leal headed qualifying with a blistering 9.53, followed by Mike Fons, who continued his good form from the World Finals and produced a 9.57. Don Nicholson ran third on 9.60, while Sox could only muster a 9.66 to sit fourth. Only 28 cars entered the Pro Stock competition, so with 32 berths, four lucky drivers were guaranteed to progress to Round 2.

Come the semifinals, it was Nicholson to face off against McCandless in the newly repainted Keystone-sponsored Sox & Martin–built Millwee/Red 'Cuda. The Ford versus Plymouth contest went the way of the big Chrysler. Meanwhile, Sox and top-qualifier Leal battled one another in the second semifinal.

A heated rivalry between the Sox & Martin and Leal camps had been developing throughout the year, and

MIKE FONS

Mike Fons arrived relatively late to the party for Chrysler's Super Stock/Pro Stock reign of terror during the 1960s and early 1970s. Indeed, it wasn't until 1971 that he first climbed aboard a Mopar Stocker, but what a Mopar it was! Fons went on to win the 1971 NHRA Pro Stock World Championship, which, on the all-time list of NHRA Pro Stock season champions, has Fons as the 1971 Champion.

Like so many hot rodders growing up in Detroit, Fons honed his skills during the mid-1960s in street racing on the infamous Woodward Avenue. He was a Chevy guy initially racing a 1962 409-powered Impala before moving to a Corvette. Fons began hanging around Dick Arons's Midwest Auto Parts store, and it was Arons who nudged him toward getting serious about his racing and taking it to the track. To that end, the pair built a 1967 Camaro for A/Modified Production.

With the Camaro, Fons ripped through the NHRA Division 3 points and won the Modified Production Eliminations at the 1969 NHRA World Championship Finals in Dallas.

Pumped by his achievements, Fons built a 1968 Camaro with which to tackle the new Pro Stock competition in 1970. While he fared well against many of the Chevy teams, invariably he was cut down by the Chrysler contingent. When Gil Kirk and Dave Koffel approached Fons about joining the new Rod Shop team, he jumped at the chance.

The Rod Shop ran a fleet of Mopars in a variety of classes with support from Dodge. Also, Fons would get to work with Ted Spehar, who'd been involved in building the 1970 *Motown Missile* Pro Stock Challenger. To that end, Fons's 1971 Rod Shop Challenger was effectively a copy of the *Motown Missile*.

Fons and the Rod Shop Challenger made their first NHRA Pro Stock appearance in Round 3 in Dallas for the Springnationals. At the following event, the Summernationals, he offered a taste of things to come by making the final,

where he faced and lost to Don Nicholson's Maverick.

Then, on October 24, at the tricky high-altitude Amarillo Raceway for the NHRA World Championship Finals, Fons put away John Hagen's 'Cuda, top-qualifier Butch Leal's Duster, and "The Boss" Ronnie Sox to reach the final. There, he faced Herb McCandless in the second Sox & Martin 'Cuda, and he stormed to an historic victory.

When the NHRA changed its weight breaks for Pro Stock in 1972, Mopar wins were harder to come by. After struggling for success, Fons left the Rod Shop team following the 1973 NHRA Gatornationals. He purchased a Plymouth 'Cuda that had been a test mule for the *Motown Missile* squad and a Plymouth Duster from Irv Beringhaus's widow Nancy after Irv had been killed in a racing accident. He campaigned the Duster through 1974 and 1975 with limited success. Following the 1975 season, he was unable to justify the costs and quit racing.

Although he'd hung up his helmet, Fons remained in the racing industry for another decade, doing chassis work and fabricating. He eventually closed it down and returned to the Fons family construction business.

The come-from-nowhere-kid Mike Fons was one of the great stories of the 1971 NHRA Pro Stock series. He won the World Championship Finals at Amarillo Dragway in Texas, beating the best of the best. That victory cemented his place in the record books as the 1971 Pro Stock Champion before the category switched to a season-long points system in 1974. (Photo Courtesy Tom West/Lou Hart)

there was little love lost between them. When Sox took down Leal during Eliminations at the Springnationals earlier in the year, a Sox & Martin spokesperson quipped, "And here we were under the impression that Butch's car would run good." Leal, meanwhile, publicly announced that he was going to beat Sox. Finally, the audience would get to see the rivalry play out.

As the pair staged, they ran a series of dry hops and lined up. When the lights flashed, it was Leal first out of the gates but only by a little. Sox then put his bumper ahead only for Leal to come back around him. It was an extremely close contest. But as they thundered across the stripe, the California Flash was barely in front. Leal ran a 9.553 to Sox's 9.558. Leal did just as he said he would, but the drama wasn't over yet. Buddy Martin lodged a protest and requested the NHRA check the front/rear weight distribution of Leal's Duster. The scales showed it to be 57.2 percent rear weight distribution. The maximum allowable was 55 percent. This rule would be dropped for 1972, but at the 1971 Supernationals, Leal was promptly disqualified. Sox faced McCandless in the final. In the end, Sox took the win (his sixth of the season) with a 9.64 at 143.31 mph.

So, Ronnie Sox won six of the eight NHRA Pro Stock finals but didn't win the championship. Had the Super Series been a points-paying system, the history books would be different. But it wasn't, and Mike Fons peaked at just the right time. Furthermore, he beat Sox in a heads-up race to win the championship. To be the best, you have to beat the best, and Fons did just that.

1971 AHRA Highlights

Beyond the excitement and drama of the NHRA series, the AHRA continued its own strong multi-race series. For 1971, it too adopted the Pro Stock name.

With the increased NHRA schedule and growing demands to stay running at the top of the Pro Stock heap, many of the faster teams chose their AHRA outings a lot more carefully than they did in 1970. As such, several of these events were won by smaller outfits in their absence. Likewise, the IHRA was also emerging as a contender, so some teams, Sox & Martin among them, opted to run in IHRA events instead.

Arlen Vanke was first to strike when he won the Winternationals at Beeline Dragway two weeks after the NHRA Winternationals took place. On April 18 at the Pro-Am Nationals, Ronnie Sox took the win. Bob Lambeck raced a 1968 Dodge Dart to victory at the Spring Nationals in June, and Tom Heller won the Gateway Nationals at St. Louis International Raceway in his Dodge Charger. The remaining races were all won by Ford or Chevrolet drivers.

It didn't get more heated than it was at Bristol for the IHRA Springnationals with Don Carlton (near) versus Ronnie Sox (far) in a mother Mopar showdown. Carlton left early, and Sox made it two in a row at Thunder Valley. (Photo Courtesy Bristol International Dragway)

1971 IHRA Highlights

Ronnie Sox went on a winning spree in the 1971 IHRA Pro Stock division, scoring victories at the Pro-Am Nationals at North Carolina Motor Speedway, Spring Nationals at Bristol International Dragway, Southern Invitational Drag Championship at North Carolina Motor Speedway, and All-American Nationals at Bristol International Dragway.

Meanwhile, Don Carlton won the U.S. Open at North Carolina Motor Speedway and the World Finals at Lakeland International Raceway.

In Conclusion

After two intense seasons of Pro Stock drag racing, Chrysler had emerged ahead of the pack. Certainly, the Sox & Martin squad had scored more victories than anyone else, but even removing this team from the equation showed just how potent Chrysler's products were in this environment. There were several Mopar campaigners snapping at the heels of Sox & Martin, and in some cases, beating them.

But really, the difference maker, the single factor that separated the Chrysler teams from everyone, was the Hemi engine. Chrysler released this incredible powerpack in 1964, and by the end of 1971, it appeared to have no equal. With performance and sporty car sales slumping and manufacturers withdrawing their support of racing, it looked like no one was about to step forward anytime soon to produce a challenger. The mighty Chrysler Hemi could go on winning for years to come.

That very scenario may well have played out, but for the NHRA, making the decision to intervene and introduce wholesale changes to the Pro Stock regulations for 1971, in its opinion, would produce a better show. It became apparent that the only way to beat the Chrysler Hemi was to simply pull the rug from under it, and that's precisely what the NHRA did.

Pro Stock drag racing would never be the same again.

CHAPTER 12

1972 AND BEYOND

From the 15 national Pro Stock races that took place during 1970 and 1971, 12 were won by Hemi-powered Chryslers. A Dodge or Plymouth reached the final in every single event. No other manufacturer even came close to that achievement. It was a full-blown trouncing.

Furthermore, the NHRA had held a total of 49 national events through to the end of 1971, and Ronnie Sox was easily the winningest driver in all competitions with 15 race wins (nearly one-third). In fact, it was even better than that. Sox made his Stock-class debut at the 1964 NHRA Winternationals, so he had actually taken part in just 37 national events when 1971 drew to a close. The next winningest driver was Top Fuel pilot Don Garlits, who sat far in arears by the end of 1971 on just 7 national victories.

Of the 15 Pro Stock national events contested throughout 1970 and 1971, Sox had won 9 of them, including 3 in 1970 and 6 in 1971. On top of that, Herb McCandless drove the second Sox & Martin car to victory at the 1970 U.S. Nationals, so in fact, this one team had recorded 10 wins from a possible 15 events. So, one team had dominated the Pro Stock division since its inception. But even with the Sox & Martin squad removed from the equation, Hemi-powered Mopars were far and away the strongest and fastest package.

Chrysler's total domination of the Pro Stock ranks was not lost on the NHRA, of course. Even as Sox scorched to yet another victory at the 1971 Supernationals in late November to round out the season, it was already well advanced in producing a total shake-up of the regulations for 1972. With those new regulations, the sands of power shifted dramatically.

To unravel the mighty Mopar domination, three new weight breaks were introduced. According to the NHRA, they were made "with an eye for increasing popularity and competition." Throughout 1970 and 1971, Pro Stock featured a relatively simple 7 pounds per ci rule, which, theoretically, would create an even playing field. The trouble was that if one manufacturer produced an engine that was better than those of rival manufacturers but was still the same size, naturally that manufacturer would be more successful. The Chrysler Hemi, Ford SOHC Cammer, and Chevy 427 Rat motor were all within a whisker of one another in terms of size, and all were right at the maximum Pro Stock size limit. Therefore, the Mopars, Fords, and Chevys all raced at the same weight. So, the NHRA started playing with the weights to manipulate the results.

Changes to 1972 NHRA Pro Stock Regulations

For 1972, the 7 pounds per ci rule remained in place but only for cars with a staggered-valve motor, such as Chevrolet's 396 and 427 big-blocks and Ford's 351 Cleveland small-block.

For the Chrysler Hemi and Ford SOHC units, the weight break was increased to 7.25 pounds per ci. A

"Akron" Arlen Vanke and Butch Leal go head-to-head in 1972. The NHRA shifted the weight breaks to cancel out the Hemi domination of Pro Stock, and as such, race wins became a tough ask for the Mopar teams. (Photo Courtesy Tom West/Lou Hart)

Melvin Yow's beautiful Dodge Challenger faces the new force in Pro Stock: Bill Jenkins's small-block-powered Chevy Vega. The little Chevy dominated in 1972. (Photo Courtesy Tom West/Lou Hart)

Irv Beringhaus continued campaigning his stunning Plymouth 'Cuda into 1972. (Photo Courtesy Tom West/Lou Hart)

It was another season for the Billy the Kid Challenger, but a new Dodge Dart would arrive in 1973. (Photo Courtesy Tom West/Lou Hart)

Don Carlton points the front wheels skyward in the Motown Missile Hemi 'Cuda. Carlton remained a leading Mopar contender. However, Pro Stock rules were rewritten for 1972, and Mopar victories became scarce. (Photo Courtesy Tom West/Lou Hart)

Even the might of Sox & Martin, who'd been so dominant during the first two years of Pro Stock competition, couldn't overcome the new NHRA weight breaks for 1972. They went winless in NHRA national events. (Photo Courtesy Tom West/Lou Hart)

Don Carlton and Ronnie Sox get set to compete. By 1972, the Motown Missile *beat the Sox & Martin machine more often than not. (Photo Courtesy Tom West/Lou Hart)*

Don Carlton drives the Mopar Missile *Plymouth Duster that replaced the team's 1972 'Cuda. (Photo Courtesy Tom West/Lou Hart)*

Dick Landy was still racing Dodge Challengers by 1974. Having won in AHRA aboard a new Dodge Dart, the AHRA adjusted its weight breaks to oust the Hemi cars, just as the NHRA had done in 1972. So, Landy built a new Dodge Challenger to run the Sportsman division. (Photo Courtesy Tom West/Lou Hart)

Lee Cameron's beautiful Super Stock Dodge Challenger continued to race well into the mid-1970s. (Photo Courtesy Geoff Stunkard Collection)

426-ci Hemi-powered Dodge or Plymouth, therefore, would have to lug roughly an extra 106 pounds of weight down the track compared to what it did in 1971. That was significant.

But there was more. Cars with a stock wheelbase of less than 100 inches and powered with a smaller wedge engine, such as Chevrolet's 302, 327, and 350; Chrysler's 340; Ford's 352; and AMC's 360, were gifted a weight break of just 6.75 pounds per ci and a minimum 2,000 pounds, provided the engine size was no larger than 366 ci.

So in essence, Chrysler was punished for designing a better engine. The NHRA, of course, was in the entertainment business, and it felt the show could be better if there were more brands winning.

But perhaps more so, the automotive market was undergoing wholesale changes, some of which were forced upon it by an impending global gas crisis and some of which were the result of soaring insurance premiums on high-performance cars.

In addition, the buying habits of new-car customers had changed to those of the mid- and late-1960s. The young Baby Boomer generation, which made the Ford

Mustang such a massive sales success in 1964 and incentivized both the pony car market and the healthy muscle car market, were in the market for a completely different type of vehicle by the early 1970s. In their place, the next generation of young car buyers had interests outside that of pure performance.

Sales and production numbers for sporty performance cars took a nosedive in the early 1970s and all but wiped out the pony car and muscle car markets. Sales of the Dodge Challenger and Plymouth Barracuda plummeted. Chrysler sold more than 76,000 Challengers in 1970 and more than 48,000 Barracudas in the same period. Those figures dipped to around 26,000 for the Challenger and a little over 16,000 for the Barracuda in 1971. The numbers were just as grim in 1972.

Likewise, General Motors sought to cull the Chevrolet Camaro and Pontiac Firebird siblings in 1972 when workers at the Norwood, Ohio, assembly plant went on strike. Norwood was the only plant to assemble GM's pony car pairing. As sales figures slumped, the strike arrived at an opportune time, and top management sought to shut down the plant and end Camaro and Firebird production

After campaigning the 'Cuda, Irv Beringhaus switched to this Plymouth Duster for 1973. It is seen here on the back of his elaborately painted hauler. Sadly, Irv was killed in January 1974 racing a newly constructed Ford Pinto at the AHRA Winternationals at Beeline Dragway. He was 39 years of age. (Photo Courtesy Grant Bittner)

Dave Wren ran his 'Cuda Super Stock in mid-1970s competition. (Photo Courtesy Geoff Stunkard Collection/Ray Mann Archive)

indefinitely. A group of enthusiasts within the company actively worked to save the models, as both prompted strong owner loyalty groups along with significant goodwill that continued throughout the GM brand.

Pint-sized Pro Stock

With buyers switching to smaller, more economical models, the NHRA felt the need to embrace the market trend. It wanted the cars competing in Pro Stock to reflect those Detroit was producing. So, its new weight breaks for 1972 Pro Stock were very much aimed at encouraging Ford Pintos, Chevrolet Vegas, Dodge Colts, and AMC Gremlins into its ranks.

Dave Boertman campaigned this Rod Shop Dodge Challenger Super Stock well into 1975. (Photo Courtesy Geoff Stunkard Collection/Ray Mann Archive)

Bruce Hawk, pictured in the ex–Lou Mancini, campaigned the big Road Runner Super Stock into the late 1970s. (Photo Courtesy Geoff Stunkard Collection/Ray Mann Archive)

The first Pro Stock racer to embrace the new 1972 regulations was Bill Jenkins. He spent the last chunk of 1971 constructing a Chevrolet Vega powered by a 331-ci small-block engine. It was a revolutionary little car, made more so by the fact it had a tube-frame chassis.

Winternationals

Jenkins debuted *Grumpy's Toy IX* at the 1972 NHRA Winternationals, where he qualified the untested Vega 17th with an unimpressive 9.90-second ET. With more testing and tuning of the chassis throughout the

When Chrysler went drag racing, it did so to the extreme. The tiny Japanese Mitsubishi Galant was sold in the United States as the Dodge Colt. It was to be the new-generation Mopar Pro Stock to tackle the latest compacts, but a spree of vicious crashes and even fatalities blunted its progress. (Photo Courtesy Geoff Stunkard Collection/Ray Mann Archive)

The Rod Shop Dodge Charger continued racing well beyond its early 1971 appearances. (Photo Courtesy C. Mike Cook)

The Nationwise Rod Shop Dodge Dart Demon of Gene Dunlap is pictured. (Photo Courtesy Charlie Suggs)

weekend, the little Vega kept going quicker. Jenkins clocked his way through round after round and into the final, where he met and beat Don Grotheer's Hemi-powered 'Cuda.

That one single Winternationals finals race summarized the change in direction the NHRA was taking Pro Stock. Grotheer's Hemi 'Cuda typified the exact type of car and engine combination that had dominated Pro Stock since its inception, and now it had just been beaten by the new breed of small-block-powered compact that was about to take the class forward into the future. With that, Jenkins just kept on winning.

Gatornationals . . . Then All Grump All the Time

Mopar racers Don Carlton (Plymouth 'Cuda) and Melvin Yow (Dodge Dart) faced one another in the final at the Gatornationals, which Carlton won. But Chrysler victories were harder to come by in 1972. Jenkins won the Springnationals (beating Grotheer in the final), Summernationals (against Dick Landy), Le Grandnational

(against Larry Breaux's Duster), World Finals (against Ken Dondero's Don Nicholson–owned/tuned Ford Pinto), and the Supernationals, where he beat Bob Glidden's Pinto. Other than the Gatornationals, the only event where Jenkins didn't take home the big prize was the U.S. Nationals, but the final result had a now-familiar look about it. Ray Allen's small-block Chevy Vega beat the similar car of Rich Miracki. Jenkins, of course, was crowned Pro Stock champion on account of his victory at the World Finals.

As 1972 rumbled forward, the grids shifted more and more toward Detroit's compact econoboxes and away from the charismatic pony cars and muscle cars that had been a feature of the category since its inception. For the racers themselves, it was a no-brainer to switch to a small-block-powered compact not only because the new regulations favored these cars but also because the greatly reduced mass aided their speed.

A 1972 Chevy Vega was 11 inches narrower than a Dodge Challenger or Plymouth 'Cuda. That's 11 inches of less girth to have to shove through the air at a high speed. But the racing had to mirror the cars adorning dealership showrooms, and these were the cars people were buying. In Stock form, a Chevy Vega couldn't

The Mike Fons Dodge Dart was originally built by Ken Fuller for Dick Landy. Fons purchased the car from Irv Beringhaus's widow after Irv was killed while racing. (Photos Courtesy Charlie Suggs)

DON CARLTON

Don Carlton sprung from virtual obscurity to being a national racing icon seemingly overnight when he was invited to drive the Chrysler Corporation–supported *Motown Missile* Dodge Challenger in 1971.

Like so many racers, Carlton scratched away for several years, building and racing his own machinery and putting any prize money he managed to win straight back into the car. But drag racing was very much an expensive hobby for him and not a profession. He worked at a furniture factory in Lenoir, North Carolina, and spent his evenings preparing the car so that he could travel and race on the weekend before traveling back home to go to work on Monday morning.

By 1969, he was making infrequent appearances at national events when the NHRA or AHRA circus was within striking distance. He made the semifinals at the 1969 NHRA Springnationals and, impressively, went to the final at the AHRA U.S. Open, losing to Hubert Platt's factory Ford Mustang.

Carlton continued the battle in 1970, the first year of Pro Stock, campaigning a 1968 Plymouth Barracuda. His efforts were noticed by Ted Spehar, who invited him to pilot the *Motown Missile* in 1971. With that, he quit his job at the furniture factory and became a full-time drag racer.

Now, with a top car beneath him and factory support, Carlton excelled and quickly established himself as a leading protagonist in Pro Stock competition. He qualified second to Ronnie Sox at the NHRA Gatornationals and progressed through to the final, where he met Sox. During Eliminations, he'd bettered Sox's time, but come the final, he accidentally clunked his transmission into second following the burnout, gifting Sox an easy win.

Carlton progressed through to the semifinals at the NHRA Springnationals and once again topped qualifying at the Summernationals, but he narrowly lost to Don Nicholson in the semifinals. He worked through to the final at Le Grandnational, but like the rest of the Pro Stock contingent, he had to play second-best to Ronnie Sox. At the U.S. Nationals, he top-qualified once more and met Sox in the semifinals, where he was victim of a bizarre start light malfunction. In IHRA competition, he won the 1971 U.S. Open and World Finals. It had been an epic debut season.

For 1972, Carlton struggled to overcome the NHRA's new weight-break system instigated to handicap the dominant Chrysler Hemi cars. Against the odds, he took his first NHRA national victory at the Gatornationals. He drove

Don Carlton launches hard in the second of the Motown Missiles, *the Plymouth Cuda that was raced in 1972. By 1972, this was the top performing Mopar team, finally eclipsing the dominant Sox & Martin outfit. Unfortunately, the* Missile *hit full stride just as the NHRA introduced its new weight breaks to scupper the Chryslers in Pro Stock. (Photo Courtesy Steve Reyes)*

the new *Motown Missile* Plymouth 'Cuda to victory at the IHRA Longhorn Nationals as well as the Dallas Nationals and the All-American Nationals. In all three contests, he faced and beat Ronnie Sox in the final. He racked up more victories in 1973 IHRA competition aboard a new *Mopar Missile* (the Motown name was dropped for 1973) Duster as well as the NHRA Springnationals.

Carlton was extremely detail-orientated and was incredibly consistent with his passes. He was completely driven to succeed.

As Chrysler transitioned out of Pro Stock racing, the *Mopar Missile* was passed to Carlton. While he continued to work with Chrysler testing the smaller Mitsubishi-based Dodge Colt and Plymouth Arrow, he raced in Competition Eliminator and Sportsman categories before returning to Pro Stock with a new Colt.

It was on July 5, 1977, during an intense multi-day test session with the Colt in Milan, Michigan, that Carlton made a hit down the track. Suddenly the car started coasting before it swerved and dug into the surface, rolling several times. Don Carlton suffered head injuries from the crash and never regained consciousness.

Thorough investigations did not identify any mechanical problems with the car that might have been a contributing factor. Members of his crew who were present on the day believe he simply passed out from dehydration during a stifling hot day and a grueling test session.

Don Carlton was just 36 years of age and died as a drag racing hero.

Roy Hill was a friend and neighbor of the Pettys, and in 1973, Petty Enterprises built Hill a Pro Stock Duster. It was only the third drag car the Pettys had built; the first two being the Barracudas raced by Richard Petty in the mid-1960s. He became a staunch Mopar supporter, running this Plymouth Duster in Pro Stock. (Photo Courtesy Charlie Suggs)

outrun a Hemi Challenger. But Pro Stock had evolved in such a way that the race cars no longer related to the vehicles they represented.

1973: More of the Same

The theme continued throughout 1973. Don Nicholson won the Winternationals and Gatornationals in his Pinto, while Carlton triumphed in the new *Motown Missile* Duster at the Springnationals. Jenkins returned to the victory lane at the Summernationals, and Butch Leal raced his Duster to the win at Le Grandnational.

Bob Glidden and Wayne Gapp faced off in the final for the U.S. Nationals aboard their Pintos. Gapp beat Jenkins in the World Finals, and as such, was declared 1973 NHRA Pro Stock Champion. He also rounded the championship off with victory at the Supernationals.

1974

For 1974, the Pro Stock championship was contested using a points system spread across the major national events. Bob Glidden took three victories in his Ford Pinto to be crowned the champion.

Glidden's diminutive Pinto was truly a far cry from the big-block heavyweights that battled for honors in the early and mid-1960s. Indeed, virtually every top team had switched to running a tube-frame small-block-powered compact purely because that was what the rules favored. The biggest cars in the field were the Plymouth Dusters and Dodge Dart Demons, which, upon release, were themselves marketed as compact cars. In the gas crunch, smog-inhibiting era of the mid-1970s, everything was getting smaller.

The NHRA retained its new 1972 weight break rules until 1982, when it switched to a mandatory 500-ci unit.

This is another of the tiny Dodge Colts. (Photo Courtesy Charlie Suggs)

Nelson Des Champs's Dodge Colt was a former Mr. Norm car. (Photo Courtesy Charlie Suggs)

Ronnie Sox and Billy Stepp teamed up for a little while running this Plymouth Arrow. The Arrow was a Japanese Mitsubishi Celeste rebranded by Chrysler for the U.S. market. (Photo Courtesy Charlie Suggs)

Creating Closer Racing at Chrysler's Expense

When the NHRA introduced its new 1972 Pro Stock regulations, its goal was to level the playing field, eliminate Chrysler's advantage, and create an even spread of winners throughout the various brands. Ultimately, that was exactly what happened.

The Dodge Charger returned to drag racing in the 1980s, in the compact fifth-generation shell. (Photo Courtesy Charlie Suggs)

By 1973, the competition between the various brands was incredibly spirited, and everyone got a slice of the pie. From the eight national races, there were six different winners in Don Nicholson, Don Carlton, Bill Jenkins, Butch Leal, Bob Glidden, and Wayne Gapp. Indeed, Nicholson and Gapp were the only multi-race winners, scoring two victories each. Ford, Chrysler, and Chevrolet brands all rolled into the winners' circle.

But the term *Stock*, by its very definition, had become blurred in the relentless drive for evolution and the quest to remain current, as well as to produce close, exciting racing. When Jenkins debuted his 1972 tube-frame Vega, he reset the Pro Stock parameters forever. This was, essentially, a fully engineered, purpose-built chassis with a Vega body draped over the top. As such, every Pro Stock car built thereafter followed a similar theme.

Pro Stock cars had evolved into pure silhouettes and were a total departure from the flying behemoths of the early 1960s that had catapulted Stock drag racing from obscurity and thrust it into the limelight. The concept of factory Stockers that an enthusiast could purchase direct from a dealer and take straight to the track and start knocking out competitive times was now but a pipe dream.

Pro Stock racing got swept up in the changing times, and, rightly or wrongly, it evolved as it had to in order to survive. The NHRA had no influence over the new car buying habits of the public. It could only control its own racing divisions and how it incorporated the tastes and trends of the evolving market. With the new generation of cars came ongoing technological evolution, and a new generation of drivers for the fans to follow and to cheer for. Indeed, nothing stands still forever.

Back to Grassroots Stock Racing

While Pro Stock continued its high-speed march away from its roots, the NHRA sought to reintroduce Stock racing in its original form. It amalgamated all its 1971 Stock classes into a new Super Stock division for 1972 and created its Strictly Stock category in which virtually any and all modifications and bolt-on performance components were prohibited.

Furthermore, racers had to drive their cars to the track. This new grassroots formula echoed that of the early 1960s, when Stock drag racing was far and away the most prominent category at any drag racing event, if not the most popular with the punters.

End of the Road for the Chrysler E-Body Cars

The 1974 season witnessed several significant nameplates fall by the wayside, including the Dodge Challenger

Roy Hill was another to switch to a Plymouth Arrow. Although still compact, the Arrow proved to be more stable in a drag racing environment than the stubby Colt. (Photos Courtesy Charlie Suggs)

With racing history comes a fascination with the cars that made that history. Thankfully, there are survivors, including Arlen Vanke's beautifully restored BO29 Barracuda. (Photo Courtesy Geoff Stunkard Collection)

evocative styling with a new general model that spanned from 1971 to 1974, as did its B-Body sibling, the Road Runner/Satellite. In 1975, racing saw the arrival of the more reserved Chrysler Cordoba on which the Charger/Road Runner (the Satellite was dropped when the new generation arrived) was now based.

The new generation of models, which tended to be focused more toward the personal luxury car theme, carried little of the flare that was so prevalent in earlier generations. When Chrysler unveiled its ultra-modern F-Body platform in 1976, the Road Runner became a trim and graphics option on the Plymouth variant: the Volare. In this form, it continued until 1980 before it was withdrawn altogether.

The Charger, meanwhile, met its demise when production of the Cordoba-based B-Body ended in 1978. However, it made a comeback in 1982 as a front-wheel-drive two-door sporty hatchback and remained in production until 1987.

The Dodge Challenger nameplate was resurrected in 1978 with the introduction of the Japanese-sourced Mitsubishi Galant. Chrysler, which owned a 15-percent stake in Mitsubishi Motors, sought to capitalize on the growing compact market while trading off the glory of a once-celebrated nameplate. Thankfully, the

and Plymouth Barracuda, as new government-enforced frontal impact regulations demanded significant redesign work be undertaken. Slumping sales figures for these models simply didn't warrant the financial investment, particularly as the U.S. automotive industry was already hemorrhaging due, at least in part, to an influx of foreign competition.

Both the Challenger and Barracuda, once the darlings of the Chrysler fleet, were quietly withdrawn from the market in April 1974, having sold barely 11,000 units of each in the year to date. It was the end of an era.

Meanwhile, the Dodge Charger, once the most dramatic-looking of all Chrysler models, continued its

Bill Bagshaw's restored Red Light Bandit *Dodge Challenger Pro Stock is shown. (Photos Courtesy Geoff Stunkard Collection)*

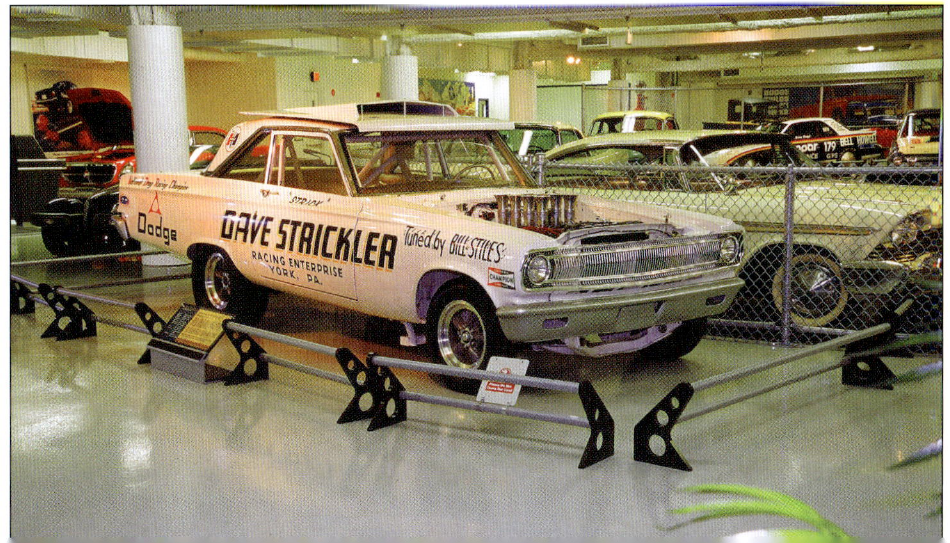

Dave Strickler's restored altered-wheelbase 1965 Plymouth Belvedere hardtop is shown here. (Photo Courtesy Geoff Stunkard Collection)

Mitsubishi-based Challenger was a short-lived venture, and it was shelved in 1983 with the arrival of the Starion-based Conquest.

Death of the Muscle Car

The American automotive industry reached its lowest ebb in the 1970s. While a changing market and government-enforced regulations stymied enjoyment and creativity, there remained a core group of genuine car enthusiasts within Chrysler Corporation that still sought to inject excitement into its products when the increasing list of restrictions allowed.

In 1978, Dodge unveiled its Lil' Red Express Truck, which was a D-100-based pickup that not only embraced the popular custom utility vehicle trend of the late 1970s but also managed to side-step horsepower-choking anti-smog regulations that helped kill the high-performance market.

Chrysler engineers explored a loophole in the government mandate that dictated motor cars must be equipped with a catalytic converter. No such directive was imposed on trucks. The Lil' Red Express Truck, therefore, was garnished in bright custom bodywork, wooden rear decking, and semitruck-inspired chrome exhaust stacks that extended up behind the cab.

Furthermore, the lack of catalytic converter allowed the 360-ci Police interceptor V-8 to breathe as it was intended, and the Lil' Red punched out a healthy (for the time) 225 hp. More significantly, it was proven to be the fastest-accelerating American-made motor vehicle in 1978, eclipsing the Chevrolet Corvette in the process.

The rate at which the American high-performance market vanished in the 1970s was staggering. Aside from the demise of the Dodge Challenger and Plymouth Barracuda, the AMC Javelin was also a victim of sluggish sales

and new frontal-impact regulations. Meanwhile, the Mustang went the way of the new breed of economy-based compacts with the second-generation model being based on the little Pinto.

For its first year of production, a V-8 engine wasn't an option. The Camaro and Firebird were truly the only survivors of the 1960s pony car revolution. Both models, while updated throughout the 1970s, actually enjoyed soaring sales toward the end of the decade.

Recapturing Past Glories by Going Full Circle

As if to finally acknowledge that Detroit got it right in the 1960s but had failed to recapture that magic in the years and decades that followed, Ford launched its retro-styled fifth-generation Mustang to widespread acclaim in 2005. The Mustang, while a modern car, borrowed heavily on the 1960s' aesthetics.

In 2008, Chrysler resurrected the Dodge Challenger, which again embraced numerous styling cues from the original 1970–1974 model. Sadly, Plymouth was unable to do the same with the Barracuda, as Chrysler had withdrawn the brand in 2001 as it sought to streamline its business model.

The new Dodge Challenger injected a new level of excitement into the Dodge fleet. It has since reintroduced some of the great performance packages from its past, including R/T, T/A, Scat Pack, and Demon. There have been specific track models created for quarter-mile competition, and likewise, there are completely insane high-horsepower variants, including the 707-hp SRT Hellcat that launched in 2015, limited-edition 2016 Hellcats producing 745 and 750 hp, and the 840-hp SRT Demon of 2017. There have been special Mr. Norm Challengers and Richard Petty Challengers. The Scat Pack 1320 is a model designed specifically for Stock and Super Stock drag racing competition.

Among the most prized of early Pro Stock cars are those built and raced by Sox & Martin. (Photo Courtesy Geoff Stunkard Collection)

The annual Muscle Car and Corvette Nationals (MCACN) event celebrates the history of the muscle car in all its forms. Naturally, vintage drag cars play an important role. Here, the Don Carlton-piloted Motown Missile Challenger and Mopar Missile Duster are displayed as is the newly restored Butch Leal 1975 Dart, the staunch Rod Shop Dart, and Reid Whisnant's Daytona. (Photos Courtesy Todd Farnum)

So, Chrysler relaunched the Dodge Charger in 2006, albeit, as a four-door sedan that bears no resemblance to the original models. Like the latest generation of Challengers, the Charger has been invigorated through the resurrection of the great Mopar performance packages of the past.

Chrysler Corporation is, quite literally, trading off its past glories—and rightly so. But in doing so, it has introduced its rich heritage to new generations while also appeasing those who were there the first time around. It is celebrating and fully embracing its own history, and what an incredible history it is. This is a car manufacturer that has always been a little unorthodox. Sure, it is a global conglomerate whose bottom line is always to sell more units. But at its core, this is a company of car enthusiasts who still love to design and create products that, quite simply, make people smile. The motor car can and should be so much more than an unremarkable transportation device that carries people and goods from one point to another. It can be something fun that can bring enjoyment by its very nature. Chrysler gets that.

The popular Stock, Super Stock, and Pro Stock battles of the 1960s and early 1970s truly encapsulated the excitement that abounded in the vehicles Detroit was producing. The regulations set out by the NHRA, the AHRA, and other governing bodies prompted the creation of some of the most outlandish, memorable, and now collectable factory hot rods ever built. Throughout this period, while being more outlandish and more daring than its rivals, Chrysler Corporation was rooted at the top of the competition pile.

In Conclusion

Pro Stock, of course, continues to this day. The cars themselves are technical marvels that are enormously efficient at what they do and perfectly encompass what the regulations allow. But they lack the charisma of the cars that competed in Stock, Super Stock, early Funny Car, and Pro Stock during the 1960s and early 1970s. It's hard to imagine a young race fan falling in love with one of today's cars as they might have done over Billy Stepp's gleaming candy-mix Dodge Challenger or a car named the *Melrose Missile*, or a *Motown Missile*, a Ramcharger, a *Red Light Bandit*, a *California Flash*, a *Drag-On Lady*, a silver Dick Landy Dodge, or a patriotic red, white, and blue Sox & Martin Plymouth. These were cars that had character; each was unique and bristling with personality, like true living monsters.

But such is the price of evolution. Indeed, racers are always looking to evolve and to move forward. Pro Stock has been a part of that evolution. Many of the original people who helped write history have since passed, but fortunately, the memories they created survive, as do a healthy number of the cars they built and raced. Even today, those cars shimmer with the ghosts of those who built and raced them, the pure joy that came from winning, the pure frustration that came from losing, and the blood, sweat, tears, and sleepless nights that got them there in the first place.

History was made so that we can enjoy it for what it is and to celebrate the heroes of the past and the incredible technicolor flying machines they created.

Naturally, original Dick Landy cars are highly coveted by collectors. This is a beautifully restored LO23 Landy Dart. (Photo Courtesy Geoff Stunkard Collection)

Restored vintage altered-wheelbase monsters include Bud Faubel's Hemi Honker *hardtop* on the left and Charlie Allen's Atlantic Dodge Flyer on the right. (Photo Courtesy Geoff Stunkard Collection)

Jere Stahl's 1966 Super Stock Hemi Plymouth is shown here. (Photo Courtesy Geoff Stunkard Collection)

Below: The beautifully restored 1965 Hemi Plymouth Super Stock of Butch "the California Flash" Leal poses here. (Photo Courtesy Geoff Stunkard Collection)

Below: Looking as sinister now as it did in 1965 when it first wowed the crowds is Dick Landy's glorious altered-wheelbase Hemi Dodge. Like so many of his generation, the Mopar legend is no longer with us, but the history he created lives on and continues to be celebrated. (Photo Courtesy Geoff Stunkard Collection)

Additional books that may interest you...

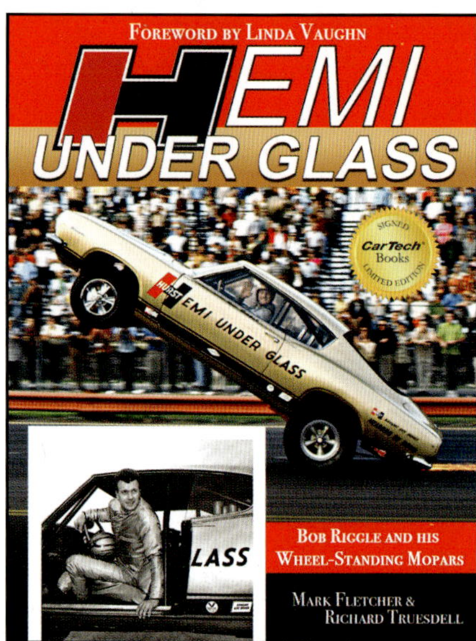

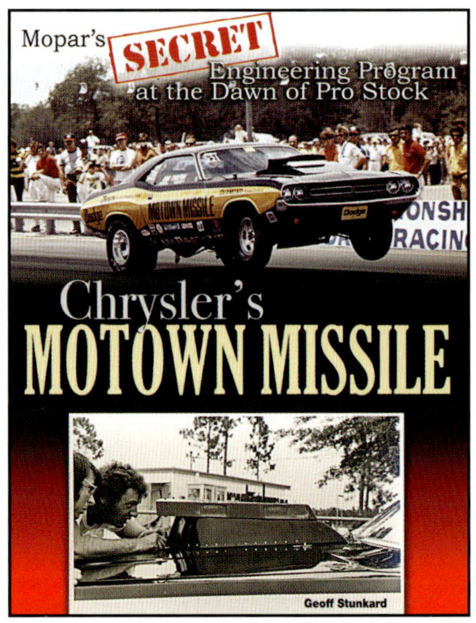

HEMI UNDER GLASS: Bob Riggle and His Wheel-Standing Mopars - Autographed Edition
by Richard Truesdell & Mark Fletcher
The First 200 Orders Receive Autographed Copies!
Bob Riggle is the most renown wheel-stander in the history of drag racing and has campaigned wheel-standing Mopars for more than 60 straight years. 8.5 x 11", 160 pgs, 358 photos, Sftbd. ISBN 9781613257463 Part # CT670S

CHRYSLER'S MOTOWN MISSILE: Mopar's Secret Engineering Program at the Dawn of Pro Stock
by Geoff Stunkard
The drama of 1970s Chrysler Pro Stock drag racing unfolds in this new book, which focuses on the racing and technological evolution of the legendary Motown Missile and Mopar Missile racing programs from 1970 to 1977. 8.5 x 11", 176 pgs, 299 photos, Sftbd. ISBN 9781613254752 Part # CT655

HURST EQUIPPED - REVISED & UPDATED EDITION: More than 50 Years of High Performance
by Rich Truesdell & Mark Fletcher
In this softcover edition, *Hurst Equipped: Revised and Updated Edition* captures the complete story from the production cars and race cars to the performance parts. 8.5 x 11", 192 pgs, 400 photos, Sftbd. ISBN 9781613255933 Part # CT676

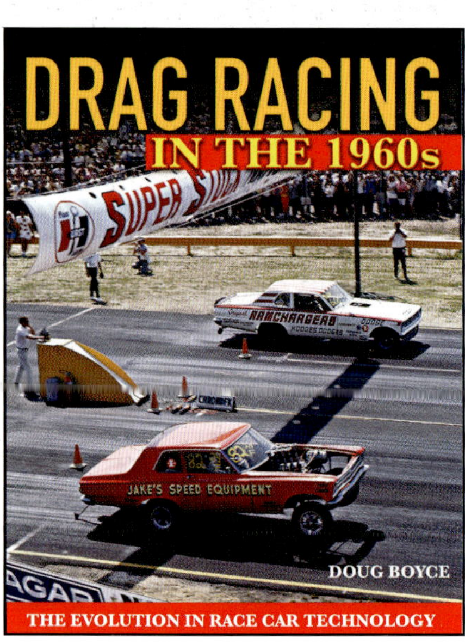

DRAG RACING IN THE 1960s: The Evolution in Race Car Technology
by Doug Boyce
In this book veteran author Doug Boyce takes you on a ride through the entire decade from a technological point of view rather than a results-based one. 8.5 x 11", 176 pgs, 350 photos, Sftbd. ISBN 9781613255827 Part # CT674

www.cartechbooks.com or 1-800-551-4754